D1267740

Urban Economics and Urban Policy

Challenging Conventional Policy Wisdom

Urban Economics and Urban Policy

Challenging Conventional Policy Wisdom

Paul C. Cheshire

London School of Economics and Political Science, UK

Max Nathan

London School of Economics and Political Science and National Institute of Economic and Social Research, UK

Henry G. Overman

London School of Economics and Political Science, UK

Edward Elgar

Cheltenham, UK • Northampton, MA, USA

Published by
Edward Elgar Publishing Limited
The Lypiatts
15 Lansdown Road
Cheltenham
Glos GL50 2JA
UK

Edward Elgar Publishing, Inc.
William Pratt House
9 Dewey Court
Northampton
Massachusetts 01060
USA

Paperback edition 2015
Paperback edition reprinted 2016

A catalogue record for this book
is available from the British Library

Library of Congress Control Number: 2013957782

This book is available electronically in the ElgarOnline.com
Economics Subject Collection, E-ISBN 978 1 78195 252 8

Printed on elemental chlorine free (ECF)
recycled paper containing 30% Post-Consumer Waste

ISBN   978 1 78195 251 1 (cased)
       978 1 78347 525 4 (paperback)

Typeset by Servis Filmsetting Ltd, Stockport, Cheshire
Printed and bound in the USA

Contents

Figures

Tables

Acronyms and abbreviations

ABI	Area Based Initiative
AONB	Area of Outstanding Natural Beauty
BIB	Business Increase Bonus
BIS	Department for Business Innovation and Skills
DTI	Department for Trade and Industry
BRR	Business Rate Retention
CABE	Commission on Architecture and the Built Environment
CIL	Community Infrastructure Charge
CO	Cabinet Office
CLG	Communities and Local Government
DCLG	Department for Communities and Local Government
DETR	Department for Transport and the Regions
DOE	Department of the Environment
EU	European Union
EZ	Enterprise Zone
FUR	Functional Urban Region
HMT	HM Treasury
LA	Local Authority
LEP	Local Economic Partnership
LPA	Local Planning Authority
LSE	London School of Economics
MAA	Multi-Area Agreements
MSA	Metropolitan Statistical Area
MTO	Moving to Opportunity
NHB	New Homes Bonus
NAO	National Audit Office
NPPF	National Planning Policy Framework
OECD	Organisation for Economic Co-operation and Development
ODPM	Office of the Deputy Prime Minister
ONS	Office of National Statistics
RDA	Regional Development Agency
RSS	Regional Spatial Strategy
SERC	Spatial Economics Research Centre

SSSI	Site of Special Scientific Interest
TCF	Town Centre First
TTWA	Travel to Work Area
UBR	Uniform Business Rate
VOA	Valuation Office Agency

Foreword

The world's cities are a precious resource. They are engines of economic prosperity and founts of cultural innovation. They provide pathways from poverty into prosperity, and bring together the crowds that can topple dictatorships.

But it is somewhat remarkable that our cities have been so successful despite the many shortcomings of urban politics and government. These shortcomings appear in rich and poor countries. The cities of the developing world often lack the basics – clean water and safe streets. The successful cities of the west perpetuate policy errors that make housing too expensive and commuting too time-consuming. Our poor urban policies are too often prisoners of overly conventional thinking that has stymied innovation.

In this bold, exciting and eminently readable volume, Paul Cheshire, Max Nathan and Henry Overman illustrate the insights that economic research brings to urbanism. Cities do not belong to a single discipline. Architects provide new visions of urban form. Engineers construct that infrastructure that makes density durable. Public health experts fight the contagious disease that can move so readily across crowded streets.

But economists have spent centuries thinking about how policies impact complex social structures, and how good policymaking anticipates behavioural responses. Since cities are themselves so complicated, it is impossible to implement wise policies without anticipating how those policies will alter human behaviour.

The problem of congestion provides a classic example of how behaviour responses can either amplify or undo a policy intervention. The naïve approach to traffic congestion is to build more roads. After all, the conventional logic goes, if we provide more open asphalt to a fixed number of drivers, then traffic speeds really do improve. But when we build more roads, the number of drivers increases – behaviour responds to policy. The empirical work of Gilles Duranton and Matthew Turner finds the vehicle miles travelled increase roughly one-for-one with highway miles built. The onrush of new drivers means that building new highways does not eliminate urban traffic jams, it only encourages an even more car-oriented society.

By contrast, London's congestion charge – implemented by Mayor Ken Livingstone, but first envisioned by the economist Willion Vickrey – works by anticipating the behavioural response. Instead of spending billions on new highways, a congestion charge pushes drivers to use the existing highways more efficiently by charging them for the social costs of their driving. Every important urban policy elicits a significant behavioural response and that is why the tools of the economist – so amply displayed in this book – are so vital.

The three core themes stressed by this book are both enduring and timely. Market forces are enormously powerful and they rarely lead to an even distribution of economic activity over space. America has spent 50 unsuccessful years trying to reverse the trend from the Midwestern Rustbelt to the cities of sunshine in the south and west. The result of all that work is that Detroit has entered into bankruptcy.

If my own country had only shown more realism and respect for the power of economic forces, I believe that much of the worst suffering might have been avoided. America's declining manufacturing cities should have focused more on providing their children with the skills that are so central for urban and personal success, instead of evicting families to erect new highly mechanized, manufacturing plants. They should have planned for decline, funding future retirement obligations during flush times, rather than leaving terrible debts to future, smaller city populations. They should have recognized that the hallmark of declining places is an abundance of structures and infrastructure relative to the level of demand: building a monorail to glide over empty streets is pure folly.

The plight of Britain's older industrial cities is not as dire as those in the US. The English population is less mobile, and the distances are shorter. Manchester and Liverpool face no climactic disadvantage, relative to London, comparable to those that bedevil Cleveland and Detroit. Still, the first step in Britain as in the US in providing sensible urban policy is to respect and understand the powerful economic forces that shape our changing urban geographies. The first chapters of this book help us to understand why economic growth has emerged so unevenly across space.

The second step is, as they write, to recognize the ineffectiveness of many current urban policies. Attempts to restrict urban growth, whether in London, Boston or Mumbai, can have terrible, unforeseen consequences. When we make it hard for an attractive city to enlarge its housing stock, that city becomes expensive and risks turning into an overpriced theme park for the global rich. I, too, love London and would never wish to see its historic beauty demolished, but we must never forget that any time we say 'no' to new building, whether in the city centre or on the edge, we are saying 'no' to families that want to experience the magic of urban life. We also ensure that every other family that lives in the city is paying more for their own homes.

Cities that build become more affordable. Chicago's magnificent lake-front real estate is priced reasonably, precisely because the city's leaders unleashed the cranes. One of the reasons why the American Sunbelt has grown so much is that it has done an exceptional job of providing massive amounts of affordable housing – through private construction, not public subsidy – for middle-income Americans. The authors are dead right in urging a reconsideration of Britain's urban planning policies.

But their third theme is the most important, and in many ways the most revolutionary. All policies need to be judged by the impact on people, not places. I have seen too many American mayors cheer at the opening of some sparkly downtown skyscraper and declare that their city has come back. But their city's people never needed that skyscraper and did not benefit from its construction. A shiny new museum in a declining industrial town may make a neighbourhood glossier, but unless it materially improves the lives of the city's residents, it is a waste of public funds.

The real city is never its skyline. The real city is the humanity that populates the structures. Those people do need good buildings and decent transportation, but every investment needs to be evaluated by its impact on humanity. That is, ultimately, the most important insight of Adam Smith's *The Wealth of Nations*, economics' seminal tome. Smith knew that the real wealth of nations was not the gold possessed by its sovereign, but the prosperity shared by its citizenry. That humanistic orientation is the finest aspect of economics, and it is the most important contribution that this book makes to the ongoing debate about urban policy.

I have learned much over the years from the work of these authors. They are exceptional urban economists who combine excellent empirical skills with incisive economic theory and a profound grasp of the realities of urban life. I am delighted that they have put together this splendid analysis of urban policy, and honoured to have been asked to write this foreword.

Edward Glaeser
Fred and Eleanor Glimp Professor of Economics and Director
of the Taubman Center for State and Local Government,
Harvard University, USA

1. Introduction

Just like cities themselves, urban economics is undergoing a period of resurgence. Yet urban economists have to date contributed very little to the development and evaluation of real-world urban policy. Both historically and currently urban policy has been much more influenced by the disciplines of engineering, architecture, design and planning than economics or other social sciences.

To us this is both surprising and worrying. Cities are social and economic constructs – 'organised complexity', as Jane Jacobs puts it in *The Death and Life of Great American Cities* (Jacobs 1961). As Ed Glaeser suggests, cities are probably our greatest invention.[1] Other great inventions – the wheel or writing – arguably derive much of their value from the economic and social success of cities. Take writing: the complexity of urban life makes the efficient coding of information a necessity rather than a luxury, while the economic surplus created by cities in turn allowed the full cultural rewards of writing to be realised. Cities also amplified the impact of the wheel: to feed growing urban populations it was essential to overcome the 'tyranny of distance' (Bairoch 1988). Because of that success there were advantages in being able to support an urban population, and because they were more productive those early citizens demanded and could pay for better transport.

Such technological changes have helped cities to grow. But cities also help generate the ideas that make technological progress possible in the first place (Marshall 1918). Cities, however, do not 'work' simply because of the technology embodied in their infrastructure, their buildings or layouts. As Alfred Marshall sets out, cities 'work' because of the way in which they encourage and support specialisation, social interaction and the exchange of ideas. Infrastructure, buildings and urban form can be a means to these ends, but they are not ends in themselves.

As complex organisms, cities are made visible in their built form – and this is one reason why so much urban policy has been focused on the built

---

[1] For a lively, informed if picaresque account of the critical role cities have played in human history and economic growth readers should consult Hall (1998). For a lucid and engaging view of cities from the perspective of an urban economist see Glaeser (2011) and Moretti (2012).

environment. One result of this is that many key urban programmes have been largely uninformed by economic insights. The prime movers in developing land use planning, for example, were Ebenezer Howard (unsuccessful farmer, journalist and proofreader for Hansard), Sir Patrick Geddes (an academic zoologist who studied mining) and Sir Patrick Abercrombie (an architect). Sir Anderson Montague-Barlow, main author of the *Barlow Report* (1940) and one might say the originator of regional policy, was a lawyer turned politician. Baron Haussmann, the planner of 19th-century Paris, was a lawyer, turned administrator. The inspiration and intellectual roots of the 'new urbanism', people like Leon Krier or Christopher Alexander or the drafters of the *Ahwahnee* Principles, were all architects. The one great exception to this list (and the only woman) is Jane Jacobs, pioneer of urban re-use and mixed use – nominally a sociologist but in practice a polymath, drawing on a vast range of disciplines and ideas. Even here, Jacobs' original thinking on how neighbourhoods and cities operate has often been distilled into fairly arid design principles, with little apparent understanding of the underlying dynamics.

What we might term 'physical urbanism' has not just influenced urban policy in Britain and France but all over the world. It has also shaped the education and habits of thinking about cities and regional differences of generations of urbanists, policymakers and practitioners. As a result, it often appears that urban policy is hardly influenced by economic thought. There is no single 'right' way to understand cities and make policy for urban areas. The best examples of urbanism recognise this, and bring multiple perspectives to the analysis (for instance, see Hall 1998, 2013 and Storper 2013). Nevertheless, economically informed perspectives on urban policy also need further exploration and development. This book is one attempt to do this, distilling policy lessons from the growing global body of urban economics and economic geography, and particularly from the work done at the Spatial Economics Research Centre (SERC), which was established at the London School of Economics in 2008.

Why does this matter? If conventional urban policy was generally successful in meeting its declared policy objectives it might not. Unfortunately, the evidence we have suggests that this is largely not the case. As this book will set out, many (though not all) of the key tools in the urban policy box have had limited or little positive effect on the economic and social outcomes we all care about. Equally, some of these tools – in the UK, notably land-use planning – have generated substantial economic and social costs for large groups of people. And until recently, a lack of robust evaluation has exacerbated these problems, by leaving ineffective or counterproductive interventions in place.

Making effective policy for cities is extremely challenging. We strongly believe that urban policy could be improved by bringing a stronger economic understanding into policy design and delivery. In particular, urban policy informed by economic insight can help improve policymaking for individual cities and urban systems as a whole. Of course we also recognise that city leaders and urban policymakers need to balance economic, social and environmental welfare. But we suggest that in at least some cases – planning, again – applying insights from urban economics can improve outcomes across all of these domains.

Three themes recur in this book: the need for realism in the face of strong market forces that drive unevenness; the ineffectiveness of many current urban growth policies and other interventions; and the importance of focusing on outcomes for people not places. The book is organised in three parts that develop these ideas, with Part IV providing some conclusions.

In the first part, Chapters 2 and 3 establish our basic building blocks. Cities both arise from and generate agglomeration economies: people and firms are more productive, all else equal, when they live and work together in cities. Agglomeration economies, as we show in Chapter 2, increase with city size. Although there are also diseconomies of size – mainly congestion, pollution and increasing space costs – recent research strongly suggests these costs have tended to be overestimated and after a certain size rise only slowly. Space costs rise with the size of a city only because it is worth paying extra to live or work there – that is because of the gain in productivity and higher incomes bigger cities generate. Workers and firms trade-off the productivity and amenity benefits of cities against these congestion costs when thinking about where to live, produce and work. Urban economics provides a powerful conceptual tool – spatial equilibrium – for thinking through the implications of these interactions for the development of the urban system as a whole.

The evidence shows that agglomeration economies are much more important in some economic sectors than in others: for example, they are some four times as important in financial or business services as in the manufacturing of wood products (Table 2.5); on average they are almost three times as important in services as in manufacturing. The sector where they are most critical of all seems to be public services: echoing one of the original functions of cities as centres of administration.

More generally, these sectoral differences in agglomeration economies make for one very powerful reason for urban resurgence – especially in larger cities and cities with more skilled and educated populations – seen over the last 20 years. The most rapidly growing sectors in advanced economies have a competitive edge in these locations. Unlike manufacturing, services and the public sector tend to use less physical space, so are relatively less constrained by higher land or property costs. With less need to ship raw materials and goods, they are also less affected by congestion – although their workforces need effective transport systems to commute.

Service activities have also differentially benefited from one of the most significant technical innovations of the past 25 years, the internet (Ioannides et al. 2008). Online technologies have hugely decreased the costs of finding and sharing information, and this has helped many service sector firms spread their businesses across multiple locations (McCann and Acs 2011). However, services also depend on face-to-face interaction: between firms and their customers and with their specialist suppliers (such as legal services, advertising or finance) and subcontractors. Cities, especially the largest urban cores, help keep these costs down by enabling contact and ideas flow on a grand scale.

Cities are places of culture and leisure, as well as centres of production. And just like workers' productivity, consumption of 'leisure goods' expands and becomes more rewarding with city size. As cities grow, the market for any given cultural activity grows with it: this allows specialisation and enhances choice. As Georg Simmel observed in 1903, city life supports multiple scenes, cliques and subcultures in which attention is part of the currency (Simmel 2013). Culture requires an audience: that is what a city provides. The larger the city (and the better its physical infrastructure), the larger audience it will generate. To put it more formally, choice of cultural pursuit and entertainment is both dependent on cities and is a positive function of their size.

As Chapters 2 and 3 acknowledge, the causes of urban resurgence are still not fully understood. In turn, this makes predicting urban futures a perilous business.[2] We can probably safely say that many of the economic changes we have been observing over the past 20 years are going to continue. Unless something fundamental changes, large-scale manufacturing will have almost no place in the economies of larger cities in rich countries in 2030, certainly not in their urban cores. Emerging technologies such as 3D printing are likely to accelerate this trend. Skills will be even more important than they are now, and economic penalties for the low-skilled will be even greater.

In Chapter 3 we examine how, within cities, the land, labour and housing markets all interact and generate fine-grained sorting between neighbourhoods. This process generates residential segregation, but at the same time, specialised neighbourhoods which often provide benefits to their residents. In some sense these are another manifestation of

---

[2] Many of the world's key cities are low-lying, coastal or both: they face increasing environmental uncertainty due to climate change. See Smith (2011) for an overview of these issues.

agglomeration economies – not in production but in consumption. In turn this has important implications for policies designed to produce 'mixed neighbourhoods'. They can have costs in both resource terms and perhaps in terms of one of the attractions cities offer – the ability (subject to income) to choose to live in congenial neighbourhoods with compatible neighbours. Recent evidence also increasingly suggests that policies to mix neighbourhoods may be wholly ineffective at reducing economic inequality. In essence, Chapters 2 and 3 make the case that a better understanding of how city economies function – in particular the importance of the three-way interaction between agglomeration benefits, congestion costs and the sorting of workers across cities and neighbourhoods within those cities – helps explain both how global trends play out spatially and the role that the spatial economy plays in driving national and global macro trends.

A key argument in this book is that urban policy needs to work better with the grain of markets. That does not mean letting markets rip: cities contain many endemic market failures, especially in land and property, where it is often in the wider social interest to override market signals. To do this effectively, however, implies building market signals into the underlying policy framework.

The second part of the book, Chapters 4–6, explores these issues in detail. Congestion and pollution are classic examples of market failure and this diagnosis suggests obvious solutions. The most obvious of all, congestion pricing, has not really been widely applied (certainly not in its 'pure' form with prices varying to reflect congestion levels) despite the politically brave effort of Ken Livingstone, the first modern London mayor. But as we argue in Chapters 4 and 5, some of the UK's most powerful urban policies have the unintentional effect of increasing the costs of urban size while at the same time constraining their growth. The incredible difference in prices across South East England between farmland and land on which it is permitted to build is in effect a signal of foregone agglomeration economies: people and firms would be willing to pay such prices to build if they could, both to gain access to income-earning locations and to popular places to live. In 2010 (the latest data at the time of writing), housing land in the South East was worth 430 times its value as farmland. On the fringes of London, that figure rises to 925 times. So these foregone agglomeration economies are likely to be large. Dealing with this problem in Britain, as elsewhere, will require radical reform of the planning system, a thorny problem that we deal with in some detail in Chapter 6.

In the third part of the book we turn to the governance of cities, and to the evaluation of urban policies. In the UK, one of the most centralised countries in the world, planning powers are part of the package of policy levers being slowly devolved from Whitehall to city leaders. Ministers hope that devolution will unleash urban economies in a way that helps to narrow spatial disparities. As Chapter 7 makes clear, however, the evidence of any link from governance to economic performance is weak, and international experience is rather mixed. In countries like the UK, there are good reasons to think that devolved governance can improve economic and social outcomes, as city leaders apply local knowledge and develop bespoke interventions. However, there is a real risk that communities with weaker or less experienced leaderships will become worse off, not better. In turn, this implies that central government will need to carefully manage the transition to localism.

Whatever the institutional architecture, improving urban policy requires a better understanding of the causes and consequences of uneven city performance. It requires us to be more realistic about policy ineffectiveness in the face of strong market forces that reinforce unevenness. And it requires us to focus much more on the impact of policy on people rather than places. The importance of cities in shaping the lives of billions makes urban policy vitally important, but as we discuss in Chapter 8, many popular urban policies either do little to achieve their stated aims or have unintended and counterproductive consequences. Our conclusions may appear discouraging. When dispassionately evaluated, the evidence suggests policy can in truth do relatively little to change the basic trajectory of underperforming urban areas, but misguided policies can have very bad unintended outcomes on all cities. In other words, governments have limited power to directly improve urban economies and a great deal of capacity to damage them. Hence, one of the key themes of this book is that policies need to be realistic about the causes of spatial disparities and the lack of effectiveness of many popular policies. In terms of causes, we argue that this means understanding that differences that may appear to be spatial are, in reality, often driven by differences between people rather than places. Realism about both causes and policy effectiveness does not mean there are not lots of very useful things policy can do but the useful things are often not so glamorous: efficient public administration, simple and transparent regulation, policies to reduce the costs that increase as cities get bigger.

Like all scholars, scientists or authors we have learned from and rely on the work of others. This is particularly true of this work. It started out as an attempt to edit the set of SERC *Policy Papers* into a coherent book form.[3] As we did this we found we had to update, discard and edit so much that it has evolved into an authored book. Some chapters had clear lead authors (Cheshire on 3, 4 and 6, Nathan on 7 and Overman on 8), one had

---

[3] http://www.spatialeconomics.ac.uk/SERC/publications/policy_papers.asp.

joint-leads (Nathan and Overman on 2) while we are jointly responsible for 1, 5 and 9. Getting to the final versions has, of course, involved substantial editing of each other's material throughout.

Large parts of the book draw heavily on – even use verbatim – many of the original *Policy Papers*. So we should particularly thank and apologise to the authors of those papers: Steve Gibbons, Ian Gordon, Patricia Rice and Paul Steeples who gave us permission to shamelessly plunder their work. We should also thank the numerous research officers and research assistants – mainly postgraduate students – who have worked on SERC projects. Most of all we should thank Kirsty Kenney, Teresa Schlueter and Sevrin Waights who have helped us directly with material and given outstanding editorial assistance. Finally we would like to acknowledge the inspiration provided by the work of Ed Glaeser. While many great scholars have contributed to the rapidly expanding body of urban economics research, Ed's boundless energy, economic insight and love of cities have been central to recent efforts to take insights from that research to a wider, non-specialist audience.

As with everything in life that is complex, there are few simple right or wrong answers when it comes to urban policy. We strongly believe that urban economics provides many pointers as to how the policy mix might be improved. But some of these recommendations are contentious. Indeed, there are a number of issues on which even we three authors disagree – on aspects of brownfield development and mixed communities policy, for instance – and where we have had to apply the principle of 'majority rule'.

Neither do we claim anything like perfect knowledge. Given the acknowledged gaps in the evidence base, some of these recommendations might not work, hence our emphasis on experimentation and rigorous evaluation to help inform the development of future urban policy.

REFERENCES

Bairoch, P. 1988. *Cities and Economic Development: From the Dawn of History to the Present.* Chicago, IL: University of Chicago Press.

Glaeser, Edward. 2011. *The Triumph of the City.* London: Pan Macmillan.

Hall, Peter. 1998. *Cities in Civilisation: Culture, Innovation and Urban Order.* London: Weidenfeld and Nicholson.

Hall, Peter. 2013. *Good Cities, Better Lives: How Europe Discovered the Lost Art of Urbanism.* Abingdon: Routledge.

Ioannides, Yannis M., Henry G. Overman, Esteban Rossi-Hansberg and Kurt Schmidheiny. 2008. 'The effect of information and communication technologies on urban structure'. *Economic Policy* 23, 201–242.

Jacobs, Jane. 1961. *The Death and Life of Great American Cities.* London: Pimlico.

Marshall, Alfred. 1918. *Principles of Economics*. New York: Macmillan.

McCann, Philip and Zoltan J. Acs. 2011. 'Globalization: countries, cities and multinationals'. *Regional Studies* 45, 17–32.

Moretti, Enrico. 2012. *The New Geography of Jobs*. Boston MA: Haughton Mifflin Harcourt.

Simmel, Georg. 2013. 'The Metropolis and Mental Life', in J. Lin and C. Mele (eds), *The Urban Sociology Reader*. Abingdon: Routledge.

Smith, Laurence. 2011. *The New North: The World in 2050*. London: Profile Books.

Storper, Michael. 2013. *Keys to the City: How Economics, Institutions, Social Interaction, and Politics Shape Development*. Princeton, NJ: Princeton University Press.

PART I

How do urban economies work? Theory and
evidence

2. Urban economic performance[1]

1. INTRODUCTION

As is well known, for the first time in history more than half of the world's population is now living in cities (UN Population Division 2010). But this apparently relentless global trend hides a much more nuanced picture for the world's more developed urban systems that are the broad focus of this book. As a closer look at the data makes clear, long-term urbanisation rates are broadly stable for more developed countries. But within many of these countries, the experience is one of recent urban resurgence after a long period of relative decline. Even then, this resurgence is often profoundly uneven within the urban system. Some cities are experiencing population growth and improved economic performance, especially those that have proved attractive to higher skilled workers or to industries that employ those workers: London and New York provide the premier examples. Other cities, particularly small industrial cities in the shadow of relatively more successful cities, continue to stagnate or decline. The experiences of Sunderland compared to Newcastle, or Charleroi relative to Brussels, provide good examples (Buck et al. 2004; Office of the Deputy Prime Minister 2006).

These disparities in urban economic performance have proved persistent and seemingly resistant to policymakers' attempts to reduce them. Clearly, understanding urban economic performance is central to improving our understanding of spatial disparities and the impact of policy. This chapter considers these issues, looking at spatial disparities in population, employment and wages and their causes – drawing on theory and evidence from Britain and around the world, though our focus is cities in more developed countries.

We argue that, as in other OECD countries, the recent economic performance of British cities is largely driven by two interconnected phenomena. First the long-term structural changes in Britain's international comparative advantage – driven by shocks in technology and trade, for example – has shifted Britain towards economic activities that tend to benefit more

---

[1] This chapter draws on Rice, P. and H.G. Overman (2008) Resurgent Cities and Regional Economic Performance, SERC Policy Paper No 1.

from urban locations. This is true of both the general shift from manufacturing to services, and of shifts within those broad categories. Second, at the same time as cities have become more important as places of production, they have also become more important as places of consumption. In particular, as consumption patterns in Britain (and other developed countries) have shifted towards 'experiences', cities have become important locations for retail and leisure activity, as well as high value production.

The fact that these structural shifts have tended to benefit more skilled workers means that these two changes have reinforced one another: successful cities have attracted higher-skilled workers, who in turn have helped make those places more successful. Indeed, as we explain below, these two factors help explain not only the resurgence of a number of British cities, most especially London, but also their resilience to the downturn and their likely economic future.

These trends highlight a crucial policy dilemma that is a main focus of this book. If the concentration of skilled workers in specific cities is key to driving both local and national economic performance, what can policy do to improve city economic performance across the urban system, and how should policy address the resulting trade-off between growth and 'spatial equity'? In the context of uneven city performance this trade-off occurs because stronger growth in some cities may be good for national growth, but at the same time may widen spatial disparities. This trade-off is sharpened further if policy can do little to address the problems faced by cities that continue to stagnate or decline. Historically, much of the literature on urban and regional policy has assumed away this dilemma by suggesting that spatial disparities are the results of inefficiencies – arising from both market and government failures – and that 'clever' policy mixes should be effective in improving the economic performance of struggling cities (Barlow Report 1940; Lipsey 1960; The National Economic Development Council 1963). In this version of the world, narrowing spatial disparities is both possible and also good for growth. But recent economic performance, as well as new research, is making both academics and policymakers question these traditional assumptions.

The situation is often further complicated (as in Britain) by the unevenness of city performance – even for cities such as Manchester and Liverpool in the North West of England, that are both geographically close and have strong economic links (for example large commuting flows). In short, while cities per se might play an important role in raising national economic growth, the relative performance of different cities will determine both (i) what happens to the gap in growth rates between the poorest and richest sub-national regions and (ii) what happens to spatial disparities within those regions.

Of course, this policy dilemma may be eased if government interventions can easily improve economic performance in struggling cities. Unfortunately, as we discuss below (and in more detail in Chapter 8) this does not appear to be the case, at least for policy interventions that have historically proved popular with policymakers. As a result, improved national economic performance may come at a cost in terms of widening spatial disparities either at national or regional level. We argue that effectively addressing this trade-off will require greater policy focus on managing both decline and growth and on the implications for individual welfare rather than 'average' area outcomes.

In short, our main arguments are that a combination of market forces and relative policy effectiveness mean that it is difficult (if not impossible) for policymakers to erase spatial disparities, and 'turn around' the performance of 'struggling' places. However, as we argue below, the spatial disparities inherent in urban systems should be seen as a second order problem relative to the first order issue of the implications for individual welfare and what, if anything, policy can do to address any negative effect on the latter. That is, discussions of urban policy should focus first and foremost on the impact of policy on people, not places. After all, the ultimate objective of (most) urban policy is surely to improve the lives of current and future populations.

The need for realism in the face of strong market forces that drive unevenness, the ineffectiveness of many urban growth policies and the importance of focusing on outcomes for people not places are the three central themes that run through the chapters that follow. Those chapters provide more rigorous evidence to underpin the basic arguments presented here and show how they apply to different policy areas and at different spatial scales.

2. RESURGENCE, PERSISTENCE AND RESILIENCE (THE GEOGRAPHY OF POPULATION, WAGES AND EMPLOYMENT)

This section describes the recent demographic and economic performance of British cities and provides international comparisons where appropriate. We start by discussing population trends over the last two decades. Urban economists often use population as a good summary statistic for capturing the overall economic performance of cities drawing on the idea that 'good places to live' will tend to attract population, while 'bad places to live' will tend to lose population (see Glaeser (2008) for further discussion). As we will discuss further in Chapters 4 and 5, in many places

Urban economics and urban policy

Table 2.1   Population growth rates for largest British cities (1991–2011)

TTWA	Population 1991	Growth 1991–2001 (%)	Growth 2001–2011 (%)	Growth 1991–2011 (%)
London	7,676,415	7.2	13.1	21.2
Manchester	1,760,141	−1.0	9.3	8.2
Birmingham	1,573,515	0.5	7.9	8.4
Glasgow	1,162,786	−2.2	2.0	−0.2
Newcastle & Durham	1,079,425	−0.2	4.4	4.2
Liverpool	989,147	−2.1	1.4	−0.7
Bristol	829,461	5.1	9.2	14.8
Leeds	827,607	5.6	5.3	11.2
Sheffield & Rotherham	785,178	1.1	6.0	7.1
Warrington & Wigan	761,219	0.0	4.2	4.2
Leicester	740,319	6.4	10.7	17.8
Nottingham	725,927	2.9	7.5	10.6
Cardiff	671,493	3.8	7.9	12.0
Guildford & Aldershot	668,034	5.2	5.9	11.4
Luton & Watford	622,530	5.4	8.3	14.1
Edinburgh	574,904	6.6	6.1	13.1
Southampton	570,364	10.2	7.1	18.0
Portsmouth	562,833	3.5	6.6	10.4
Southend & Brentwood	552,893	1.2	6.0	7.3
Maidstone & North Kent	530,916	4.5	9.4	14.2
Stoke-on-Trent	515,902	−0.1	3.2	3.1
Coventry	508,188	3.0	5.0	8.2
Wycombe & Slough	506,171	3.9	8.5	12.7
Great Britain	54,854,179	4.1	7.5	11.9

Notes: Authors' own calculations based on Census data for 1991, 2001 and 2011.

(including Britain) this relationship can be distorted by planning restrictions that mean popular places may end up expensive, rather than big. With this caveat in mind, however, population trends illustrate many of the features of the British urban system that we highlighted in the introduction.

Table 2.1 reports population for the largest British Travel to Work Areas (TTWA) with a population above 500,000 in 1991.[2] Official

[2] TTWA are areas constructed so that 75 per cent of the resident population work within the same area and 75 per cent of the jobs are taken by workers who live in the area. They are designed to capture 'local' labour markets and provide an approximation to US style Metropolitan Statistical Areas.

population data for TTWAs are not available, so we constructed these using Census data from 1991 to 2011 for smaller areas aggregated to the TTWA level. The figures for Britain as a whole appear in the final row.

Several messages emerge from these figures. The first is the overall improvement in the fortunes of the largest TTWA in the decade to 2011 relative to the period 1991–2001.[3] All of these cities recorded positive population growth rates in the second period, in marked contrast to the earlier decade when many saw their population stagnate or even decline. In terms of individual cities, second period growth rates were higher than first period (sometimes significantly so, for example Manchester), with three exceptions (Leeds, Edinburgh and Southampton) seeing falls from relatively high positive growth rates in the first period. Admittedly, all of this comes against a background of higher population growth overall, but a majority of cities saw increases that exceeded that overall increase (either in relative or absolute terms). In short, the last decade has seen relatively strong absolute and relative population growth in Britain's largest cities, in marked contrast to the previous decade.

Another message to emerge clearly from Table 2.1 is that, despite overall higher population growth, growth rates continue to differ markedly across cities. For example, contrast Liverpool's 1.4 per cent growth rate in the second period to London's 13.1 per cent. This is not just a London versus the rest, or a north–south, phenomenon. As we suggested in the introduction, growth rates can differ quite considerably between cities located quite close to one another. Table 2.2 provides some comparisons for selected cities to highlight this pattern. Over the two decades from 1991 to 2011, Birmingham saw overall population growth of 8.4 per cent while nearby Stoke-on-Trent experienced only 3.1 per cent growth. The contrast for Manchester and Liverpool is even more striking. While the former experienced population growth of 8.2 per cent over the two decades, the latter saw its population decline over the same period. Similarly, Newcastle experienced 4.2 per cent growth while nearby Sunderland experienced a cumulative 4.8 per cent decline. In short, there is considerable diversity in terms of the recent population growth experience across British cities, even for neighbouring cities within the same region. As we show below, this diversity of experience is also evident for other economic indicators such as employment growth.

---

[3] Just as – all British modesty aside – one of the authors predicted back in 1995 (Cheshire, 1995). A careful analysis of changing patterns of urban development across Western Europe as a whole between 1971 and 1991 provided evidence that the impact on the cities of Northern Europe of what was then called 'de-industrialisation' was coming to an end and, in London, effectively had ended. The importance of the growing service sector was already apparent in many skill-rich cities.

Table 2.2　Varying population growth rates for 'neighbouring' cities

	Region	Population 2011	1991– 2001 (%)	2001– 2011 (%)	1991– 2011 (%)
Great Britain		61,371,315	4.1	7.5	11.9
London		9,307,182	7.2	13.1	21.2
Birmingham	West Midlands	1,706,466	0.5	7.9	8.4
Stoke-on-Trent	West Midlands	531,741	−0.1	3.2	3.1
Manchester	North West	1,904,901	−1.0	9.3	8.2
Liverpool	North West	981,848	−2.1	1.4	−0.7
Newcastle	North East	1,125,206	−0.2	4.4	4.2
Sunderland	North East	367,374	−3.5	−1.3	−4.8
Leeds	Yorkshire	920,267	5.6	5.3	11.2
Sheffield	Yorkshire	841,191	1.1	6.0	7.1
Grimsby	Yorkshire	200,387	0.2	2.2	2.4
Leicester	East Midlands	872,418	6.4	10.7	17.8
Nottingham	East Midlands	802,737	2.9	7.5	10.6
Cambridge	East of England	435,178	13.0	14.1	28.9
Southend	East of England	593,054	1.2	6.0	7.3
Oxford	South East	499,515	12.3	7.8	21.0
Portsmouth	South East	621,143	3.5	6.6	10.4
Southampton	South East	673,104	10.2	7.1	18.0
Bristol	South West	952,175	5.1	9.2	14.8
Plymouth	South West	373,403	1.4	5.6	7.0
Cardiff	Wales	751,976	3.8	7.9	12.0
Newport	Wales	345,996	2.3	4.7	7.1
Edinburgh	Scotland	650,178	6.6	6.1	13.1
Glasgow	Scotland	1,160,555	−2.2	2.0	−0.2

Notes:　Authors' own calculations based on Census data for 1991, 2001 and 2011.

Comparing growth rates for 1991–2001 and 2001–2011 across cities in both Tables 2.1 and 2.2 suggest a final stylised fact – relative performance is quite persistent across the two decades. Figure 2.1, which plots growth rates in the second decade against growth rates in the first, illustrates this point more clearly. Cities with relatively high population growth rates in 1991–2001 tend to have higher population growth rates in 2001–2011. There is certainly some variation in relative positions, but the correlation coefficient at 0.6 is high and significant.

In demographic terms, then, British cities show resurgence (that is a move from weak to stronger population growth), divergence (that is a diversity of performance) and persistence (that is high positive correlation

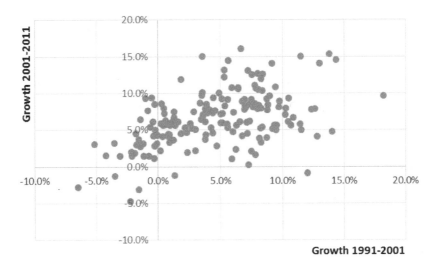

Notes: Relative population growth rates for all TTWA with population greater than 100,000. *Data source:* as for Tables 2.1 and 2.2.

Figure 2.1   Persistence in population growth rates 1991–2001, 2001–2011

in relative growth rates). As we now show, the same broad picture holds for wages and employment too, both in the short term and over long periods.

We start with resurgence where data availability means that long run evidence is, sadly, fairly limited. Champion and Townsend (2009) do provide some evidence on employment growth for a long time period, but for only a small selection of cities: specifically, the eight English 'core cities' between 1984 and 2007. The core cities – Newcastle, Leeds, Sheffield, Manchester, Liverpool, Nottingham, Birmingham and Bristol – comprise the largest English conurbations outside London. These cities added 963,000 full-time equivalent (FTE) jobs over these two decades, and as Table 2.3 shows, with accelerating job growth in the late 1990s, a period of physical, demographic and economic renaissance in many urban cores (Nathan and Urwin 2006). As the table also shows, however, despite an improvement, employment growth in the largest (core) cities has been generally below the national level, and behind job growth in London.

We have much better evidence on the other two trends evident in the population data – large spatial variation in performance and high persistence over time. Indeed, at the regional level, we have some quite long run evidence of persistence. For example, Table 2.4, drawn from

Table 2.3   Annual FTE employment rate change in large urban areas,
1984–2007

	1984– 2007	1984– 1989	1989– 1993	1993– 1998	1998– 2002	2002– 2007
Birmingham CR	0.31	0.71	−2.39	2.05	0.38	0.28
Bristol CR	1.20	2.03	−1.02	1.55	2.77	0.53
Leeds CR	0.82	1.45	−1.32	1.57	1.39	0.69
Liverpool CR	−0.04	−0.31	−1.84	−0.13	1.84	0.24
Manchester CR	0.60	1.26	−1.73	1.24	1.20	0.70
Newcastle CR	0.51	0.01	−0.68	0.80	1.51	0.87
Nottingham CR	0.42	0.66	−2.08	1.78	−0.52	1.59
Sheffield CR	0.21	−0.32	−2.50	1.31	0.79	1.35
All 8 CRs	0.50	0.75	−1.75	1.36	1.11	0.70
London CR	0.64	0.53	−2.78	3.10	1.07	0.70
Rest of England	1.16	1.91	−1.52	2.51	1.01	1.34
England	*0.81*	*1.15*	*−1.94*	*2.52*	*1.06*	*0.97*

Notes: Unless otherwise specified, units are city-regions (CRs). Employment covers all
sectors except farming, forestry and fishing. Changes expressed as compound rate.

Source: Champion and Townsend (2009).

Table 2.4   Persistence of regional unemployment differentials: correlation
over time

Date	UK	Germany	Italy	France	Japan	USA
1980	0.98	0.92	0.91	0.93	0.95	0.32
1975	0.92	0.54	0.87	0.46	0.91	−0.21
1970	0.86	0.40	0.89	. . .	. . .	0.29
1965	0.75	0.21	0.19	. . .	0.88	0.19
		1994 with 1980				
	0.77	0.85	0.88	0.66	. . .	0.39

Note: Rank order correlations of regional unemployment rates in each year with
corresponding rates in 1987. Some historical data series are incomplete.

Source: Armstrong and Taylor (2000).

Armstrong and Taylor (2000), shows the correlation of five-year regional
unemployment differences in the UK and five other advanced economies
over a 30-year period. We can see that in almost all cases, differences in
regional unemployment rates are highly persistent. In the US, the relative

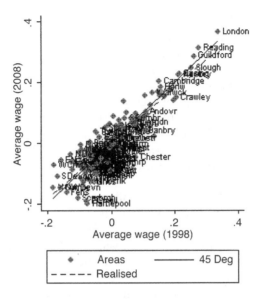

Horizontal axis shows area wages relative to mean area in 1998. Vertical axis
shows relative wages for 2008. Data is from the Annual Survey of Hours and Earnings.
Further details are provided in Gibbons et al. (2010).

Figure 2.2   Persistence of wages, 1998–2008

lack of persistence may be explained by higher levels of internal labour
mobility (Blanchard and Katz 1992). Other analysts have looked further
back in time; writing in the mid-1970s, Cheshire (1973) finds that regional
unemployment disparities across the UK were largely unchanged since the
1920s.

At the city level, evidence on persistence is generally available for a
shorter time period. For example, Figure 2.2 taken from Gibbons et al.
(2010) compares hourly wages across British TTWA in 1998 and 2008
and shows both substantial variation, as well as little change in relative
positions over time. The figure is constructed so that if there had been
no change at all in wage disparities, areas would fall along the 45-degree
line. The dashed line showing what actually happened to relative wages
suggests that there may have been some slight convergence – although in
practice this is indistinguishable from 'churn', or reversion to the mean.
This certainly should not detract attention from the most striking features,
which are the large variation across space and the high persistence over
time.

As with regional unemployment disparities, these large, and persistent, local differences in wages can be found in a number of other countries. European studies, such as Combes et al. (2008) for France, Groot and De Groot (2011) for the Netherlands, and Mion and Naticchioni (2009) for Italy – also highlight similar findings. In the US, Moretti (2010) reports that average nominal wages for high school graduates vary by 60 per cent between the 1st and 99th percentiles of the distribution of metro areas; for college graduates the difference is 112 per cent, almost twice as large. Further, these wage gaps have been visible since the 1980s; there has been no sign of mean reversion, and if anything they have risen slightly over this period.

Outcomes for employment show similar spatial variation and time series persistence. Employment also tends to be higher in places with higher wages. In other words, employment and wages are positively correlated. Indeed, it is this positive link between wages and employment that leads economists to conclude that city size must confer some productivity benefit. Of course, a positive correlation between high employment levels and wages could still be consistent with a negative correlation between employment rates and wages if unemployment or participation tended to be worse in large cities. Figure 2.3 shows, however, that this is not the case. While it is true that London has a relatively low employment rate given its very high wages, this turns out to be the exception rather than the rule: wages, employment and employment rates are all positively correlated. Notice, too, that the figure shows, once again, that there is high variation across cities: employment rates vary from just over 60 per cent of the working age population (Hartlepool) to just under 80 per cent (Gloucester, Aberdeen).

It seems unlikely that the recent recession will significantly affect these long-run trends – historically, recessions and other shocks to the business cycle do not appear to undo these spatial differences. Indeed, as Jackman and Savouri (1992, 1996) point out, if anything recessions generally tend to widen area disparities. In Britain specifically, while this was not the case in the 1989–92 recession and the 2000–01 dotcom downturn which hit London and the South East hardest; these appear to have been exceptions to the rule. Given that the most recent recession's origins were in financial markets, there were predictions that London's labour markets would be hardest hit this time too (see, for example, MoneyWeek 2007; Drury 2008; *Financial Times* 2008; Seager 2008; Stewart et al. 2008). In fact, London – relatively speaking – 'got away with it', with smaller UK cities and communities experiencing much greater economic shocks (Overman 2011). Average wages in the capital fell 2.5 per cent in 2008–09, well below the national average (with only the North West and North East experiencing smaller falls). Employment shocks to the major conurbations have been

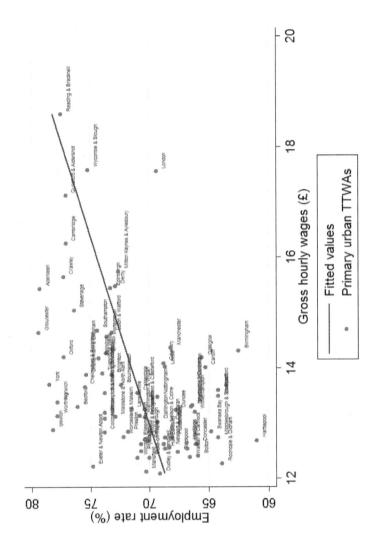

Notes: Nominal wage data comes from ASHE and is aggregated to TTWAs using postcode weighting. Employment rate data comes from the Annual Population Survey. Urban and non-urban TTWAs organised as above.

Figure 2.3 Average wages and employment rates, primary urban TTWAs, 2012

substantially worse than for London: between 2007 and 2010 the core cities (and Glasgow) lost over 320,000 FTE jobs – a drop of 4.9 per cent, compared with 2.2 per cent for London over the same period, and 3.5 per cent for Britain as a whole (Champion and Townsend 2012). The big conurbations outside London also experienced the highest rises in claimant unemployment during this period (Lee et al. 2010).

To summarise, after a period of decline a number of British cities have seen much improved growth rates – both economic and demographic. This 'resurgence' has not been felt in all cities, however, and the data show considerable variation even for cities that are geographically close. Further, wages and employment (both levels and rates) tend to move together so that the highest wage places also have the highest employment and vice-versa. These wage and employment differences have also proved remarkably persistent, even in the face of large macroeconomic shocks. Most, if not all, of these trends would be repeated in many developed countries and provide the overall context for everything that follows.

3.   UNDERSTANDING SPATIAL DISPARITIES

One possible explanation of these features of the urban system is that they are simply the local manifestation of national and international forces. Certainly, we know that a number of deep trends have influenced recent wage and employment movements in Britain and other countries. First, the past few decades have seen substantial shifts in labour demand, driven both by technological progress and by an increasingly open world economy (see *inter alia* Krugman 1997; Storper 1997; Goldin and Katz 2010; McCann and Acs 2011; Moretti 2012). These type of structural evolutions in national economies are not new – over many years economists such as Bowley (1930), Beveridge (1936) and Brown (1969) have argued that regional labour market differences in Britain owe much to industrial transformation and changes in international comparative advantage.

As part of this shift, skill-biased technical change has helped push up wages and employment for higher-skilled workers, while directly decreasing the demand for lower-skilled workers (Nickell and Bell 1995; Autor et al. 2003; Goldin and Katz 2010). Most manufacturing and logistics firms in Britain are now highly efficient, but much less labour-intensive; some lower-value manufacturing and service activity has been relocated to cheaper locations, both in the UK and abroad (Sako 2006). The process of structural economic change – or de-industrialisation – may create its own labour market challenges: losing a major employer will have knock-on effects in the rest of the local economy. And for some ex-industrial workers, there is clear evidence that the long-term scarring effects of unemployment will make it harder to get new jobs (see for example Beveridge 1936; Blanchard and Summers 1987; Gallie and Paugam 2000; or Martin 2012).

Second, profound changes in labour market institutions have occurred alongside these structural shifts. Goos and Manning (2007) highlight a number of factors that have produced labour market polarisation in Britain. The growth of part-time and temporary employment, weaker labour unions and labour market deregulation have helped loosen established wage structures, as well as changing the patterns and quality of employment experiences for those in entry-level and intermediate activities. So-called 'lousy' jobs may be less attractive to low-skilled workers; and there are some suggestions that net immigration is linked to these shifts, with some employers increasingly depending on migrant workers to fill less skilled entry-level positions (Wills et al. 2010).

Third, many of these long-term shifts may also be amplified by shorter-term shocks in the business cycle. Some commentators already worry that the recent recession has reduced younger workers' employability, especially in the places most affected (Lee et al. 2010). A combination of public and private sector pay restraint, plus rising commodity costs, has been eroding living standards across the country (Resolution Foundation 2012). Short-term national policy decisions may also have unintended local impacts. The UK government's 2009 bailout of UK banks saved the big five banks around £107bn interest costs (Haldane 2010). Since banks (and banking jobs) are disproportionately concentrated in London, it seems plausible that this helped cushion parts of London's labour market – although it seems highly unlikely that this fully explains London's relatively strong performance in the last recession (Overman 2011).

These 'big picture' changes have had profound effects at the local level. From the 1950s onwards, cities were declining, with counter-urbanisation the dominant trend (Champion and Townsend 2012). Now, these global shifts have given new impetus to urban development and, as discussed above, triggered new interest in the 'resurgent city'. More service-dominated economies have increased the economic importance of larger cities and led to new layers of urbanised 'knowledge economy' activity (see, for example, Glaeser (2011), McCann and Acs (2011) and Moretti (2012) for detailed discussions of these issues).

Spatial economics and economic geography also help us to see how spatial factors can both influence and be influenced by these trends (Massey 1984; Fujita et al. 1999). This implies that understanding the inter-relationship between global and local factors requires us to understand the underlying spatial drivers of city growth and urban economic performance.

Economic activity is very unevenly distributed across space. It is inconceivable that this marked unevenness can be explained by appealing purely to inherent differences in physical geography (for example climate or natural resources). Instead, it must be that, over time, the workings of the economic system amplify and reinforce differences to generate historically persistent patterns of spatial disparity. For this to happen there must be self-reinforcing benefits from the spatial concentration of activity. Spatial economists and economic geographers identify a number of possible mechanisms that may give rise to these agglomeration economies (or externalities) (Marshall 1918; Jacobs 1969). In a world of economies of scale in production and trade costs, firms reduce their costs by producing at larger scales close to their larger markets. Locating close to other firms also allows the sharing of large fixed costs, for example in providing infrastructure such as ports and airports. Added to this, large markets often operate more efficiently than small markets. For example, locating with other firms helps facilitate access to intermediate goods needed in production. Similarly, the larger the pool of labour that a firm can access, the more likely it is to find skills that precisely match its production requirements. At the same time, workers are more willing to invest in acquiring specialist skills if they are able to access many potential users of these skills. Finally, knowledge spillovers – through labour mobility, by face-to-face social contact between workers, or by observing the practices of other firms – are easier between proximate firms than remote ones. (Duranton and Puga (2004) summarise these channels respectively as 'sharing', 'matching' and 'learning' economies.) What evidence there is indicates that these agglomeration economies operate over relatively small spatial scales, favouring dense, highly urbanised environments (Rice et al. 2006; Graham 2007; Arzaghi and Henderson 2008).

Of course, there are a number of costs from agglomeration that work to offset these benefits. As economic activity concentrates, the price of scare resources, notably land, increases. The greater number of firms increases competition and reduces profitability. Finally there are the negative externalities associated with greater congestion of roads and public transport and increased pollution. In a modern economy, it is the trade-off between these costs and benefits that determines which areas are rich and which are poor; which grow fast and which grow slowly; and how activities shift within areas, from cores to peripheries and vice-versa (Fujita et al. 1999).

Technological progress, international economic integration, national and international policy and a whole host of other factors, lead to changes in these costs and benefits, and hence the nature of this trade-off. The response to these changes is not instantaneous but rather plays out over many years as people and organisations slowly adjust to the different forces at work. There are also important dynamic components: geographic concentration is often characterised by feedback loops and path-dependence, so that existing agglomerations often have first-mover advantage (Krugman and Obstfeld 2003). The combination of technological innovations and sectoral responses can also produce discontinuities or 'jumps', for example from higher to lower cost regions (Venables 2006). These might be driven by underlying structural changes but are often hard to predict, introducing apparently random elements in the evolution of urban systems.

How does this evidence on the underlying drivers of city growth refine our understanding of the way in which global structural trends are changing the economic geography of Britain? One crucial link arises because the extent to which different activities benefit from agglomeration economies (that is the productivity benefits of being located in larger urbanised environments) varies considerably across sectors. If structural shifts in the economy move us towards activities that benefit more from agglomeration economies then we would expect to see significant growth in cities that are relatively specialised in those activities, accompanied by decline elsewhere. That is, this shift can help us understand both resurgence and divergence within the urban system. The shift from manufacturing to services provide an important example of one such change because, as shown in Table 2.5 and documented in, for example, Graham (2007) and Combes et al. (2008), service industries generally benefit much more than manufacturing from agglomeration economies. As the table shows, when weighting by employment service sector activity has an agglomeration elasticity that is roughly three times that of manufacturing. Exceptions to this general trend tend to be either high technology manufacturing industries (such as manufacture of radio, television and communications equipment) or low-tech or transport-intensive service industries (such as wholesale and retailing).

Thus, variations in the role of agglomeration economies help determine how shifts in the overall structure of the economy play out across the urban system. At the same time, however, changes in agglomeration economies also drive change in the structure of the economy as a whole – reinforcing growth in particular cities (and decline in others). For example, the general rise in skill levels has increased the benefits to employers and workers of locating in 'thick' labour markets (offering lots of diverse opportunities either in terms of different occupations or in terms of different employers within the same occupation). This effect is compounded by the greater prevalence of dual-earner households in which two adults are seeking skilled employment. As highlighted by Costa and Kahn

Table 2.5   Agglomeration economies for different types of activities

Industry group	Agglomeration elasticity
Manufacturing	
Manufacture of food products and beverages	0.084
Manufacture of wood and wood products	0.069
Publishing, printing and reproduction of media	0.105
Manufacture of radio, television and communication	0.382
Employment weighted average *all* manufacturing	0.077
Services	
Wholesale and retail	0.041
Hotels and restaurants	0.224
Transport services	0.325
Finance and insurance	0.251
Real estate	0.034
Business and management consultancy	0.298
Architecture and engineering	0.066
Advertising	0.137
Public services	0.292
Motion picture, video and TV	0.222
Employment weighted average *all* services	0.197

Notes: The table reports urbanisation agglomeration economies (that is based on effective density of all activity) that are estimated as positive and significant in the UK. Based on Tables 2 and 4 in Graham (2007). The averages are employment weighted averages based on all industry groupings. Based on these weighted averages, one can see that the shift in the UK economy from manufacturing to service activities increases the importance of agglomeration economies.

(2000), these effects become particularly important for so called 'power-couples' – households where two highly educated workers both want to develop specific careers (rather than simply find employment). For such couples, very large cities like London and New York provide far more opportunities likely to satisfy both partners' career aspirations. Other changes have contributed to a strengthening of agglomeration effects including the shift from rail to road and the increasing use of information communication technologies. See Cheshire (1995), Overman and Leunig (2008) and Ioannides et al. (2008) for further discussion and evidence. Clearly changes to congestion costs (that work to offset agglomeration benefits) have similar effects. London's new 'Crossrail' east–west transport link, for example, will reduce congestion costs and increase agglomeration economies in London and we might expect similar effects in Liverpool, Manchester, Sheffield and Leeds for the 'Northern Hub' rail package.

Finally, if cities offer economies of production to firms, they also offer economies of consumption to residents – that is, access to a critical mass and variety of goods, services and experiences in a small area. In the UK and US, recent centre-city repopulation suggests a growing appetite – at least among the young and single – for such 'city living' experiences (Nathan and Urwin 2006; Unsworth and Nathan 2006). As Storper and Manville (2006) point out, alongside the preferences of firms – the focus of most research on agglomeration economies – we also need to consider 'the preferences of people'. An increasing number of empirical studies do this: Glaeser et al. (2001) provide some suggestive evidence that the success of cities hinges more and more on their roles as centres of consumption while Glaeser and Gottlieb (2006), notably model cities as gigantic 'romantic markets' for future partners. The role of increased variety and choice in terms of the characteristics of neighbourhoods to live in, the amenities that they have to offer and how this increases with city size is discussed in Chapter 3.

Taken together, it is these shifts that most likely explain much of the growth that we are seeing in successful cities. Indeed, these factors may well continue to drive growth in these cities as the economy continues to shift towards sectors that benefit more from agglomeration economies at the same time as these agglomeration economies themselves continue to strengthen. Note that while these forces may, on average, increase the importance of urban economies, they are likely to play out rather differently in different locations within the urban system, as the data in section 2 suggests is happening in Britain. There are also important country-level differences even in geographically close regions (see Dijkstra et al. (2012) for a recent discussion of urbanisation and counter-urbanisation in EU member states, for example).

Economic theory also implies that at some population size, the benefits to economic actors from further increases in population and economic activity in more successful cities will be outweighed by the higher costs of scarce resources, particularly land, congestion and pollution. However, recent evidence from Combes et al. (2012) suggest that, at least for French cities, costs increase fairly slowly with city size so the point at which costs exceed benefits may be consistent with very large cities. This point need not even be stable if, for example, agglomeration economies continue to strengthen and smart technologies and other infrastructure investments continue to mitigate the costs of growth. If these findings generalise to Britain, then the changes that we have described above may be consistent with continued growth for more successful cities for some time to come.

To summarise, the recent economic performance of British cities is largely driven by two interconnected phenomena. First, as in other rich countries, long-term structural changes have shifted Britain towards economic activities that tend to benefit more from urban locations. At the same time, agglomeration economies have strengthened for some of these activities more than others. Second, cities have also become more important as places of consumption. As we said in the introduction, the fact that these structural shifts have tended to benefit more skilled workers means that these two changes have reinforced one another: successful cities have attracted higher skilled workers, who in turn have helped make those places more successful.

4.   DECOMPOSING SPATIAL DISPARITIES

If spatial disparities are partly the result of the clustering of highly skilled workers and agglomeration benefits from geographical concentration working in tandem, this raises a further set of questions about the mechanisms through which those interactions take place. Economic theory suggests a number of channels that connect urban agglomeration to individual outcomes – which in turn help to explain clustering of highly skilled workers and area-level outcomes. For example, urban areas support innovative activity by individuals and firms: in part this operates through cities' economic diversity, which provides entrepreneurs and companies with good access to a rich set of activities, suppliers and collaborators, and facilitates both new ideas and the recombination of existing ideas. As Jane Jacobs put it, these features of cities help their citizens generate 'new work' – both new employment and high-value, well-paid new roles (Jacobs 1969; Moretti 2012). Equally, big cities can act as 'nurseries' to start-ups and entrepreneurs, helping them convert new ideas into new businesses (Duranton and Puga 2001). In turn, these benefits to entrepreneurs, inventors and skilled workers encourage these groups to relocate to the most innovation-friendly urban areas.

Theoretical work on these channels is still in relative infancy; empirical analysis is more developed, and it is to this that we now turn. One way to understand the relative contribution of agglomeration benefits and sorting of skilled workers to real world disparities is to 'decompose' them. Specifically, researchers explore how far local variation in employment and wages boils down to differences between people (in the same place), or to differences between places (Gibbons et al. 2010; Gibbons and Overman 2012; Combes et al. 2008). We refer to the first of these as 'sorting' of individuals, and the second as 'area effects'.

How would these two effects work in practice? Our individual skills, capabilities and experience clearly play an important part in our chances of finding employment, the type of work we can get and the wage we can hope to earn (Combes et al. 2008). But this may not be the whole story. Both spatial economic theory and intuition tell us that jobs and job opportunities are concentrated in and around urban areas. As the previous section has made clear, exogenous differences between urban and rural locations – such as physical features or climate – cannot fully explain this (Moretti 2010). Agglomeration economies evidently have important roles to play too, as in the innovation example sketched out above.

All of which means that individual sorting and area effects are not easy to identify separately. For one thing, as already discussed, the benefits of agglomeration vary substantially across and within industries – we know, for example, that much service sector activity is more location-sensitive than manufacturing activity, not least because job roles vary in their need for face-to-face interaction (Charlot and Duranton 2004; Venables 2006; Combes et al. 2009). So an area's industry and occupational mix may vary a great deal, with implications for employment mix and salary levels (see Melo et al. (2009) for UK empirics on this). For another, people tend to 'sort' across space to take advantage of opportunities, so that more able workers may select into the more productive markets for them.

There is substantial empirical evidence that agglomeration economies do influence productivity, and thus wages and employment levels at urban and regional levels (see Combes et al. (2008) and Melo et al. (2009) for the UK, Rosenthal and Strange (2004) for the US, Mion and Naticchioni (2009) for Italy and De La Roca and Puga (2011) for Spain among many others). Once these area-level differences are explored in more detail, two distinct, but closely related points emerge. First, most of the individual disparities are directly explained by individual differences rather than area effects. For example, in analysis for the Spatial Economics Research Centre (SERC) Gibbons et al. (2010) using data from 1998–2008, find that area effects explain less than 1 per cent of Britain's overall wage variation. Put simply, labour market disparities are explained much more by who you are than by where you live.

Second, although who you are is the most important factor, where you live does also influence what you earn and possibly how fast your income grows over time. This is why workers in cities tend to earn more than their identically skilled, non-urban counterparts (Glaeser and Maré 2001). In short, as theory and empirical evidence both suggest, area characteristics, individual characteristics and individual sorting, all interact to influence future area disparities.

These results confirm previous analysis for the UK: for example Duranton and Monastiriotis (2002) found that regional wage inequality in the UK was largely driven by differences in individual skills and education levels. They also echo a number of other international studies: for example, Baum-Snow and Pavan (2012) for the US, Combes et al. (2008) for France and Groot and De Groot (2011) for the Netherlands all find individual skills explain the largest part of local wage differences, but that agglomeration effects also play a role.

5.   SPATIAL EQUILIBRIUM, LINKAGES, CONSEQUENCES

The idea that interaction between agglomeration benefits, congestion costs and the geographic concentration of different types of firms and workers help explain urban economic performance is one of the fundamental insights of spatial economics. A second central idea – the concept of 'spatial equilibrium' – allows us to think through the implications of this interaction for the urban system as a whole. Spatial equilibrium is achieved when households and firms are indifferent between locations. This is a useful concept because it helps us think through how people and firms sort across cities as they trade off wages, amenities and the local costs of living and producing. Underpinning this concept is the highly reasonable assumption that – at least in equilibrium and given the costs of moving – people and firms will move until they cannot improve their conditions by living somewhere else. A crucial implication of such a spatial equilibrium is that differences in nominal wages and costs are a basic feature of the system – since higher wages in one city can be balanced by a higher cost of living in that place and/or worse local public goods, environmental quality or amenities.

There is some empirical support for these predictions: for instance, Gibbons et al. (2011) show that for Britain real wage differences (that is nominal wages adjusted for living costs) are substantially lower than nominal wage disparities. Does this mean that policymakers do not need to worry about the impact that spatial disparities have on inequality? Not necessarily. In practice, adjustments towards spatial equilibrium do not tend to run smoothly (Storper 2011; Partridge et al. 2012). Conditions in some areas will adjust faster than others: the experience of many British cities in the 1980s and 1990s suggests that industrial change and its aftereffects can take many years to work through urban labour markets. Firms may face informational and financial constraints; or managers may choose to locate in (say) prestigious rather than objectively optimal locations (Helmers 2010). Labour mobility is also imperfect: some groups may face informational and financial barriers to moving; others' family circumstances and ties may also reduce mobility. In the UK and Europe levels of mobility between cities are lower than in the US,[4] but even in the latter there is evidence that internal labour flows are slowing, so that labour market adjustment is becoming 'stickier' (Dustmann et al. 2008; Molloy et al. 2011; Partridge et al. 2012).[5]

These caveats aside, thinking about the urban 'system' when agents are free to move between places raises the broader question of what determines the nature of the economic linkages between places. These linkages work through three main channels. First, firms buy and sell goods and services across space. Second, workers can live in one place and commute to work in another place. Third, workers and firms can move between places. A general analysis of the implications of these channels for the nature of linkages between places is beyond the scope of this chapter. But it is useful to think through their implications in the specific circumstances where a major economic shock – of the kind outlined in section 3 – hits the spatial economy, or where policymakers seek to influence urban economic development.

The role of supply and demand linkages between firms has been emphasised by proponents of the New Economic Geography (Fujita et al. 1999; Combes et al. 2005 and Moretti 2010). Imagine that a major technological innovation raises the productivity of workers in an industry clustered in a particular city (call it city A). If we ignore, for the moment, the possibility that firms and workers can move between locations then expanding the number of firms operating in city A has two contrasting effects on firms elsewhere. To the extent that these new or expanded firms increase their demand for goods and services from elsewhere, this will provide a positive linkage between places. At the same time, lower production costs and increased competition among firms in city A may lead to cheaper sources of inputs for firms located in other parts of the region. Again, this effect will provide a positive linkage between places. However, if these new or expanded firms compete for customers with firms located elsewhere then this will work in the opposite direction and imply a negative linkage between places. In reality, both the positive and negative linkage will be at work and the impact on firms elsewhere is theoretically ambiguous. We do not know of any literature that has been able to measure the relative strength of these two different effects empirically, although there is

---

[4] Adjusting for the size of units Cheshire and Magrini (2009) concluded that the rate of inter-regional migration per 1,000 population was about 15 times higher in the US than in Western Europe despite measured regional disparities being smaller in the US.

[5] There is little consensus on the causes of this slowdown, although some factors can be ruled out. Molloy et al. (2011) find relatively small roles for housing market contraction and the Great Recession in explaining mobility patterns. Partridge et al. (2012) also find little role of the recession.

evidence that the balance of these two forces helps determine the wages that firms are able to pay in different locations (Redding and Venables 2004).

As economic activity concentrates in city A, these demand and supply 'linkages' change the relative profits that firms can make in different locations in the region. Other economic forces also come into play. Agglomeration economies further increase firm profitability in city A as the amount of activity there expands. Offsetting this, increased competition in the markets for their goods and services can decrease the profits of individual firms as the overall number of firms expands. In addition, increased competition for scarce local resources (particularly workers and land) drive up firms' costs in city A as the number of firms expands. If the combined effects of greater agglomeration economies (better access to suppliers and customers, better labour markets, more productive workers, increased knowledge spillovers) outweigh the effects of increased competition and increased costs of doing business as city A expands then growth can be self-reinforcing (Krugman 1991; Fujita et al. 1999).

What happens to other cities as firms and workers are drawn to city A? According to traditional 'neo-classical' economic analysis, the increase in the supply of labour to city A tends to reduce wages and increase house prices and other living costs. In other cities, wages increase and house prices are expected to fall as the population declines. The net result is that real wages in the city A fall relative to those in other cities and this reduces the incentives for further migration.

However, if agglomeration economies are sufficiently strong then the impact of migration on wages can be very different. In the presence of strong agglomeration economies, as the population of city A grows, productivity and hence wages increase still further, while declining population in other cities leads to lower productivity and wages. Whether or not we regard this as a good thing will depend on whether we look through the prism of people or places. If we focus on places, what we tend to see is average population, wages and house prices increasing in the growing city and falling in other cities (Overman et al. 2009). This clearly looks pretty bad if you are a politician (especially one representing the less successful city) where wages and house prices are falling (and vice versa for policymakers in the more successful city).

If the outcome is clear from a place perspective, what about from the perspective of the people who live in these different places? For instance, if growing cities succeed in attracting yet more economically successful firms and people, what impact may this have on their more deprived residents?

The answer to this question is much more nuanced. Within the growing city, the increase in wages on average more than offsets the increase in housing (and other living) costs. Average real wages and hence living standards are higher – if this were not the case then workers would not be moving to the expanding city. However, this is not to say that everyone is better off as a result of the changes. Individuals who remain outside the labour market and are dependent on fixed incomes from the state or other sources may be worse off due to rising housing costs. This is one of the reasons why deprivation measures can be high in high housing cost cities. Rising housing costs may lead to worse outcomes also for those workers, like nurses and teachers, whose wages are set nationally and are not very responsive to changes in local economic conditions. This effect is partly responsible for the arguments about 'key' workers and for the 'affordability' issues that face low-paid public sector workers who live in expensive cities. In other words, in terms of the people resident in the growing city, the picture is more mixed than the aggregate wage and house price data might suggest.

The available empirical evidence tends to confirm this, and indicates significant disparities for different groups even within 'winning' cities. Global cities like London and New York are characterised by substantial labour market polarisation (Sassen 2001; Buck et al. 2002; Massey 2007). Growing shares of high-value 'innovation economy'-type activity help support lower-value local services – but this consumer demand channel also exacerbates wage gaps, by generating both very well paid and low-paid work. Kaplanis (2010a, b) finds some empirical support for these trends in UK cities: a rise in the local share of workers with degrees is linked to rising employment and rising wages for workers in the bottom occupational quintile. However, higher returns to skilled workers mean their wage gains are higher than for lower-skilled workers, widening wage gaps.

In the cities that are losing firms and population, this story of winners and losers is repeated. Individuals who move to city A are better off because their real wage rises. For those workers who are unable or unwilling to move, wages are lower. Lower housing costs may partially offset the effects of lower wages for some, but the consequences of lower house prices will vary across households depending on whether or not they own their home. Finally, in the reverse of what happens in city A, workers outside the labour market or on fixed or nationally wages may actually be better off in real terms as their costs of living fall. This, in turn, reduces the incentives for these groups to relocate to city A where demand for their services is increasing.

As is the case for the majority of significant economic changes, the story is one of gainers and losers. However, it is important to remember that the net result of the increased spatial concentration of economic activity is likely to be higher productivity and higher real income as a whole. Hence, from an aggregate perspective, the benefits to the gainers should outweigh the costs to the losers. But as we noted at the start of the chapter, this creates real difficulties for policymakers looking to improve economic outcomes for everyone. We return to this issue at the end of the chapter.

An alternative to both people and firms moving to city A is that firms move, but workers stay put and commute. Commuting, rather than relocating, may dampen the positive effects on wages and house prices in the growing city and the negative effects in other cities. It is for this reason that some commentators focus on improving transport networks as a means of 'spreading out' the benefits from growth in resurgent cities (Lucci and Hildreth 2008). There are a number of caveats to this conclusion, however. First, encouraging large-scale commuting between places may not help with environmental impacts, specifically regarding carbon emissions and global warming. Second, if large commuting flows are driven by the fact that housing supply is unresponsive in growing cities (perhaps as a deliberate result of policy) then this will have the effect of making some people living in less successful places worse off – namely those who would have chosen to move in the absence of the restriction on housing supply but now opt to commute. Commuting further costs both money and time. Restricting housing supply actually restricts the extent to which people in other places can benefit from growth in other cities even if it helps protect those places from falling wages and house prices.

More broadly, moves into and out of cities across the lifecycle also appear to have some impact on local labour market disparities. Researchers are starting to test whether the urban wage premium stays with people over time, and in particular, if people maintain it when they leave a city. It is not hard to see how this could work. As Glaeser (2011) suggests, cities could 'help us become smarter', if workers in cities learn from each other through multiple interactions in dense environments. They can then bargain this expertise and experience into systematically higher wages in other places. Changes in circumstances – such as starting a family – are often triggers for moves from big cities to smaller, less dense places. Peri (2002) suggests there is an economic rationale too: younger workers learn more from each other than older workers, so gain more from living in cities. As they age, knowledge spillovers become less important, and so they relocate to non-urban communities. If wage premia are mobile too, this will make moves easier.

There is now some evidence for these dynamic learning effects. Glaeser and Maré (2001) find that US workers keep 'a significant fraction of the urban wage premium' when they move out of cities. De La Roca and Puga (2011) find similar evidence for Spain: former urban workers keep at least some of the urban wage bonus, especially for those previously resident in big cities. Using propensity score matching, Newbold and Brown (2012) find suggestive evidence of a productivity gain for in-migrants to Toronto. For the UK, Gordon (2012) finds suggestive evidence of an 'elevator' effect for workers moving into big cities, and an 'escalator effect' which helps workers maintain higher wages over time. Gordon also finds that workers in lower-demand labour markets experience some bumping down in the occupational distribution, lowering their own pay. So moves across the lifecycle may help individual workers – but reinforce labour market disparities between places.

All of this discussion ignores two additional complications. First, it is possible that disadvantaged households might gain from being located with more successful households. This would further exacerbate any negative effects on those 'left-behind' as people move from less successful to more successful places. Fortunately, the evidence for these additional indirect costs to those left-behind is quite weak – as we discuss extensively in the next chapter. The second complication is that this discussion ignores externalities – for example in terms of pollution or loss of open space – that may occur as a result of spatial concentration. We discuss these issues extensively in Chapters 4 and 5.

6. POLICIES TO NARROW SPATIAL DISPARITIES

As we have just seen, urban economics – with its focus on agglomeration benefits, congestion costs, sorting and spatial equilibrium – provides a very useful framework for thinking about the impact of urban policy. More recently, research in the field has turned its attention to the question of the robust analysis of the impact of specific urban policies on urban economic performance. We consider some of this evidence in detail in Chapter 8. Here, however, we want to give a flavour of the overall message that emerges from that more detailed discussion – specifically, that on this evidence, traditional policies aimed at narrowing spatial disparities by 'turning around' declining places have largely proved to be depressingly ineffective. It is for this reason that much of this book (Chapters 4 to 6) focuses on planning – an area where policy levers are strong (that is highly effective) but where policymakers understanding of their impact on urban economic performance is weak.

As Storper (2011) points out, there are two basic ways to structure a response to spatial disparities. If policymakers believe that wage and employment 'gaps' reflect area differences – the 'place-based' view – they should aim to achieve area convergence in economic outcomes, and take steps to support the economies of 'struggling' places. However, if policy-makers believe disparities reflect differences between people, the strategy should be to improve individuals' labour market opportunities – and (say) use active labour market policy to raise human capital and soft skills. This is the 'people-based' approach favoured by Glaeser and Gottlieb (2008) among others.

In practice, regional and local economic development policies in the UK and elsewhere have tended to combine both elements, reflecting political aspirations both to improve individual life-chances, and to achieve 'spatial equity'. Notably, this commitment to both people and place-based approaches has survived several shifts in the underlying conceptual 'base' (Hildreth and Bailey 2013). The prominence of the place-based element has, though, varied over the years. Probably the high point of such policy in Britain was in the late 1960s when incentives for investment in disadvantaged regions were reinforced with subsidies on employment (the Regional Employment Premium) and direct controls restricting development in the most prosperous areas.

Attachments to place-based approaches also run across party political lines. The 1997–2010 Labour government set up Regional Development Agencies, conducted a root-and-branch review of economic development policy and established fledgling city-regional structures as discussed in Chapter 7 (see also Pike and Tomaney 2008, 2009). It also set up a high-level 'Public Service Agreement' target to both raise the average growth rate of all regions, and to narrow regional disparities between those regions (HM Treasury 2007).[6]

The Coalition Government elected in 2010 has removed much of Labour's institutional architecture, and introduced a greater role for the private sector in delivery. However, it still shares some of the same objectives: while the explicit aim of narrowing area-level disparities has gone, it arguably remains implicit in the current policy mix. For instance, Ministers have explained their desire to 'create a fairer and more balanced economy . . . [with] new business opportunities across the country . . . the Government is . . . determined that all parts of the country benefit from sustainable economic growth' (Department for Business Innovation and Skills 2010). To help achieve this, the Coalition introduced a series of City Deals (see Chapter 7) and implemented the recommendations of the 2012 Heseltine Review, introducing a £2bn/year Single Local Growth Fund in order to 'dramatically advance the process of decentralisation [and]

---

[6] As various commentators on all sides pointed out at the time, it was not obvious how both sides of this target could be met.

unleash the potential of local economies' (HM Treasury and Department for Business Innovation and Skills 2013).

What do 'people'- and 'place'-based interventions involve? Area Based Initiatives (ABIs) have typically involved subsidies to firms (to locate in a given community, or for existing businesses to reduce costs), or physical interventions (such as clearing contaminated land, or construction of new buildings). The Local Enterprise Growth Initiative (Department for Communities and Local Government (DCLG) 2010) and Regional Selective Assistance (Department for Business Enterprise and Regulatory Reform 2008) are examples of the former; the Thames Gateway programme an example of the latter, involving multiple site developments along the Thames estuary (DCLG 2007).

People-focused interventions encompass both formal education and training programmes (school, higher education and adult skills programmes) and active labour market policies, or 'welfare to work' programmes. In the UK, welfare to work has evolved from a range of training and employment schemes in the 1980s and early 1990s, to the New Deal and Flexible New Deal programmes under Labour (Department for Work and Pensions 2007, 2008a, b), to the Coalition's Work Programme (Department for Work and Pensions 2011). These programmes share the same aims: targeted at the long-term unemployed, they aim to raise individual employability, improve labour market matching, and (to varying extents) help those matched stay in work, through continued in-work support.

As Storper's analysis implies, these interventions reflect a mix of equity and efficiency rationales. The equity argument for 'people' policies is clear enough – the need to improve individual life-chances, especially in the face of deep changes to national and local economic structures. The efficiency argument is that as economies adjust to these 'big shifts' they generate a series of co-ordination problems in the labour market for workers and firms; equally, the skill-biased nature of these changes requires many people to improve their human capital or lose out.

The efficiency argument for ABIs is less straightforward. There may be direct job creation effects from reducing business running costs, or physical regeneration programmes. Proponents have also justified such interventions by appealing to indirect effects – if physical regeneration sends a signal that government is 'investing' in an area, this might trigger further private sector investment, bringing new employment (see Peter Tyler's chapter in Lawless et al. (2011)). In cases such as the Thames Gateway – 'Europe's largest regeneration project' – the ultimate aim is to trigger large-scale re-urbanisation and shifts in the industry mix (DCLG 2007). From an equity point of view, the argument for ABIs is either that they help redistribute economic activity to less successful places; or, by raising the 'indigenous capacity' of these places, help trigger convergence with more successful areas. In both cases, the aim is to achieve a form of 'spatial equity'.

Against this, there are reasons to think that Area Based Initiatives may have limited effects – particularly when they attempt to treat areas rather than individual workers or firms. As Moretti (2010) points out, to the extent that workers and firms are mobile, workers and firms in the treated area are unlikely to capture the full benefit of the intervention. Other workers will commute in to take new jobs; firms may shift into the treatment zone from neighbouring areas. In both cases, the net business base or employment benefits from the programme will be small, as activity is largely displaced from other locations. Physical regeneration programmes tend to raise property and land values so landowners and landlords gain, but these groups are generally not the target audience for the policy.

Empirical evidence largely bears out the negative predictions. (We discuss this material in more detail in Chapter 8, but give a flavour of the findings here.) For example, evaluations of the UK's 1980s Enterprise Zones suggest they have largely shifted jobs around, rather than creating much net additional employment (Office of the Deputy Prime Minister 1995; Larkin and Wilcox 2011; Sissons and Brown 2011). Analysis of the structurally similar LEGI programme, introduced in 2006, suggests similarly poor employment outcomes (Einio and Overman 2013). Evaluations of Enterprise Zones in the US (Neumark and Kolko 2010) and France (Mayer et al. 2012) also suggest little or no net jobs effect once displacement effects are taken into account. By contrast, the Regional Selective Assistance (RSA) programme, which targeted individual companies, had some positive employment effects (Criscuolo et al. 2012). The post-2010 Coalition worryingly revived Enterprise Zones, which share many features of their 1980s predecessors; it also introduced a Regional Growth Fund, which like RSA targets firms, but has a budget of only £2.4bn over three years (Department for Business Innovation and Skills 2010); but this is only slightly higher than the annual budget of the Regional Development Agencies.

If worker mobility is limited, ABIs may be more effective – but in ways that are hard to predict. The US Empowerment Zone programme, which combined physical area improvements with firm-level incentives, appears to have successfully raised wages and employment rates for low-skilled local people (Moretti 2010; Busso et al. 2013). The major reason for this result seems to be that workers in the treated neighbourhoods did not want to work in other areas; and neither did workers in nearby neighbourhoods want to commute in. These outcomes are, however, hard to spot in advance, and are likely to reflect area-specific conditions that may not be shared in other countries. This suggests some caution in policy transfer.

Importantly, the experience of US Empowerment Zones and RSA also suggests that even ABIs that have succeeded on their own terms have not done much to roll back national patterns of spatial disparities. Given what we know about spatial economic systems, this should not be a surprise – these are micro programmes working against megatrends. It is now difficult to conceive of a 'big push' type ABI which could fundamentally reorganise a country's economic geography (Moretti 2012). (Certainly, the Thames Gateway programme has not managed to shift the fundamentals of the Greater South East.) All of this suggests that current policy ambitions to spatially rebalance UK labour market opportunities are unlikely to succeed.

7. POLICIES TO INCREASE GROWTH

Economic development policies in the UK and elsewhere have historically been based both on the desire to improve individual life-chances, and to achieve area-level convergence. These latter reflect both efficiency arguments, and more fundamentally, concerns about spatial equity. The discussion so far highlights four big challenges for this point of view.

First, disparities between areas are large, historically persistent and show no signs of disappearing in years to come. Second, these disparities are as much (if not more) about differences in individual characteristics ('people' factors) as they are about area-level ('place') factors, although area and individual effects also interact. Third, big structural shocks – such as those rooted in technology and trade – tend to reinforce wage and employment disparities between places, as people sort between cities and as new forms of urban work are generated. The agglomeration processes that help cities to form and grow over the long term are themselves self-reinforcing. Fourth, traditional policy tools have not proved very effective at turning around declining places.

None of this is to say that urban policy is powerless – far from it. But the extent of the challenge in 'turning around' declining places has led some to call for a greater policy focus on more successful cities. In practice, as we will see in Chapters 4 to 8, this will require both reforms to the planning system and a greater focus on particular types of policy interventions in particular places. In this chapter, we set aside details on how this might happen and focus instead on two broader questions: the likely effectiveness of urban growth policy that seeks to 'build on success' as well as concerns about how to ensure that as many people as possible can share in that success. We start by briefly considering the first of these questions. The argument in favour of building on success as an effective way of raising growth rates comes in two steps. The first is to provide evidence that there is considerable potential for continued growth in our more successful cities. The second is to demonstrate that policy can play an important role in ensuring that these cities achieve this potential; and equally can do much to prevent it.

One way to think about the potential for continued growth is to compare the British urban system to that found in other countries. Such comparisons are complicated. At a simple level, countries differ hugely in terms of underlying population. Further, as we explained in section 3, the shape of a given urban system is the outcome of multiple, dynamic processes. However, despite this complexity, it may be possible to compare the size of cities across countries. Indeed, statistical analysis for a wide range of countries suggests that the relative size of cities often satisfies an empirical regularity known as Zipf's law (Zipf 1949). A version of this law which is particularly easy to understand is known as the rank–size rule. In a group of cities that obey the rank–size rule, the second largest city is half the size of the largest city, the third largest city is a third the size of the largest city, and so on.

An easy way to see whether a group of cities obey the rank–size rule is to draw the scatterplot of the (natural) logarithm of city size against the (natural) logarithm of its rank. Starting from the point on the vertical axis that corresponds to the largest city, we then draw a line with slope –1. If the group of cities obeys the rank–size rule then all the cities in the group will lie along this line. Numerous cross-country studies and comparative international evidence provide support for Zipf's law (see Gabaix and Ioannides (2004) and Rozenfeld et al. (2011) for recent contributions). A recent study of 73 countries by Soo (2005) finds an average value for the slope of the Zipf line of –1.17 with a standard deviation of 0.26.

Figure 2.4 shows such a Zipf plot for English cities, and corresponds to similar analysis for Great Britain by Rozenfeld et al. (2011). Medium-sized cities in England are, roughly speaking, about the size Zipf's law would predict given the population of London, the largest city. Smaller cites are, if anything, too big (the line sits below the points for these cities). But England's 'second tier' of cities appear to be too small, as can be seen from the fact that their points lie some way below the Zipf line (a similar point can be made for a few smaller cities at the far right hand side of the figure).

It is important to note that this feature does not appear to be a consequence of London being 'too large'. If we had predicted the population of England's largest city by drawing the Zipf line through the medium-sized

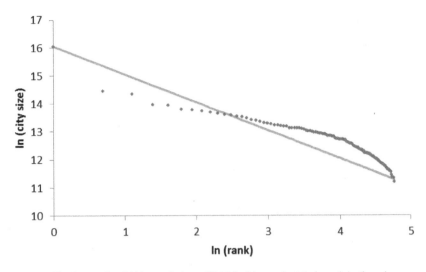

Notes: The figure plots 2011 population of British cities against their rank in the urban hierarchy. The fact that the second tier of cities appear to be too small can be seen from observing that they lie below the Zipf line (which roughly summarises the relationship between the size and rank of cities that holds across many different countries). In contrast, note that medium-sized cities sit above the Zipf line. Data is from the 2011 Census.

Figure 2.4   Zipf plot for British cities showing Britain's 'second tier' cities are undersized

cities and projecting to the y-axis then we would obtain a figure not much different from that of the actual population of London (if anything, it would be larger). Of course, such a simplistic exercise comes with a number of important caveats (not least that the exact definition of urban areas will affect their relative sizes). But the Zipf plot is at least indicative of the fact that, for Britain, relative to many other countries, second-tier cities may be too small. Planning and other government policies (see Chapters 4, 5 and 8) all have a role to play in explaining this pattern, suggesting that there is considerable potential for growth in (some of these) smaller cities – if we were willing to make appropriate changes to policy.

   While Britain may be somewhat unusual in its deviation from Zipf's Law, a more generalizable way of thinking about the scope for further growth in particular cities is to look at price signals provided by land markets. Land prices indicate the amount that firms and workers are willing to pay to produce and work in different places. These prices show an incredible amount of variation across space, as Figure 2.5 indicates for commercial land in Britain. Of course supply, as well as demand from

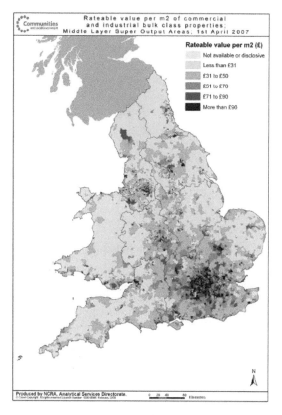

Notes: Floorspace and rateable value of commercial and industrial properties, 1 April 2007, England and Wales (the most recent data available at the time of writing). A number of factors determine rateable value, but one can reasonably expect spatial variations in rateable value to be quite highly correlated with spatial variations in land values.

Source: CLG/ONS Statistical Release (February 2008).

Figure 2.5   The UK has very marked spatial variations in land prices

firms and households, is a key determinant of the price of land. In some circumstances, land prices will be high because of the existence of an unexpandable natural local amenity, for example, a sea view or beautiful countryside that makes an area desirable. These local amenities will explain some of the high land prices in rural areas that are visible in Figure 2.5.

But across urban areas, spatial variations in prices are less likely to be driven by natural amenities. Instead, they tend to reflect the fact that the supply of land is heavily restricted in the areas which are experiencing the strongest increases in demand for land. This is most obvious in London and the South East, but also applies more widely across Britain where the price of land in some cities is significantly above that of others nearby. We would reach a similar conclusion if we considered residential land, although the picture is complicated by both the role of natural amenities and peoples' commuting patterns.

Land prices, like the prices of other goods and services, are useful to policymakers because they provide a signal telling them where millions of individuals want to live and work, even if housing and land use policies currently prevent them from doing so (see Chapter 4). In many markets, there is a very strong case for simply following these signals, but this is not the case when it comes to land use for the simple reason that individual decisions on land use impose externalities on other individuals. When houses are built in previously undeveloped areas, it negatively affects those individuals who currently derive benefit from this undeveloped land (perhaps because they use it for recreation or because their houses overlook it). The fundamental economic rationale for a planning system is to ensure that these externalities are taken into account when making decisions about land use. Unfortunately, for a variety of reasons, there has been a historical tendency for spatial planning in Britain to go to the other extreme when it comes to market signals, that is, to require that planners ignore prices when making decisions on land use (Barker 2006). Recent reforms have suggested that the system should take some account of land prices (although, ironically, just as the government has stopped publishing any information or data on them). See Chapters 4 to 6 for further discussion.

A growth policy based around successful cities could make use of these price signals to identify cities (possibly within broader sub-national regions) with the strongest potential for market-led growth. The main role of policy would then be to ensure that conditions prevail that allow this potential to be achieved. In many countries, including Britain, possibly the most important policy decisions will be around planning, ensuring that land is made readily available for new or altered commercial and residential uses in these cities, that the rules permitting development are simple and transparent and that appropriate infrastructure and utilities are provided, and so on. But many other policy areas, including the provision of skills training and support to businesses need to play a role.

There are two stylised reactions to these differences in city growth patterns in terms of their implications for meeting growth objectives and for the evolution of spatial disparities. The first is to suggest that we need to build on success stories and that growth in these successful cities will then spill over to benefit other nearby cities. The second, contrasting reaction, argues for a policy focus on less successful cities on the grounds that policy interventions here will be more effective, and moreover, this is where intervention is most needed given that spillover benefits are minimal. Given the strength of conviction of those on both sides of this argument, it is perhaps surprising to find that there is relatively little evidence to fully justify either of these assertions. What evidence we do have suggests that the proponents of 'building on success' strategies are probably right in thinking that this is the most realistic and effective way of delivering on the objective of raising national growth rates. However, it is possible that they overemphasise the extent to which these benefits may then spill over to surrounding places and, more importantly, to people living in those surrounding places. Unfortunately, we still know very little about how these different effects play out in practice: certainly, there are likely to be winners and losers to such a strategy, and additional interventions will be required to mitigate these distributional impacts.

Also note that the observation that some second-tier cities may be too small does not imply that the policy focus should be on all those locations that currently fill these positions in the ranking. That is, the ranking of British cities should not be regarded as immutable. The strategy should, instead, take greater account of what areas market signals (for example land prices) suggest have the greatest potential for productivity gains through growth. This may imply that some medium-sized cities overtake some traditional second-tier cities in the longer term. Finally, strategies that focus on relatively successful cities outside of the most successful sub-regions (the South East in the British context) might be working against market forces at the national level (otherwise it would not be necessary to intervene to achieve spatial disparity objectives), but they are at least working with market forces within sub-regions. It is for all these reasons that we conclude that focusing on relatively successful cities may offer the best chance of meeting economic growth objectives.

How much do we know about how all of these different effects play out in practice? The answer is, unfortunately, very little. On balance, the evidence suggests that growth strategies based around relatively successful cities are most likely to deliver on growth objectives. Further, it is highly likely that the overall benefits to people who move to, or commute to, the growing cities will outweigh the losses to people who are unwilling or unable to do so. But as the discussion in this section makes clear, new evidence will be needed to help quantify the magnitudes of gains and losses to different people in different places. On the basis of what we currently know, however, it is likely that there will be winners and losers to such a strategy, even if the size of any effects remains unknown.

8. CONCLUSIONS

This chapter has considered recent urban economic performance in Britain and explained how that performance can be characterised as showing resurgence (that is a move from weak to stronger population growth), divergence (that is a diversity of performance) and persistence (that is high positive correlation in relative growth rates). We have explained how part of the explanation for these trends belongs to 'big picture' global shifts in both technology (for example skill-biased technological change) and institutions (for example labour market reform and globalisation). But we have also made the case that a better understanding of how city economies function – in particular the importance of the three-way inter-action between agglomeration benefits, congestion costs and the sorting of workers across cities – helps explain both how these global trends play out spatially and the role that the spatial economy plays in driving national and global macro trends.

In addition to thinking about the functioning of individual cities, urban economics provides us with a powerful conceptual tool – that of spatial equilibrium – for thinking about how the urban system as a whole responds to shocks and develops over time. We have shown how this concept can be used to carefully think through the implications for both people and places when major technological innovations or policy inter-ventions favour one particular city over others. If we focus only on the average outcomes for different cities, what we would tend to see is average population, wages and house prices increasing in the growing city and falling in other cities. But from the perspective of people who live in these different places, the economic impact is much more nuanced. Indeed, as is the case for the majority of significant economic changes, the story is one of gainers and losers in all cities (including the city that grows as a result of this favourable 'shock'). As we will see time and again through this book, thinking about the impact of urban policy requires us to distinguish carefully between outcomes for people and for places. As we have tried to demonstrate in this chapter, urban economics provides a useful set of tools for doing this. Chapter 3 will show how these concepts also allow us to think through the mechanisms that lead to residential segregation within cities and the likely consequences of this segregation.

We have also briefly considered the evidence on the relative effectiveness of some popular urban policy interventions. Many of these interventions have not proved very effective at reducing spatial disparities or improv-ing urban economic performance. As we explain in much more detail in Chapter 8, urban economics can often help us to understand this policy ineffectiveness. This highlights one of our other central messages – that the most effective urban economic strategies are based on the actual workings of local economies, rather than how some policymakers would like them to behave. It is for this reason that a significant part of this book focuses on the impact of restrictive land use regulation. If policymakers have only weak tools for directly affecting the productive side of the urban economy then they need to pay careful focus instead on the cost side – an area where they have strong policy levers which have profound implications for the functioning of our urban system. We consider these issues in much more detail in Chapters 4 to 6.

What would happen if policymakers became more realistic about policy effectiveness and their inability to counteract strong market forces? In this chapter we have tried to sketch out some answers and think through some of the implications for the urban system as a whole if policymakers switched their focus from a traditional emphasis on turning around declining places to a more realistic policy of building on success. While planning reform might be central in this context (at least in Britain), more generally urban economics stresses the importance of focusing on improving local fundamentals – such as individual skills, connectivity, business capacity and the physical environment (Manchester Independent Economic Review 2009). Given that wage and employment disparities largely reflect individual differences, we would particularly highlight the importance of the individual-focused components of this policy mix.

This raises a related set of questions about implementation – beyond the question of local delivery discussed earlier. If local wage and employment patterns are partly the product of local history, demography and industrial structure, does this require locally tailored strategies – that is, transfer of policy design, budgets and management to local actors? Theory suggests devolution could provide benefits by unleashing local knowledge and policy innovation; on the other hand, economies of scale could be lost. We have little hard evidence either way, as we discuss further in Chapter 7, but good reasons to think that in countries like the UK, devolution could deliver net benefits at local and national level.

One likely result of more policy realism is that people in 'struggling' places will move elsewhere. As we have discussed above, if we care most about improving individual life chances, this is no bad thing (Webber and Swinney 2010). This raises the question of whether policymakers should also consider more active interventions that raise individual mobility across the UK. In the US, economists such as Glaeser (2005) and Moretti (2012) have forcefully argued this case. In the UK such an approach is much more controversial, with angry reactions to one recent think-tank report (Leunig and Swaffield 2009).

Policy realism also argues in favour of 'managed decline' for people and places 'left behind'. Unfortunately, for those in favour of 'managed decline', the awkward truth is that we have little hard evidence about what might work. And there would likely be substantial social and personal costs for many households involved, as well as huge political challenges for those trying to implement such a policy at national level. Certainly, it is hard to reconcile with devolution or localism: it is striking that in the US, strategies to remodel 'shrinking' or 'legacy cities' – such as Detroit or Flint, Michigan – have been taken forward by locally elected leaders rather than national policymakers (who have stayed well away from such debates) (Nathan 2010).

In short, even as our evidence base improves, urban policymaking remains challenging. As this chapter and the rest of this book demonstrates, urban economics provides tools and evidence for helping address these challenges but it certainly does not provide all of the answers.

REFERENCES

Armstrong, Martin and Jim Taylor. 2000. *Regional Economics and Policy*. Oxford: Wiley-Blackwell.

Arzaghi, Mohammad and J. Vernon Henderson. 2008. 'Networking off Madison Avenue'. *Review of Economic Studies* 75, 1011–1038.

Autor, D.H., F. Levy and R.J. Murnane. 2003. 'The skill content of recent technological change: An empirical exploration'. *Quarterly Journal of Economics* 118, 1279–1333.

Barker, K. 2006. 'Barker Review of Land Use Planning: Final Report – Recommendations'. London: HMSO.

Barlow Report. 1940. 'Royal Commission on the Distribution of the Industrial Population', Cmd. 6153.

Baum-Snow, Nathaniel and Ronni Pavan. 2012. 'Understanding the city size wage gap'. *The Review of Economic Studies* 79, 88–127.

Beveridge, W. 1936. 'An analysis of unemployment'. *Economica* 3, 357–386.

Blanchard, Olivier J. and Lawrence F. Katz. 1992. 'Regional evolutions'. *Brookings Papers on Economic Activity* 23.

Blanchard, Olivier J. and Lawrence H. Summers. 1987. 'Hysteresis in unemployment'. *European Economic Review* 31, 288–295.

Bowley, A. 1930. *Some Economic Consequences of the Great War*. London: Thornton Butterworth.

Brown, A.J. 1969. 'Surveys of applied economics: regional economics, with special reference to the United Kingdom'. *The Economic Journal* 79, 759–796.

Buck, Nick, Ian Gordon, Alan Harding and Ivan Turok. 2004. *Changing Cities: Rethinking Urban Competitiveness, Cohesion and Governance*. London: Palgrave Macmillan.

Buck, Nick, Ian Gordon, Peter Hall, Michael Harloe and Mark Kleinman. 2002. *Working Capital: Life and Labour in Contemporary London*. London: Routledge.

Busso, M., J. Gregory and P. Kline. 2013. 'Assessing the incidence and efficiency of a prominent place based policy'. *American Economic Review Papers and Proceedings* 103, 897–947.

Champion, Tony and Alan Townsend. 2009. 'The Fluctuating Record of Economic Regeneration in England's Second-Order City Regions, 1984–2007', Spatial Economics Research Centre (SERC) Discussion Paper 0033. London: SERC.

Champion, Tony and Alan Townsend. 2012. 'Great Britain's Second-Order City Regions in Recessions, 1978–2010', SERC Discussion Paper 0104. London: SERC.

Charlot, Silvie and Gilles Duranton. 2004. 'Communication externalities in cities'. *Journal of Urban Economics* 56, 581–613.

Cheshire, P.C. 1973. *Regional Unemployment Differences in Great Britain*. Regional Papers II. Cambridge: Cambridge University Press.

Cheshire, Paul. 1995. 'A new phase of urban development in Western Europe? The evidence for the 1980s'. *Urban Studies* 32, 1045–1063.

Cheshire, P. and S. Magrini. 2009. 'Urban growth drivers in a Europe of sticky people and implicit boundaries'. *Journal of Economic Geography* 9(1), 85–115.

Combes, Paul-Phillipe, Gilles Duranton, Laurent Gobillon, Diego Puga and Sébastien Roux. 2009. 'The Productivity Advantages of Large Cities: Distinguishing Agglomeration from Firm Selection', SERC Discussion Paper 0027. French. London: SERC.

Combes, Pierre-Philippe, Gilles Duranton and Laurent Gobillon. 2008. 'Spatial wage disparities: sorting matters!' French. *Journal of Urban Economics* 63, 723–742.

Combes, Pierre-Philippe, Gilles Duranton and Laurent Gobillon. 2012. 'The Costs of Agglomeration: Land Prices in French Cities', IZA Discussion Paper No. 7027. French. Bonn: IZA.

Combes, Pierre Philippe, Gilles Duranton and Henry G. Overman. 2005. 'Agglomeration and the adjustment of the spatial economy'. *Papers in Regional Science* 84, 311–349

Costa, Dora L. and Matthew E. Kahn. 2000. 'Power couples: changes in the locational choice of the college educated, 1940–1990'. *Quarterly Journal of Economics* 115, 1287–1315.

Criscuolo, Chiara, Ralf Martin, Henry G. Overman and John Van Reenen. 2012. 'The Causal Effects of an Industrial Policy', SERC Discussion Paper 0098. London: SERC.

DCLG. 2007. 'Thames Gateway Delivery Plan'. London: DCLG.

DCLG. 2010. 'National Evaluation of the Local Enterprise Growth Initiative Programme: Final report'. London: DCLG.De La Roca, Jorge and Diego Puga. 2011. 'Learning by Working in Dense Cities', Centre for Economic Policy Research Discussion Paper No. 9243. London: CEPR.

Department for Business Enterprise and Regulatory Reform. 2008. 'Evaluation of Regional Selective Assistance (RSA) and its Successor, Selective Finance for Investment in England (SFIE)'. London: BERR.

Department for Business Innovation and Skills. 2010. 'Local Growth: Realising Every Place's Potential', Cmd. 7961. London: HMSO.

Department for Work and Pensions. 2007. 'In Work, Better Off: Next Steps to Full Employment'. London: HMSO.

Department for Work and Pensions. 2008a. 'The longer-term impact of the New Deal for Young People', DWP Working Paper 23. London: DWP.

Department for Work and Pensions. 2008b. 'Phase 1 – Flexible New Deal Provision Specification and Supporting Information'. London: HMSO.

Department for Work and Pensions. 2011. 'The Work Programme'. London: DWP.

Dijkstra, Lewis, Enrique Garcilazo and Philip McCann. 2012. 'The economic performance of European cities and city regions: myths and realities'. *European Planning Studies* 21, 334–354.

Drury, Ian. 2008. 'The recession map of England: London and South-East to lose one in 12 jobs over next 18 months', *The Daily Mail*, 18 November, retreived from: http://www.dailymail.co.uk/news/article-1086527/The-recession-map-En gland-London-South-East-bear-brunt-recession-loss-12-jobs-18-months.html.

Duranton, Gilles and Vassilis Monastiriotis. 2002. 'Mind the gaps: the evolution of regional earnings inequalities in the UK, 1982–1997'. French. *Journal of Regional Science* 42, 219–256.

Duranton, Gilles and Diego Puga. 2001. 'Nursery cities: urban diversity, process innovation and the life cycle of products'. *American Economic Review* 91, 1454–1477.

Duranton, Giles and Diego Puga. 2004. 'Micro-Foundations of Urban Agglomeration Economies', in J. V. Henderson and J.-F. Thisse (eds), *Handbook of Regional and Urban Economics Volume 4*. The Hague: Elsevier, pp. 2063–2117.

Dustmann, Christian, Albrecht Glitz and Tommaso Frattini. 2008. 'The labour market impact of immigration'. *Oxford Review of Economic Policy* 24, 477–494.

Einio, Elias and Henry Overman. 2013. *The Effects of Spatially Targeted Enterprise Initiatives: Evidence from UK LEGI*. London: LSE.

Financial Times. 2008. 'Recession Britain: Grim down South', *The Financial Times*, 12 November, retreived from http://www.ft.com/cms/s/0/77612efa-b0f0-11dd-8915-0000779fd18c.html..

Fujita, Masahisa, Paul Krugman and Anthony J. Venables. 1999. *The Spatial Economy: Cities, Regions, and International Trade*. Cambridge, MA: MIT Press.

Gabaix, Xavier and Yannis M. Ioannides. 2004. 'Chapter 53: The Evolution of City Size Distributions', in J.V. Henderson and T. Jacques-François (eds), *Handbook of Regional and Urban Economics*. The Hague: Elsevier, pp. 2341–2378.

Gallie, Duncan and Serge Paugam. 2000. *Welfare Regimes and the Experience of Unemployment in Europe*. Oxford: Oxford University Press.

Gibbons, S. and H. Overman. 2012. 'The Decomposition of Variance into Individual and Group Components with an Application to Area Disparities'. Mimeo. London: LSE.

Gibbons, Stephen, Henry G. Overman and Guilherme Resende. 2011. 'Real Earnings Disparities in Britain', SERC Discussion Paper 0065. London: SERC.

Gibbons, Steve, Henry G. Overman and Panu Pelkonen. 2010. 'Wage Disparities in Britain: People or Place?', SERC Discussion Paper 0060. London: SERC.

Glaeser, Edward. 2005. 'Should the government rebuild New Orleans, or just give residents checks?' *The Economists' Voice* 2, 4.

Glaeser, Edward. 2008. *Cities, Agglomeration and Spatial Equilibrium*. Oxford: OUP.

Glaeser, Edward. 2011. *The Triumph of the City*. London: Pan Macmillan.

Glaeser, Edward and Joshua D. Gottlieb. 2006. 'Urban resurgence and the con-sumer city'. *Urban Studies* 43, 1275–1299.

Glaeser, Edward and Joshua D. Gottlieb. 2008. 'The economics of place-making policies'. *Brookings Papers on Economic Activity* 2008, 155–239.

Glaeser, Edward L. and David C Maré. 2001. 'Cities and skills'. *Journal of Labor Economics* 19, 316–342.

Glaeser, Edward L., Jed Kolko and Albert Saiz. 2001. 'Consumer city'. *Journal of Economic Geography* 1, 27–50.

Goldin, Claudia and Lawrence F. Katz. 2010. *The Race between Education and Technology*. Cambridge, MA: Harvard University Press.

Goos, Maarten and Alan Manning. 2007. 'Lousy and lovely jobs: the rising polarization of work in Britain'. *Review of Economics and Statistics* 89, 118–133.

Gordon, Ian. 2012. 'Ambition, Human Capital Acquisition and the Metropolitan Escalator', SERC Discussion Paper 0107. London: SERC.

Graham, Daniel. 2007. 'Identifying urbanisation and localisation externalities in manufacturing and service industries'. *Papers in Regional Science* 88, 63–84.

Groot, Stefan and Henri De Groot. 2011. 'Wage Inequality in the Netherlands: Evidence, Trends and Explanations', CPB Discussion Paper 186. The Hague: CPB Netherlands Bureau for Economic Policy Analysis.

Haldane, Andy. 2010. 'The $100 Billion Question', speech at Institute of Regulation & Risk, Hong Kong, 8 March. London: Bank of England Publications.

Helmers, Christian. 2010. 'Choose the Neighbour Before the House: Agglomeration Externalities in UK Science Parks', in SERC Urban and Regional Economics Seminar. London: LSE.

Hildreth, Paul and David Bailey. 2013. 'The economics behind the move to "localism" in England'. *Cambridge Journal of Regions, Economy and Society* 6, 233–249.

HM Treasury. 2007. 'Public Service Agreement 7: Improve the Economic Performance of all English Regions and Reduce the Gap in Economic Growth Rates between Regions'. London: HM Treasury.HM Treasury and Department for Business Innovation and Skills. 2013. 'Government's Response to the Heseltine Review'. London: HMT and BIS.

Ioannides, Yannis M., Henry G. Overman, Esteban Rossi-Hansberg and Kurt Schmidheiny. 2008. 'The effect of information and communication technologies on urban structure'. *Economic Policy* 23, 201–242.

Jackman, Richard and Savvas Savouri. 1992. 'Regional migration in Britain: an analysis of gross flows using NHS Central Register Data'. *The Economic Journal* 102, 1433–1450.

Jackman, Richard and Savvas Savouri. 1996. 'Regional Migration and the Hiring Function: An Examination of Distance and Contiguity Effects in Great Britain, 1975–92', in R. Schettkat (ed.), *The Flow Analysis of Labour Markets*. London: Routledge, Pp. 272–287.

Jacobs, Jane. 1969. *The Economy of Cities*. London: Vintage.

Kaplanis, Ioannis. 2010a. 'Local Human Capital and Its Impact on Local Employment Chances in Britain', SERC Discussion Paper 0040. London: SERC.

Kaplanis, Ioannis. 2010b. 'Wage Effects from Changes in Local Human Capital in Britain', SERC Discussion Paper 0039. London: SERC.

Krugman, Paul. 1991. *Geography and Trade*. Cambridge, MA: MIT Press.

Krugman, Paul. 1997. *Pop Internationalism*. Cambridge, MA: MIT Press.

Krugman, Paul and Maurice Obstfeld. 2003. *International Economics: Theory and Policy*. Boston, MA: Addison Weasley.

Larkin, Kieran and Zach Wilcox. 2011. 'What would Maggie do? Why the Government's Policy on Enterprise Zones Needs to be Radically Different to the Failed Policy of the 1980s'. London: Centre for Cities.

Lawless, Paul, Henry G. Overman and Peter Tyler. 2011. 'Strategies for Underperforming Places', SERC Policy Paper 006. London: SERC.

Lee, Neil, Katy Morris, Jonathan Wright, Naomi Clayton, Ian Brinkley and Alexandra Jones. 2010. 'No City Left Behind? The Geography of the Recovery – and the Implications for the Coalition'. London: The Work Foundation.

Leunig, Tim and James Swaffield. 2009. 'Cities Unlimited'. London: Policy Exchange.

Lipsey, Richard G. 1960. 'The relation between unemployment and the rate of change of money wage rates in the UK, 1862–1995: a further analysis'. *Economica* 27, 1–31.

Lucci, Paula and Paul Hildreth. 2008. 'City Links: Isolation and Integration'. London: Centre for Cities.

Manchester Independent Economic Review. 2009. 'The Review'. Manchester: Manchester Enterprises.

Marshall, Alfred. 1918. *Principles of Economics*. New York: Macmillan.

Martin, Ron. 2012. 'Regional economic resilience, hysteresis and recessionary shocks'. *Journal of Economic Geography* 12, 1–32.

Massey, Doreen. 1984. *Spatial Divisions of Labour: Social Structures and the Geography of Production*. New York: Metheun.

Massey, Doreen. 2007. *World City*. Bristol: Polity Press.

Mayer, Thierry, Florian Mayneris and Lorian Py. 2012. 'The Impact of Urban Enterprise Zones on Establishments' Location Decisions: Evidence from French ZFUs', Centre for Economic Policy and Research (CEPR) Discussion Paper 9074.

McCann, Philip and Zoltan J. Acs. 2011. 'Globalization: countries, cities and multinationals'. *Regional Studies* 45, 17– 32.

Melo, Patricia, Daniel Graham and Robert Noland. 2009. 'A meta-analysis of estimates of urban agglomeration economies'. *Regional Science and Urban Economics* 39, 332–342.

Mion, Giordano and Paolo Naticchioni. 2009. 'The spatial sorting and matching of skills and firms'. *Canadian Journal of Economics* 42, 28–55.

Molloy, Raven, Christopher L. Smith and Abigail Wozniak. 2011. 'Internal migration in the United States'. *Journal of Economic Perspectives* 25, 173–196.

MoneyWeek. 2007. 'Credit crunch will squeeze London'." *MoneyWeek*, 12 September, retreived from http://www.moneyweek.com/home/news-and-charts/ economics/credit-cruch-will-squeeze-london.

Moretti, Enrico. 2010. 'Local Labor Markets', in O. Ashenfelter and D. Card (eds), *Handbook of Labor Economics.* Amsterdam: Elsevier, pp. 1237–1313.

Moretti, Enrico. 2012. *The New Geography of Jobs*. Boston: Houghton Mifflin Harcourt.

Nathan, Max. 2010. 'Shrink to Fit', in, *Squareglasses blog*.

Nathan, Max and Chris Urwin. 2006. 'City People: City Centre Living in the UK'. London: Centre for Cities.

Neumark, David and Jed Kolko. 2010. 'Do enterprise zones create job? Evidence from California's enterprise zone program'. *Journal of Urban Economics* 68, 1–19.

Newbold, K. Bruce and W. Mark Brown. 2012. 'Testing and extending the escalator hypothesis: does the pattern of post-migration income gains in Toronto suggest productivity and/or learning effects?' *Urban Studies* 49, 3447–3465.

Nickell, Stephen and Brian Bell. 1995. 'The collapse in demand for the unskilled and unemployment across the OECD'. *Oxford Review of Economic Policy* 11, 40–62.

Office of the Deputy Prime Minister (ODPM). 1995. 'Final Evaluation of Enterprise Zones', Urban Research Summary No. 4. London: ODPM.

Office of the Deputy Prime Minister. 2006. 'State of the English Cities Report'. London: Office of the Deputy Prime Minister.

Overman, Henry. 2011. 'How Did London Get Away With it? The Recession and the North–South Divide', London: LSE Works.

Overman, Henry and Tim Leunig. 2008. 'Spatial patterns of development and the British housing market'. *Oxford Review of Economic Policy* 24:1, 59–78.

Overman, Henry G., Patricia Rice and Anthony J. Venables. 2009. 'Economic linkages across space'. *Regional Studies* 44, 17–33.

Partridge, Mark D., Dan S. Rickman, M. Rose Olfert and Ying Tan. 2012. 'When Spatial Equilibrium Fails: Is Place-Based Policy Second Best?' University Library of Munich.

Peri, Giovanni. 2002. 'Young workers, learning, and agglomerations'. *Journal of Urban Economics* 52, 582–607.

Pike, Andy and John Tomaney. 2008. 'The Government's Review of Sub-National Economic Development and Regeneration: Key Issues', SERC Discussion Paper 0008. London: SERC.

Pike, Andy and John Tomaney. 2009. 'The state and uneven development: the governance of economic development in England in the post-devolution UK'. *Cambridge Journal of Regions, Economy and Society* 2, 13–34.

Redding, Stephen and Anthony J. Venables. 2004. 'Economic geography and international inequality'. *Journal of International Economics* 62, 53–82.

Resolution Foundation. 2012. 'Gaining from Growth: The Final Report of the Commission on Living Standards'. London: Resolution Foundation.

Rice, Patricia, Anthony J. Venables and Eleonora Patacchini. 2006. 'Spatial determinants of productivity: analysis for the regions of Great Britain'. *Regional Science and Urban Economics* 36, 727–752.

Rosenthal, Stuart and William Strange. 2004. 'Evidence on the Nature and Sources of Agglomeration Economies', in V. Henderson and J.-F. Thisse (eds), *Handbook of Urban and Regional Economics Volume 4.* Amsterdam: Elsevier, pp. 2119–2171.

Rozenfeld, Hern D., Diego Rybski, Xavier Gabaix, and Hern A. Makse. 2011. 'The area and population of cities: new insights from a different perspective on cities'. *The American Economic Review* 101, 2205–2225.

Sako, Mari. 2006. 'Outsourcing and offshoring: implications for productivity of business services'. *Oxford Review of Economic Policy* 22, 499–512.

Sassen, Saskia. 2001. *The Global City: New York, London, Tokyo.* Woodstock: Princeton University Press/Blackwell.

Seager, Ashley. 2008. 'The dark underbelly of London's boom', *The Guardian*, 12 February, retrieved from http://www.guardian.co.uk/commentisfree/2008/feb/12/londons.dark.underbelly

Sissons, Andrew and Chris Brown. 2011. 'Do Enterprise Zones Work?"' London: The Work Foundation.

Soo, Kwok Tong. 2005. 'Zipf's Law for cities: a cross-country investigation'. *Regional Science and Urban Economics* 35, 239–263.

Stewart, Heather, Nick Mathiason, Tim Webb, Zoe Wood and Caroline Davies. 2008. 'It's grim down south', *The Observer*, 19 October, retreived from http://www.guardian.co.uk/business/2008/oct/19/creditcrunch-marketturmoil-recession-london.

Storper, Michael. 1997. *The Regional World: Territorial Development in a Global Economy*. New York: Guilford.

Storper, Michael. 2011. 'Justice, efficiency and economic geography: should places help one another to develop?' *European Urban and Regional Studies* 18, 3–21.

Storper, Michael and Michael Manville. 2006. 'Behaviour, preferences and cities: urban theory and urban resurgence'. *Urban Studies* 43, 1247–1274.

The National Economic Development Council. 1963. 'Conditions Favourable to Faster Growth'. London: HMSO.

UN Population Division. 2010. United Nations World Urbanisation Prospects: The 2010 Revision Population Database'. United Nations.

Unsworth, Rachael and Max Nathan. 2006. 'Beyond city living: remaking the inner suburbs'. *Built Environment* 32, 235–249.

Venables, Anthony. 2006. 'Shifts in Economic Geography and Their Causes', CEP Discussion Paper 767. London: LSE.

Webber, Chris and Paul Swinney. 2010. 'Private Sector Cities: A New Geography of Opportunity'. London: Centre for Cities.

Wills, Jane, Kavita Datta, Yara Evans, Joanna Herbert, Jon May and Cathy McIlwaine. 2010. *Global Cities at Work: New Migrant Divisions of Labour*. London: Pluto Press.

Zipf, George K. 1949. *Human Behavior and the Principle of Least Effort*. Cambridge, MA: Addison-Wesley.

3. Residential segregation and people sorting within cities[1]

1. INTRODUCTION: RESIDENTIAL SEGREGATION AND INEQUALITY

Tackling poverty and the relationship between poverty and place have both become key issues for policy (Hills 2007). They are also one of the central focuses of this book. In the last chapter, we talked about the role that sorting – the tendency of different types of people to live in different places – played in driving spatial disparities in economic performance across cities. This chapter changes spatial focus to look at residential segregation and sorting within cities. In Chapter 2 we identified three channels through which spatial linkages worked: trade, commuting patterns (and changes in them) and migration of people or relocations of firms. The second of these is very low cost; workers can easily change their patterns of commuting as the spatial patterns of job availability change. So spatial adjustment between neighbourhoods within cities is relatively low cost and highly responsive to differential opportunities.

The result is that within cities, sorting plays an even more important role in understanding spatial disparities than it does across cities. This has fundamental implications for both our understanding of disparities and for the formulation of effective urban policy. It is extremely worrying, therefore, that the role of sorting is so poorly understood in both popular and policy debate. Indeed, given the popular discussion of social facts which reflect segregation it would seem that explanations other than sorting are all but universally assumed to be 'true'. How else can one explain the outrage greeting every new report of what in Britain is known as 'postcode lottery unfairness'? In a matter of a few days in June 2013 two stories of such apparent geographical injustice were major news in Britain.

On 1 June the BBC news website reported that the Health Secretary, Jeremy Hunt, found: 'The local variation in early death rates revealed

---

[1] This chapter draws on SERC Policy Paper No. 2. This was jointly authored with Steve Gibbons and Ian Gordon. Their ideas and generosity are gratefully acknowledged.

in a new league table for England ... "shocking".' The league table in question reported premature death rates for English Local Authorities (LAs).[2] Two London boroughs, Richmond on Thames and Kensington and Chelsea had among the lowest premature death rates; another, Tower Hamlets, was close to the other extreme (ranking 137th out of the 150 LAs listed). The commentary on the website itself was more nuanced, concentrating on the way in which some more deprived places were not among the least healthy and vice-versa. Still the focus of public discussion was on the shocking – even scandalous – geographical inequality the data revealed.

Only two days earlier the British newspaper *The Guardian* carried a 'postcode' scandal about unequal entrance to the two top British universities. The story was headlined:

Controversy over class at Oxbridge is nothing new: Oxford and Cambridge argue strenuously that it is attainment and not geography that influences admissions decisions.

The paper reported that figures obtained under the Freedom of Information Act had

revealed a golden triangle centred on Oxford, Cambridge and London that contributes a disproportionately large number of undergraduates to the universities, raising questions over whether they are doing enough to encourage those from other parts of the country to apply.

Three London boroughs, Richmond on Thames, The City of London and Kensington and Chelsea headed the list of 'lucky' local jurisdictions, all with more than 27 successes at Oxbridge per 1,000 of their 16/17-year-olds. Not given emphasis in the scandal of the 'golden triangle' splash was that among the places with the lowest admission success to Oxbridge there was also a group of London boroughs – but of course poorer ones like Havering and Barking and Dagenham.

These two examples highlight a widely held perception of geographic unfairness. It also demonstrates – witness 'shocked' senior politicians – that it is not just the media that often implicitly assumes issues of inequality, of many kinds, are essentially about where people live, and the nature of those neighbourhoods. In this world view, the problems of inequality largely or wholly stem from the character of the neighbourhoods in which people live. Indeed something that might be called a 'policy industry' has

---

[2] Public Health England's Longer Lives http://longerlives.phe.org.uk/.

developed based on the presumption that it is the character of these disadvantaged (or distressed) neighbourhoods in which 'disadvantaged' people are concentrated that causes their disadvantages (OECD 1998; ODPM 2005).

If we care about understanding or reducing inequality the fundamental issue is one of causation. There is clearly evidence of an association between living in a deprived neighbourhood, and poor economic and social outcomes. It is much less clear that deprived neighbourhoods actually cause these outcomes for their residents. We believe that improving the quality of public debate in this area requires two things. First, we need a clear and accurate understanding of how and why such deprived neighbourhoods arise. Why are poor people concentrated in poor neighbourhoods in cities while the rich are in rich neighbourhoods? This involves understanding better how cities function. Second, we need good quality evidence on whether disadvantage (as experienced by residents) is significantly caused or exacerbated by the characteristics of the neighbourhood (particularly the concentration of other poor residents), rather than simply reflecting sources of disadvantage operating at the individual or family level.

The aim of this chapter is to consider both these issues. We start by examining the growing evidence we have – and to which SERC researchers have contributed – as to the causes of 'residential segregation'; in particular why neighbourhoods within cities tend to have particular characteristics especially in terms of the income and associated characteristics of the people who live within them. One of our central points is that the most important causation runs from personal characteristics to incomes to the characteristics of the neighbourhoods in which people live and maybe not the other way round at all. A great proportion of the variation in earnings and incomes across individuals and households can be explained by their characteristics, such as health, ability, age, experience, background or motivation and drive. And these characteristics are correlated. Better educated people tend not only to earn more, for example, but they tend to be healthier and less likely to have criminal records; their children are more likely to get into good universities, and so on. So higher incomes go together with a host of other advantageous personal characteristics. Recognising this, it is easy to see that understanding spatial disparities in a number of dimensions requires us to understand why people with similar incomes tend to concentrate in similar neighbourhoods.

A central insight of urban economics, captured in the monocentric urban model of land use, provides an answer: people will pay through the housing market for nicer neighbourhoods, with better access to better jobs and income earning possibilities. As the supply of housing is limited in these neighbourhoods (often, as is explained in Chapter 4, policies amplify any natural restriction) this, in turn, means that access to better neighbourhoods is 'capitalised' in land markets. We all know that there are some neighbourhoods which are much 'nicer' to live in, for a variety of environmental and social reasons, and that their desirability makes it more expensive to live there. Research evidence – much of it produced, in the British context, by SERC researchers – now shows quite how much more it can cost to access many desired neighbourhood characteristics, from green space to 'better' schools; less crime to lower pollution and noise disturbance.[3] The evidence, in our judgement, quite clearly demonstrates that poor people get to be concentrated in worse neighbourhoods primarily because living in cheap neighbourhoods costs less (whether in private or social housing). 'Nice' neighbourhood amenities are not free, so those with less purchasing power tend to end up in less 'nice' places – either through the urban housing market or in some cases, via the social housing system (see next section).

If this mechanism explains much of the sorting of people with low incomes into disadvantaged neighbourhoods, the consequences of this sorting for inequality depend crucially on whether living in such neighbourhoods is in itself a significant additional source of disadvantage, adding to the overall incidence of poverty. That is, are 'neighbourhood effects' on individual outcomes significant? If the evidence suggests not, then policy really should concentrate on helping poor people and not be concerned with where they live or with 'neighbourhood mix'. Indeed it would suggest policies trying to socially engineer 'mixed neighbourhoods' by moving poorer people to richer neighbourhoods are at best a diversion: at worst counterproductive. The evidence on neighbourhood effects is the focus of the second substantive section of this chapter.

2.   WHAT CAUSES RESIDENTIAL SEGREGATION?

The differentiation of neighbourhoods in terms of their population, by ethnic composition, education, class, family status and lifestyle factors, comes about in various ways. But in market economies there are two key factors. The first is the varying preferences of different groups in terms of the locational and neighbourhood characteristics that matter most for them. Given that these more desirable characteristics of neighbourhoods are reflected in the cost of houses, then the second key factor is the

---

[3] For example, Ahlfeldt and Mastro (2012); Cheshire and Sheppard (2004b); Gibbons (2001, 2004), Gibbons and Machin (2005), Gibbons and Silva (2008) or Hilber (2010).

differences between households in their purchasing power. As with other desirable 'goods' (meals out, short-break holidays or season tickets to Premier League football) income constrains a household's ability to purchase them. One might think that public housing would act as a significant third factor. But at least in England, social housing is only 17.5 per cent of the total housing stock in 2012.[4] Also, as we shall discuss, structural features of the social housing system seem to reinforce rather than offset the market forces that help produce residential segregation.

There are many things which add greatly to one's quality of life or future earning power to which one only has access when one lives in a particular location. That is, living in a particular neighbourhood – even on a side of a particular street – provides access to specific packages of goods and amenities. It is useful to divide these into two classes: consumption or quality of life amenities such as access to parks, entertainment, low crime, places of worship or language communities; and life chances or productivity amenities such as better schools or jobs. The evidence overwhelmingly shows that the values of all desirable amenities, or locational attributes, of this type are reflected (capitalised) in house and land prices. This evidence has accumulated from an ever-increasing number of hedonic studies of housing markets: that is studies which break down the total price of housing into the prices paid for the particular attributes of the house including the amenities to which its location gives access.

These studies show an amazing range of locational attributes are reflected in the price of houses. There are studies which show that local crime rates are reflected in local house prices (Gibbons 2004) as is the value of access to parks of different types (for example, Cheshire and Sheppard 1995; Anderson and West 2006). But the value of access to parks interacts with local crime rates. In the highest crime rate neighbourhoods nearby parks turn out to have a negative price! Instead of providing better opportunities for recreation or exercise they provide better opportunities for muggers (Troy and Grove 2008). High quality local architecture is reflected in local house prices (Ahlfeldt and Mastro 2012; van Duijn and Rouwendal 2013). We also know that ambient noise is reflected in house prices and the source of that noise – trains, road or aircraft – generates different prices (see, for example, Day et al. 2006). Even intangible attributes of a neighbourhood, such as its level of social capital, seem to be reflected in house prices (Hilber 2010).

There is a strongly significant price paid for an extra m² of garden space,

---

[4] According to DCLG housing statistics table 100 local authority accounted for 7.3 per cent and housing associations and other social providers 10.2 per cent of the total stock of housing in 2012.

but all else equal a garden of a given size is more valuable if it is squarer (Cheshire and Sheppard 2004b). Housing markets work in subtle and sophisticated ways to value all these local public goods and locational amenities which, in turn, get capitalised into the price of land (Cheshire and Sheppard 1995; Hilber 2010; Cheshire et al. 2011).

Moreover, even within the same city, houses in the best and most desirable neighbourhoods do not just command a premium, they command a very substantial premium indeed. Again quoting Cheshire and Sheppard (2004b), 'moving' a house which in other respects had the characteristics of the sample mean, from the worst primary school to the best primary school catchment area was associated with an increase in price of 33.5 per cent. The impact of secondary schools was less but a similar move from the worst to best secondary school catchment area added an estimated 18.7 per cent to a house's price. These price effects were also very non-linear with respect to school quality. Buying the last 10 per cent of primary school quality cost nearly three times as much as moving from the worst to a school at the 90th percentile in the distribution of quality; for secondary schools the premium paid for accessing the best school in the urban area was even higher (Cheshire and Sheppard 2004b). This non-linearity of the price of schools with respect to their quality was also found in a recent study of the US (Chiodo et al. 2010). Home owners interested in using the housing market to 'buy' better quality education seem to be trying to buy access not to just a decent state-funded school but to the best in their area.

The prices paid for these locational attributes appear not just to reflect their current value but expected future changes as well. For example a study by Irwin (2002) showed that the value paid for a view over open countryside increased with the probability that the countryside in question would not be built on in the future. Cheshire and Sheppard (2004b) showed that the price paid through the housing market for school quality in Reading, England, reflected not just the current measure of the school's quality but the recent variability in that quality (a risk discount) and the likelihood that the house would remain zoned to that particular school in the future.

Residential Segregation is Self-Reinforcing

There are many amenities that all households value, such as clean air, easy access to jobs, better views or parks, where income differences alone generate residential segregation. Here segregation produces clearly unequal outcomes entirely generated by unequal incomes. But residential segregation also arises because preferences for particular neighbourhood attributes vary across households; as a result of differences in culture, age, lifestyle or just tastes. To the extent that this is important, preferences alone would produce segregation. Most of these preference-driven sources of residential segregation involve 'consumption/quality of life' attributes: associated with, for example, ethnic neighbourhoods or areas where young singles or the older and richer concentrate.[5] But some preference differences may also be correlated with income, such as a taste for specialist delicatessens versus discount stores, or easy access to betting shops compared to music venues. There may also be some neighbourhood attributes for which preferences vary in ways correlated with incomes that relate to 'production/life chance' issues, as with the informal local social networks used particularly by less-skilled workers to access information about relevant job opportunities (Blau and Robins 1992).

In other words, both income inequality and differences in preferences lead to residential segregation. But segregation would exist in cities even if incomes were all equal providing preferences differ or, if incomes varied, preferences were uniform. The patterns we actually observe reflect varying combinations of both these causal factors and the localised concentration of demand for any given attribute which an initial sorting generates is self-reinforcing. If more people who care about education are attracted into a neighbourhood because there is a good local school, then the schools get better; if picturesque architecture attracts those who value how an area looks then the appearance of the area will get nicer still; a few Sikh families might establish a place to worship, drawing in more Sikhs to the neighbourhood so creating a local market for shops or restaurants selling specialities. At the very bottom of the social ladder, however, there are some neighbourhoods with little to attract those who can afford to live elsewhere. Housing in such neighbourhoods tends to be among the very cheapest, attracting 'problem' families who, in turn, further drive down prices. Transport links to better paying jobs will be poor in such neighbourhoods since, as we have already seen, accessibility to jobs is capitalised into house prices. Those without jobs or job prospects cannot afford to pay the housing market costs of better transport links. Moreover given their low skills or poor health and so their poor prospects of getting better jobs, they are likely not quite so badly off living in less accessible but cheaper areas. In short, residential segregation is self-reinforcing.

---

[5] Anderson and West (2006) find that access to golf courses is particularly valued by the over 50s living in richer neighbourhoods. This is not surprising but is just one more example of how the housing market prices and so allocates access to valued attributes of neighbourhoods.

The Social Housing System

If market mechanisms lead to self-reinforcing residential segregation then to what extent can social housing counter these forces? In principle, social housing could provide a strong offsetting mechanism. However, in practice it does not because social housing is itself divided into more and less privileged neighbourhoods and, whilst there are exceptions, social housing itself is concentrated in poorer areas.

Across London boroughs, for example, the correlation coefficient between the proportion of the housing stock which is local authority owned and the Index of Multiple Deprivation (IMD) is 0.64; for housing association and other social housing it is 0.50. The three most deprived London boroughs on the basis of the IMD (also, as it happens, the three most deprived local authorities in England on that measure – again see below for why) have 38 per cent of their housing stock as social housing: the two least deprived boroughs have 11 per cent. The least deprived of all – and among the least deprived in England – is Richmond upon Thames where there are no local authority houses at all. At a smaller spatial scale the correlation between deprivation and concentrations of social housing is even stronger (Weinhardt 2010). Even within social housing the poorest and most deprived tend to get concentrated by the system itself on 'sink' estates.

The Incidence of Segregation and the Distribution of Incomes

In practice, as discussed at the start of this section, the actual price paid for particular amenities – and thus their 'exclusivity' – can vary in quite complex ways, both with the characteristics of particular local areas (see, for example, Cheshire and Sheppard, 2004b; Anderson and West 2006) and with wider economic and political developments influencing either the relative supply of or demand for particular locational attributes.[6] Some amenities or local public goods to which the location of a particular house gives access may be in very inelastic supply. There are only so many houses in London looking out over the Thames, for example, or in New York with a view of Central Park. We showed above that at least in Reading, England, the demand for school quality was really more or less for access to the 'best' local state schools and there is evidence suggesting this may also be the case in the US (Chiodo et al. 2010).

---

[6] For example the system of accessing or the quality of state-funded schools, the relative supply of space or changes in the distribution of disposable incomes – the point here.

The 'best' local school will cost substantially less if local policy does not rigidly allocate school places according to home address but is flexible; or allocates in some other way, such as by lot or according to academic achievement. It will also cost less in housing markets where average incomes are lower, because demand for school quality is income elastic. In a higher income housing market, people will be spending a higher proportion of their incomes trying to buy educational quality.

The price of access to the 'best' local school – or any other localised amenity in inelastic supply – will also tend to rise if local incomes become more unequally distributed over time; or in cities with more unequal overall distributions or income. Where or when incomes are more unequal the price of attributes in fixed supply will be relatively higher and we should expect an even stricter sorting of households between nicer and more disadvantaged neighbourhoods, with the best state schools becoming even more strictly reserved for the richest local households (see Cheshire and Sheppard 2004a).

The partial segregation or sorting of rich and poor into different neighbourhoods is thus an almost inevitable consequence of individual income inequality combined with residential choice in a market system. Differences in average incomes between neighbourhoods within a single housing market area – typically a wider city-region – are essentially the spatial articulation of income inequality between individuals (or households) in that society. The substantial increase in income inequality evident in many OECD countries, particularly the UK and the US, since the late 1970s would thus be expected to have increased the incidence of residential segregation. For neighbourhoods within US cities this has been clearly demonstrated (Massey et al. 2003). For the UK, evidence is scarcer and less clear-cut. There is some evidence, however, that an increase in local income inequality is accompanied by a widening spread of local house prices, as relatively richer people pursue a strictly limited supply of opportunities to access the best amenities and local public goods. In one case for which comparative data is available – for Reading in 1984 and 1993 – a rise in the Gini coefficient for the distribution of incomes (from 0.35 to 0.53) was accompanied by a rise in the Gini coefficient for house prices (from 0.22 to 0.28). One would expect the change in house price inequality would be significantly less than that for incomes, because many features of houses contributing to their price (such as central heating or number of rooms) do not have a tightly restricted supply. Equally in societies which are more equal – such as Finland – we observe less neighbourhood differentiation – a lower incidence of residential segregation. Finland is a very equal society and Helsinki, by the standards of a London or a New York, is a city without obvious residential segregation.

Residential Segregation, Urban Size and Agglomeration

We can think of neighbourhoods which have a distinct character as just one of those features of large cities that add to the range of goods and services citizens can consume. The bigger the population, the finer can be the sorting process and the more varied the neighbourhoods. Thus, the measured incidence of residential segregation will increase as cities get bigger. In a really big city there may be enough liberal middle class professionals to fill a census tract – even a local jurisdiction. In a small country town the liberal middle class professionals might occupy just a few houses or a street. In turn, these specialised or segregated neighbourhoods represent an agglomeration economy – in consumption more than production[7] – because the bigger a city is the more likely a household of a given income is to find a neighbourhood that matches their preferences.

One central consideration, that explains the link between city size and segregation, is the need for any labour market area to accommodate somewhere within it each of the groups represented in its workforce. The boundaries of housing markets closely shadow those of labour markets because earnings are the most important source of people's ability to finance housing. Therefore, it is natural to find that the degree of segregation across communities of a given population size (for example wards, census tracts – school catchment areas or districts) is greater in larger metropolitan regions than in small towns, while the level of diversity within these communities is greater in small towns than in metropolitan regions (Gordon and Monastiriotis 2006; Krupka 2007). That explains why London – so much larger than other British cities – has boroughs within it ranked at the extremes of deprivation for all local authority areas in England. London boroughs are in population terms the size of medium-sized towns but London as a whole functional metropolitan region is so big (around 9.5 million people as a Travel to Work Area or 13.5 million as a whole functional urban region) that some boroughs approximate neighbourhoods within it. Lincoln or Canterbury, cities of the size of London boroughs, will have just a few streets and perhaps some outlying dormitory villages where the rich inhabitants who work there live: London is big enough that the Borough of Richmond upon Thames is densely populated with the rich and educated.

Not only is there more choice of neighbourhoods in larger cities (in itself an agglomeration benefit) but because of more choice there will be better

---

[7] There may be agglomeration economies of production too from specialised neighbourhoods since there is some evidence they facilitate job matching (Blau and Robins 1992; Edin et al. 2003; Bayer et al. 2005).

matching (another source of agglomeration economies). Perhaps one of the most obvious examples relates to ethnic neighbourhoods. If you are a recent immigrant and want to be able to continue to speak your original language, engage in your native culture or religion, and buy food or other items you have developed a taste for, then there are great advantages in living in neighbourhoods with concentrations of people of similar origin (Edin et al. 2003). This is one obvious source of the ethnic neighbourhoods of large American and European cities. A study of children in primary schools found 300 different language communities in London living in linguistically and culturally specialised neighbourhoods (Baker and Eversley 2000). Indeed, cities like London or New York are so big that if you are, say, Jewish, you can not only choose to live within walking distance of a synagogue but you can live with conservative, moderate or liberal co-religionists, or just culturally familiar agnostics. In London the same is true for Muslims or Hindus. There are middle-class Hindu neighbourhoods and working-class Hindu neighbourhoods; there are Kurdish, Korean or Christian Lebanese neighbourhoods (Sepulveda et al. 2011).

Such agglomeration economies in consumption are not confined to ethnic groups. People and families of similar incomes, tastes or points in the life cycle tend to consume similar goods and services and require similar amenities. Living in a neighbourhood with a local wholefood supermarket, Montessori school, gastropub or microbrewery commands a premium: neighbourhoods with pawnbrokers, a local Aldi or discount store and a takeaway are cheaper. Families with young children will find benefits of networks and facilities, and mutual support as well as information, if they live in neighbourhoods with substantial numbers of families at the same stage in life. Young singles who eat out and have a taste for urban entertainment and culture will similarly find agglomeration economies in consumption if they find neighbourhoods in which large numbers of like-minded people are concentrated. More educated people, and people working in the liberal arts, may prefer to live in neighbourhoods with concentrations of similar types, sharing leisure and cultural pursuits and seeking similar local shops; business people may equally gain consumption benefits from concentrating in neighbourhoods in which other business people live.

To sum up then: spatial differences trigger adjustment – people and firms may move. But in the context of a single city not only is movement cheaper – mainly because it is easier to get information about jobs or housing costs in other neighbourhoods in your own city than cities hundreds of miles away – but it is not necessary for anyone to move to achieve substantial spatial adjustments. If you are looking for a new local job you are most likely to find one where they are relatively most plentiful and you can just adjust your commuting pattern; equally a firm can hire anyone who lives within commuting distance – in any direction. Because this type of adjustment to localised spatial labour market differences is so cheap and easy, the constant process of job turnover rapidly brings the different neighbourhoods of a city into balance. If we add to this the overwhelming evidence that all manner of amenities and differing qualities of local public goods and services are fully capitalised into housing costs, we can see that variation across individuals and households in incomes and preferences, interacting with innate differences in certain amenities (views, open space or air quality), leads to spatial sorting and the emergence of residential segregation. Differences in income are the primary driver because the rich can always outbid the poor. Moreover this process is inevitably self-reinforcing as richer inhabitants improve precisely those local amenities they value, so making their neighbourhoods more attractive to other richer people. Social housing does little to dampen this process.

Both the patterns and incidence of social segregation are therefore primarily the spatial manifestation of societal income inequality, the 'postcode lotteries' the British seem so fixated on are mainly just an expression of underlying inequality across households and individuals. Moreover the development of 'specialised neighbourhoods' has many benefits. People's welfare is significantly affected by the compatibility of their neighbours and how good their local services and amenities are – for them. Specialised neighbourhoods allow more choice and the bigger a city is the more such neighbourhoods there are and the more specialised they can be. A great benefit of cities is that a person can choose their neighbours rather than getting landed with just those within walking distance in their village. But of course the neighbourhood choice is constrained by income: it is not so much that poor people want to live in poor neighbourhoods (though there can be advantages such as facilities specialised for low incomes), they cannot afford to live in 'nice' neighbourhoods.

3. DOES RESIDENTIAL SEGREGATION MATTER: ARE THERE IMPORTANT 'NEIGHBOURHOOD EFFECTS'?

Is this residential segregation a bad thing in terms of welfare or equity? For economists, the answer to this question boils down to whether living in concentrations of poverty make poor people worse off than they would be otherwise. This is the essential question asked by the literature concerned with the existence of 'neighbourhood effects': are there negative externalities for poor people of living together with other poor people.

Alternatively, we might ask if there are positive externalities for poor people if they could live among richer neighbours. This is the underlying logic for believing that 'mixed neighbourhoods' would produce better economic (and social?) outcomes for poor people. Remember, however, that specialised neighbourhoods allow more choice and help people live with compatible neighbours, in areas with facilities and amenities useful to them (given their tastes and incomes) so sorting may well be a source of welfare gain.[8] This implies that 'mixed communities' will only benefit the poor if any such positive externalities poor people got from living together with other poor people were outweighed by the positive externalities and the welfare gains they would get from living with richer neighbours.

In fact, credible evidence on whether neighbourhood effects exist, let alone are important, has been entirely absent until quite recently. Instead policies justifying 'mixed communities', logically predicated on neighbourhood effects being a significant source of additional disadvantage for the poor, rested exclusively on correlations. For example:

> People living in deprived neighbourhoods are less likely to work, more likely to be poor and have lower life expectancy, more likely to live in poorer housing in unattractive local environments with high levels of antisocial behaviour and lawlessness and more likely to receive poorer education and health services. Living in a deprived area adversely affects individuals' life chances over and above what would be predicted by their personal circumstances and characteristics. (ODPM 2005, p. 6)

Careful reading of this quote shows that the author(s) go directly from the observed correlations to a diagnosis of causation. Certainly residential segregation will be correlated with a range of outcomes, but those correlations tell us nothing about causation and could result entirely from the sorting processes discussed in the previous section of this chapter.

Unfortunately, as is so often the case, it is extremely difficult to identify causal effects of neighbourhood characteristics on the outcomes for their inhabitants. As was discussed in Chapter 2 (in the context of the difficulty of isolating 'place' effects from 'people' effects as causal factors in inter-regional or inter-urban differences) the most important reason for this is the difficulty in fully controlling for those other (personal or family) factors influencing people's life chances independently of where they live. The more that rigorous studies – such as those highlighted below – control for family and personal differences, the weaker, even non-existent, have 'neighbourhood effects' turned out to be; an obvious reason why they may

---

[8] There is also evidence from the US that in fact having neighbours who are richer than you are is a direct source of welfare loss – see the discussion of Luttmer (2005) below.

have proved to be difficult to find! Indeed a careful reading of the literature would not persuade anyone that the effects – if they exist at all – are either large or general. Even in careful studies (for example, Buck and Gordon 2004) they have always been small relative to those found at the individual level, somewhat uncertain or complex – and least likely to emerge from those studies with the most rigorous methods and controls. The overwhelming evidence suggests neighbourhood effects on educational or economic outcomes are small to insignificant (Weinhardt 2010; Gibbons et al. 2013). So far as there is any rigorous evidence supporting significant neighbourhood effects it seems to relate only to health (Sanbonmatsu et al. 2012) and even here the effects are small, positive as well as negative, and could be caused by other factors.

There are two rigorous methodologies which one could use to isolate neighbourhood effects. The first is to track individuals over a long period to find out whether there was any tendency for the type of neighbourhood they were living in initially to influence their current prosperity or other features relating to their welfare. So far, the weight of evidence from several independent studies of this type, in both the UK (Gibbons 2001; Bolster et al. 2007; van Ham and Manley 2010), Canada (Oreopoulos 2003) and Sweden (Edin et al. 2003) is that the character of the neighbourhood in which people lived (10, 20 or 30 years) previously had little or no significant negative impact on their educational achievements or current prosperity. Indeed, for Sweden, Edin et al. show a significant improvement in labour market success for ethnic minority individuals who had originally lived in the 'worst' neighbourhoods (that is minority ethnic, contrary to official Swedish policy to 'mix' immigrants).

The second rigorous approach to identifying the causal role of neighbourhood characteristics on personal outcomes important for welfare is social experiment; that is people in deprived neighbourhoods are randomly assigned to 'treatment' and 'control' groups (as in medical random-controlled trials) with those in the treatment group being moved to more favourable neighbourhoods or vice versa. One study of this kind, from the US, provides the most powerful evidence to date on how little living in highly deprived neighbourhoods affects people's quality of life, their economic prospects or even their health. It comes from a major experimental programme, Moving to Opportunity (MTO), conducted in five large US cities during the 1990s. The MTO programme was designed both to pilot a policy for relief of concentrated neighbourhood poverty and as a scientific experiment to test the benefits of more mixed communities.

Families in the poorest neighbourhoods were offered help – with both housing costs and professional advice – to move to a more affluent neighbourhood. The professional advice alone cost $3,000 per treated family. To help isolate the effects on poor people of moving to an affluent neighbourhood, those families who qualified for the programme were randomly assigned to one of three groups. Group 1 had professional advice and financial help to move and had to move to a low (below 10 per cent) poverty neighbourhood; Group 2 just got financial help for housing, to move as they wished; Group 3, the control group, got nothing. Some 4,600 families were accepted onto the programme.

There are still some concerns about selection effects in this study, since participation was voluntary and presumably only families who thought they might benefit volunteered. Moreover volunteering families were screened to exclude those with a criminal record or rent arrears. Finally not all those offered the opportunity to move actually took it up. As a trial for a new drug, in other words, it would not have got past first base. Such trials are sensibly required to track those who refuse to participate as well as those that do, to avoid a selection bias in favour of finding positive outcomes. If only those who think they might benefit participate in a trial, for example, it is more likely positive outcomes will appear. Nevertheless the MTO's long-term follow-up of families offers some of the most direct evidence available so far on the differential effect of low- and high-poverty neighbourhoods on outcomes for disadvantaged families. There has been extensive and sophisticated analysis of outcomes in a succession of papers: Kling and colleagues (2005, 2007) analysed outcomes after five and ten years; Sanbonmatsu et al. (2012) analysed outcomes after 10–15 years.

All study findings with respect to economic outcomes have been clear-cut and exactly reflect those of the cohort studies reported above: moving from a truly deprived to a more affluent neighbourhood has no measurable effect at all on a person's economic success in terms of income, employment or likelihood of being welfare dependent. Results with respect to educational and behavioural outcomes were slightly more mixed and complex. There was some evidence, especially from Kling et al. (2007), of worse outcomes for boys and young men but better outcomes for girls and young women as a result of moving to a better neighbourhood. The differences observed were not statistically significant, however. The main statistically significant differences involved an increased incidence of arrest for property-related crime, together with worse behaviour in schools and within the family, for adolescent boys moving to more affluent neighbourhoods.

Evidence on outcomes on some 'quality of life' aspects, particularly health, is more suggestive of neighbourhood effects playing a part, although even here results are mixed. In the most recent MTO study, following outcomes up to 15 years after the original move, Sanbonmatsu et al. (2012) claimed to find evidence of positive health outcomes for the treatment group. Even here, however, the evidence was not all that decisive. In terms of psychological health and wellbeing they measured outcomes on five indicators: those in Group 1 who had help to move, provided it was to an affluent neighbourhood, scored significantly (at the 5 per cent level) better than members of the control group on one indicator but scored worse (again significant at the 5 per cent level) on another. They also scored better than the control group on a third indicator but only at the 10 per cent significance level. However, those who received financial help but could move to any neighbourhood they liked, did if anything slightly better overall, scoring worse than the control group on no indicator and better on two. The common finding was that those who had moved from the most deprived neighbourhoods scored significantly better on the indicator for psychological distress. Given that they had wanted to move from their original neighbourhoods, and been enabled to do so (while the control group who had also wanted to move had not been able to) this is, arguably, unsurprising. It also fits with the finding from a (simpler) UK study using the British Household Panel Study, which found the one clear neighbourhood effect to be on whether people liked the area in which they lived (Buck and Gordon 2004).

Results from the MTO study for indicators of physical health also reported by Sanbonmatsu et al. (2012) yielded slightly stronger evidence of neighbourhood effects playing a part. The main significant result was that those who had been helped to move – whether to a more affluent neighbourhood or to a neighbourhood of their choice – suffered less morbid obesity than the control and suffered less from the health problems caused by morbid obesity.[9]

On the face of it, the almost complete lack of evidence that neighbourhood effects play any role in determining life opportunities may seem a bit surprising, given the fact (discussed in the previous section) that people who have the resources are prepared to pay large amounts to live in areas offering what are perceived as better schooling opportunities for their children. It also seems surprising given evidence that schools do appear to perform better in higher status neighbourhoods. For example, in England, secondary schools reported as achieving the highest levels of academic progress ('value-added') are those with the highest quality intakes, and these are found particularly in areas with better-educated, typically

---

[9] The study by Sanbonmatsu et al. (2012) identifies three gradations of obesity, diabetes and physical limitations on movement but really these seem difficult to separate since morbid obesity is a cause of diabetes and also limits mobility. This is what underlies my judgement that really there was only one clear health indicator on which the movers scored better: morbid obesity. On self-reported physical health and the incidence of asthma and hypertension there were no differences between the three groups.

middle-class parents. At the other extreme, value-added seems to be particularly depressed in (poor) neighbourhoods with concentrations of lone parents (Gordon and Monastiriotis 2006). It is consistent, however, with the findings of Weinhardt (2010) that effectively forced moves to deprived neighbourhoods and poor performing schools had no significant impact on educational outcomes once all other relevant factors were controlled for.

A part of the answer to this apparent conundrum may come from studies on the role of peer groups within schools. This question has been the subject of much research by educationists, who have been interested not only in effects on the average child, but on how effects for low achievers from mixing with high achievers compare with the effects on high achievers of mixing with low achievers. In general, just as for neighbourhoods, the influence of peer groups on individual pupil achievements has not been found to be large in well executed studies – at least not in comparison to the overall range of achievement and the influence of personal and family background characteristics. Where there are discernible effects, however, they do not appear to be entirely symmetrical. For example, while a recent study of secondary school children in England found that overall achievements of pupils at age 14 were unaffected by the prior achievements of their schoolmates, there was some evidence that the lowest achievers actually lost out from mixing with high ability peers, while those with upper-middle abilities gained (Gibbons and Telhaj 2008). In terms of child happiness, the available evidence does not suggest that disadvantaged children will do better in a school with an advantaged middle-class intake than they would in a poor school (Gibbons and Machin 2008). Some of the educational evidence specifically calls into question the assumption that mixing is always a good thing, as with Hoxby and Weingarth's US study showing that pupils benefit the most from education among other pupils of similar ability (Hoxby and Weingarth 2005).

Less radically, analyses of school-level data in England suggest first that the major differences in effects of school (and area) context on secondary school exam outcomes are to be found between the best and the average, not between the worst and the average (Gordon and Monastiriotis 2006). Second, while the most residentially segregated urban regions display the most unequal results, this is essentially because they do better at the top end, not because they do significantly worse at the bottom end (ibid.). This is consistent with the evidence discussed above on how non-linear the price paid for school quality is with respect to the range of school quality (that is the extremely high relative premium paid for housing giving access to the very best schools). Given what we do seem to know about the impact of ability mix on individual educational outcomes, it seems quite rational for middle-class families to spend substantial resources to locate in areas where schools are free of disruptive influences. At the same time children from disadvantaged backgrounds may gain less from living in contexts where these influences simply operate at a somewhat lower level.

Are there Other Positive Externalities for the Poor of Living Close to the Rich?

From our discussion so far it appears that, while there is little if any evidence of material effects from neighbourhood social mix on 'production/ life chances', at least for the disadvantaged groups which are the major focus of concern, this may not be as true for 'consumption/quality of life' factors. This relates directly to a second possible motive for promoting greater social mix, namely that everyone, whether rich or poor, would benefit from living in more diverse communities. There is, however, some evidence (from a smaller number of studies) which casts doubt on even these 'direct' benefits of mixing. On the one hand, there is the issue of how comparisons with neighbours' relative living standards affect personal welfare. The burgeoning literature on 'happiness' (Layard 2005) provides much suggestive evidence that such relativities affect both people's sense of well-being and their behaviour. A more detailed study by Luttmer (2005) even concludes that a 10 per cent increase in the earnings of everyone else in a person's neighbourhood has as great a depressing effect on their happiness as a 10 per cent fall in their own income – apparently because it tends to make the poorer-paid work longer hours, thus spending less time with their families and having less leisure. As a single study this is not enough to confidently conclude that social mix is in welfare terms a bad thing because those on low incomes are happier amongst others on low incomes, but it does call into question the assumption that putting the poor in more affluent neighbourhoods must make them happier. In the one British study of how residential composition affects individuals' attachment to their local neighbourhoods, Livingston et al. (2008) found only weak relationships with either social mix or individuals' social/tenure fit to their neighbourhood attachments. For both more and less advantaged groups, however, they did find attachments to be stronger in areas which had an affluent local population.

The second reason for scepticism about the 'quality of life' benefits of social mix stems from evidence that 'specialisation' of neighbourhoods' provides both economic and welfare benefits for their residents. In the private housing market at least, people tend to put a lot of effort into finding a neighbourhood which is both congenial and convenient for their interests and lifestyle, rather than one which is simply of higher social status. That is because people directly gain from living with compatible and complementary neighbours. Indeed, as discussed extensively in section 2, this is one of the fundamental mechanisms that help drive residential segregation.

4. CONCLUSIONS

Our main conclusion is that when it comes to determining your life chances and welfare, who you are is much more important than where you live in a city. The main cause of spatial disparities within cities is the residential sorting of households across areas. This process is largely conditioned by people's incomes, as well as preferences and policy factors, and suggests that income inequality and poverty and the family and personal characteristics which determine this are far more important in determining individual outcomes than the neighbourhoods in which people live.

Poverty arises from many sources, including the changing structure of employment. Policies themselves may have contributed to this through both the tax structure and the welfare system. As pointed out in the previous chapter, there has been an increasing polarisation in the job market and the payoff to high-level skills has risen, leaving the lower skilled and less educated behind, and it is these gaps that are manifest in the spatial patterns of income and segregation that we observe within cities in nearly all OECD countries. Redistribution of resources and opportunities from the richer to the poor seems to have had less emphasis over recent years. But this is likely to be a more effective – certainly a more cost-effective – way of helping the poor than trying to ensure that they live in more affluent neighbourhoods given the paucity of hard evidence that neighbourhood effects matter much (and seem to matter not at all for economic outcomes). That is, policies which successfully reduced societal inequality would also be a far more effective way of reducing residential segregation. So, even people who continue to believe (despite the paucity of rigorous evidence) in the importance of adverse neighbourhood effects should support redistribution of opportunities and incomes to the poor rather than insisting on directly trying to 'mix communities'. Such efforts cost real resources and there is precious little evidence that they help the really disadvantaged. We return to the implications of this diagnosis for policy responses to deprived neighbourhoods and poverty in Chapter 8.

These questions of policy aside, what is clear, however, is not only that residential segregation is a virtually universal urban phenomena – it was highly developed in Ancient Rome and is obvious in all the larger cities in the world – but that there is still more to learn about why it occurs.

The explanation offered in this chapter and supported, in our judgement, by much recent urban economics research is that it is effectively a spatial manifestation of the inequality of household incomes in the urban area interacting with variation in household preferences. The more unequal are household incomes, the more obvious is social segregation. Richer people are not only richer but they are better educated, fitter, healthier and less likely to be (at least detected) criminals. Houses in neighbourhoods which are more desirable in terms of their amenities or access to income earning opportunities cost more, much more. So the housing market ensures that richer households are concentrated in 'nicer' neighbourhoods.

It does not follow from this, however, that living in a poor neighbourhood is in any way a cause of social disadvantage. There are good reasons to be concerned about lack of social mobility, especially in Britain, and be worried by the big differences in premature death across the population. But it is not at all clear why we should be worried *per se* that the children of people living in Richmond upon Thames have a much greater chance of getting into Oxbridge than those whose parents live in Barking and Dagenham, unless, of course, it is the fact of living in Barking and Dagenham that causes them to be less likely to get into Oxbridge or die young. However, the evidence strongly suggests any causal link between the characteristics of the neighbourhood in which one lives or is raised and one's life chances is at best very weak indeed and likely nonexistent. At least within cities – residential segregation largely reflects personal inequality rather than causing it and is caused by sorting in the housing market (including social housing) constrained by ability to pay.

REFERENCES

Ahlfeldt, Gabriel and Alexandra Mastro. 2012. 'Valuing iconic design: Frank Lloyd Wright architecture in Oak Park, Illinois'. *Housing Studies* 27, 1079–1099.

Anderson, Soren T. and Sarah E. West. 2006. 'Open space, residential property values, and spatial context'. *Regional Science and Urban Economics* 36, 773–789.

Baker, Philip and John Eversley (eds). 2000. *Multilingual Capital: The Languages of London's Schoolchildren and the Relevance to Economic, Social and Educational Policies*. London: Battlebridge.

Bayer, P., S.L. Ross and G. Topa. 2005. 'Place of work and place of residence: informal hiring networks and labor market outcomes'. *Journal of Political Economy* 116, 1150–1196.

Blau, David M. and Philip K. Robins. 1992. 'Job search outcomes for the employed and unemployed'. *Journal of Political Economy* 98, 637–655.

Bolster, Anne, Simon Burgess, Ron Johnston, Kelvyn Jones, Carol Propper and Rebecca Sarker. 2007. 'Neighbourhoods, households and income dynamics: a semi-parametric investigation of neighbourhood effects'. *Journal of Economic Geography* 7, 1–38.

Buck, Nick and Ian Gordon. 2004. 'Does Spatial Concentration of Disadvantage Contribute to Social Exclusion?', in M. Boddy and M. Parkinson (eds), *City Matters: Competitiveness, Cohesion and Urban Governance*. Bristol: Policy Press, pp. 71–92.

Cheshire, Paul, Christian A.L. Hilber and Ioannis Kaplanis. 2011. 'Evaluating the Effects of Planning Policies on the Retail Sector: Or Do Town Centre First Policies Deliver the Goods?', SERC Discussion Paper 0066. London: SERC.

Cheshire, Paul and Stephen Sheppard. 1995. 'On the price of land and the value of amenities'." *Economica* 62, 247–267.

Cheshire, Paul and Stephen Sheppard. 2004a. 'Introduction to feature: the price of access to better neighbourhoods'. *The Economic Journal* 114, F391–F396.

Cheshire, Paul and Stephen Sheppard. 2004b. 'Capitalising the value of free schools: the impact of supply characteristics and uncertainty'. *The Economic Journal* 114, F397–F424.

Chiodo, Abbigail J., Rubén Hernández-Murillo and Michael T. Owyang. 2010. 'Nonlinear effects of school quality on house prices'. *Review – Federal Reserve Bank of St. Louis* 92, 185–204.

Day, B., I. Bateman and I. Lake. 2006. 'Estimating the Demand for Peace and Quiet Using Property Market Data'. CSERGE Working Paper EDM 06-03, UEA.

Edin, P.-A., P. Frederiksson and O. Åslund. 2003. 'Ethnic enclaves and the economic success of immigrants: evidence from a natural experiment'. *Quarterly Journal of Economics* 118, 329–357.

Gibbons, S. 2001. 'Paying for Good Neighbours: Estimating the Value of an Implied Educated Community', Centre for Economics, Discussion Paper 0017. London: London School of Economics.

Gibbons, S.. 2004. 'The costs of urban property crime'. *The Economic Journal* 114, F441–F463.

Gibbons, Stephen and Stephen Machin. 2005. 'Valuing Rail Access Using Transport Innovations', Centre for Economic Performance (CEP) Discussion Paper 0611. London: CEP.

Gibbons, Stephen and Stephen Machin. 2008. 'Valuing school quality, better transport, and lower crime: evidence from house prices'. *Oxford Review of Economic Policy* 24, 99–119.

Gibbons, S. and O. Silva. 2008. 'School Quality, Child Wellbeing and Parents' Satisfaction'. Centre for Economics of Education Working Paper, London School of Economics.

Gibbons, Stephen and Shqiponja Telhaj. 2008. 'Peers and Achievement in England's Secondary Schools', SERC Discussion Paper 0001. London: SERC.

Gibbons, Stephen, Olmo Silva and Felix Weinhardt. 2013. 'Everybody needs good neighbours? Evidence from students' outcomes in England'. *The Economic Journal* 123, 831–874.

Gordon, Ian and Vassilis Monastiriotis. 2006. 'Urban size, spatial segregation and inequality in educational outcomes'. *Urban Studies* 43, 213–236.

Hilber, C.A.L. 2010. 'New housing supply and the dilution of social capital'. *Journal of Urban Economics* 67(3), 419–437.

Hilber, Christian A.L. and Wouter Vermeulen. 2011. 'The Impact of Restricting Housing Supply on House Prices and Affordability: Report for NHPAU'. London: DCLG.

Hills, John 2007. 'Ends and Means: The Future Roles of Social Housing in England'. London: Centre for Analysis of Social Exclusion, London School of Economics and Political Science.

Hoxby, Caroline M. and Gretchen Weingarth. 2005. 'Taking Race Out of the Equation: School Reassignment and the Structure of Peer Effects. Working paper, Harvard University.

Irwin, Elena G. 2002. 'The effects of open space on residential property values'. *Land Economics* 78, 465–480.

Kling, J., J. Ludwig and L.F. Katz. 2005. 'Neighbourhood effects on crime for female and male youth: evidence from a randomised housing voucher experiment'. *Quarterly Journal of Economics* 120(1), 87–130.

Kling, Jeffrey R., Jeffrey B. Liebman and Lawrence F. Katz. 2007. 'Experimental analysis of neighborhood effects'. *Econometrica* 75, 83–119.

Krupka, Douglas J. 2007. 'Are big cities more segregated? Neighbourhood scale and the measurement of segregation'. *Urban Studies* 44, 187–197.

Layard, Richard. 2005. *Happiness: Lessons from a New Science.* London: Penguin.

Livingston, M., N. Bailey and A. Kearns. 2008. *People's Attachment to Place – The Influence of Neighbourhood Deprivation.* Coventry: Chartered Institute of Housing/Joseph Rowntree Foundation.

Luttmer, Erzo F.P. 2005. 'Neighbors as negatives: relative earnings and well-being'. *The Quarterly Journal of Economics* 120, 963–1002.

Massey, Douglas S., Mary J. Fischer, William T. Dickens and Frank Levy. 2003. 'The Geography of Inequality in the United States, 1950–2000 [with Comments]'. *Brookings–Wharton Papers on Urban Affairs*, 1–40.

ODPM. 2005. 'Sustainable Communities: People, Places and Prosperity', Cmd 6425. London: HMSO.

OECD. 1998. *Integrating Distressed Urban Areas.* Paris: OECD.

Oreopoulos, Philip. 2003. 'The long-run consequences of living in a poor neighborhood'. *The Quarterly Journal of Economics* 118, 1533–1575.

Sanbonmatsu, Lisa , Jordan Marvakov, Nicholas A. Potter, Fanghua Yang, Emma Adam, William J. Congdon, Greg J. Duncan, Lisa A. Gennetian, Lawrence F. Katz, Jeffrey R. Kling, Ronald C. Kessler, Stacy Tessler Lindau, Jens Ludwig and Thomas W. McDade. 2012. 'The long-term effects of moving to opportunity on adult health and economic self-sufficiency'. *Cityscape* 14, 109–136.

Sepulveda, Leandro, Stephen Syrett and Fergus Lyon. 2011. 'Population super-diversity and new migrant enterprise: the case of London'. *Entrepreneurship & Regional Development* 23, 469–497.

Troy, Austin and J. Morgan Grove. 2008. 'Property values, parks, and crime: a hedonic analysis in Baltimore, MD'. *Landscape and Urban Planning* 87, 233–245.

van Duijn, Mark and Jan Rouwendal. 2013. 'Cultural heritage and the location choice of Dutch households in a residential sorting model'. *Journal of Economic Geography* 13, 473–500.

van Ham, Maarten and David Manley. 2010. 'The effect of neighbourhood housing tenure mix on labour market outcomes: a longitudinal investigation of neighbourhood effects'. *Journal of Economic Geography* 10, 257–282.

Weinhardt, Felix. 2010. 'Moving into the Projects: Social Housing Neighbourhoods and School Performance in England', SERC Discussion Paper 0044. London: SERC.

PART II

Land use regulation: the need to be guided by markets but not obey them

4. Planning for a housing crisis: or the alchemy by which we turn houses into gold

1. INTRODUCTION

A common thread in this book is how unexpected consequences, often the exact opposite of those intended, can result if policy is formulated without allowing for the power of markets. No policy arena offers a more dramatic example of this than British planning – land use regulation – policy. In very simple terms what British land use regulation – planning – has done is restrict the supply of housing space. It restricts the amount of land available for housing and it also restricts the height of buildings. Look at the skyline of London compared to New York, where height restrictions *increase* house prices (Glaeser et al. 2005). What do economists know about the impact of these kinds of restrictions? Economists like to retain a healthy level of scepticism about everything and much in economics is uncertain and debated. But there are some things on which nearly all mainstream economists would agree. Perhaps the nearest to unanimity one could find would be the proposition that if the supply of a good does not vary much as its price changes, and if the demand for that good rises proportionally more than incomes as incomes rise but is subject to cyclical fluctuations, then the price of that good will rise over the long run relative to other prices and its price will be volatile over the cycle. That, in a nutshell, is one of the basics of market analysis, one of the fundamental elements of economic analysis with a history of research and application going back at least 200 years.

The supply of some goods is determined by nature: there is not all that much gold in the world and the amount produced from year to year cannot change very much no matter what happens to the gold price, and anyway current production does not have much effect on the supply of gold. There is an awful lot of the stuff out there mined and refined over a 10,000-year period of human interest in gold. But still, in the short term, supply is fairly restricted relative to more common metals and so over periods when demand rises the price of gold increases and gold prices are volatile.

In contrast to these natural constraints that underpin the relatively high and volatile price of gold, the high price of housing is essentially driven by policy not by natural constraints (as Figure 4.1 bears testimony). In short, the British planning system has been turning houses into gold ever since the Town and Country Planning Act came into law in 1947. Nor is Britain alone. We have been seeing land use regulation have rather similar effects in an increasing number of countries over the past 25 years or so. One can point to the US – mainly the East and West coasts – Korea, and even such 'land-strapped' countries as Australia and New Zealand. The Netherlands, by nature a country with a limited supply of land, managed to maintain the supply of new housing until quite recently but in the past 20 years has been edging towards supply restriction too.

British policy has been restricting space since 'containment' policies were imposed after the 1947 Act and those restrictions were tightened during the 1950s as Greenbelt boundaries were established and more and more land around towns and cities was taken out of the effective land supply in just those places where demand has grown most strongly over the years. Planners (and newspapers) assume demand for housing is driven by the numbers of households, but analysis shows that this has surprisingly little impact on demand. What has really increased the demand for houses is rising incomes: as people get richer, they try to buy more space and bigger gardens – the supply of which is exactly what British planning policies restrict. So what policy has done more effectively in Britain than in almost any other country is turn a good whose long-term supply should be responsive to price (the supply of building materials and builders is in the long run expandable at more or less constant cost and the unit cost of building houses actually falls the more are built on a given site) into a good whose supply is almost fixed. The results for land and house prices over the very long term (illustrated in Figure 4.1) demonstrate exactly what happens. As economics predicts, the volatility of the housing market and the real price of both houses and land for houses has increased dramatically since the mid-1950s. This is one inevitable outcome. Another is that the size of new houses has got ever smaller (it is space we are rationing) and housing affordability has seriously worsened. Our planning system has turned houses into the economic equivalent of gold except that, of course, houses have become very superior gold. We all want to buy houses and more housing space as we get richer but we can manage with very little gold. In the rest of this chapter we explain and document these problems and show how the problems in Britain compare with and seem to be spreading to other countries.

All rich countries in the OECD have systems of land use regulation. There are good reasons for this. Land markets suffer from endemic

problems of 'market failure': land and housing markets left to their own
devices would not produce socially optimal outcomes. The most obvious
reason for this is that the value of and enjoyment derived from any parcel
of land is highly dependent on the uses of and activities on all neighbouring parcels – whether that is heavy industry, a beautiful garden or a convenient metro station. The value – positive or negative – associated with
such uses is not appropriately reflected in prices in unregulated markets.[1]
Then there are public goods such as, habitat, open space, historic cityscape or potential problems of monopoly. As is argued at greater length in
Chapter 6, we need a system for regulating land markets.

The British do this through a regulatory system constructed by the
Town and Country Planning Act in 1947 and essentially unchanged since.
The act set out to contain urban areas and stop them spilling out into surrounding countryside and preserve amenities of various kinds including
separating land uses which might be incompatible (for example industry
from residential). At the same time the aim was to provide lower density
and greener living conditions in the new towns. As is discussed in more
detail below, the British system therefore controls, independently of prices,
the amount of land available not just for housing but for all urban uses of
land including for offices, retail or commercial use. That is, it 'rations' the
supply of space for development. As it has developed, the British system
is remarkable in the degree to which it restricts development and renders
housing supply (indeed supply of property for all purposes) almost completely insensitive to price changes, that is highly price-inelastic. But such
restrictiveness is spreading around the developed world. With that spread,
as we show below, comes rising real house prices, falling affordability and
increasing price volatility. In short, understanding the impact of the highly
restrictive British planning system is important in the context of UK urban
policy. But the British experience also provides some idea of what the
future might hold for other countries as planning systems become increasingly restrictive.

The 1947 Act was conceived in a world which believed in the efficiency
and wisdom of state control of markets, had an idealistic vision of a benign
socialism and was enthused with a commendable aspiration to build a
better future. Without a quite detailed understanding of political and social
history it is difficult to appreciate how different that Fabian world view was
from our present and how much it owed to the political and administrative

---

[1] As explained in Chapter 3, even the most elementary hedonic exercise tells us, such 'goods'
as access to metro stations or 'bads' such as pollution from heavy industry, are reflected in
house prices. Such values are fully capitalised into land prices. The market failure is that,
in the absence of regulation, it is not the person responsible for producing these localised
goods or bads who benefits or pays.

experience of a quasi state-run economy during two world wars. The planning system bequeathed to us by the 1947 Act is the last element of that period of post-World War II reconstruction which has not been at least substantially reformed to take into account market realities. There have been many modifications since 1947 but the act established an approach and framework that has not been superseded. The policy framework and aspirations it created derived from design and engineering intellectual traditions; and were informed by a belief in the efficacy of state planning.

British planning policy, analysis and implementation were, and still are, focused on physical units of housing: areas of land and densities of buildings. Decisions – despite the attempted reform with the National Planning Policy Framework (NPPF) of 2012 – have taken no notice of market signals or the real drivers of demand or supply. Indeed until 2007[2] decisions about housing numbers, or the supply of any other category of real estate, were explicitly prevented from considering the impacts of decisions on prices. Prices were not a 'material consideration' within the statutory framework governing planning. Following a 2004 report for the UK Treasury (Barker 2004), at least the system was supposed to take into account the impact of plans on housing affordability; and with the introduction of the 2012 NPPF there is an injunction to 'take account of market signals' (paras 17 and 22) but the word 'price' appears only once in the 47 pages of the main document and the role of markets in signalling shortages is almost invisible. In contrast the phrase 'Greenbelt' appears 46 times and never in a critical context. The British planning system also completely ignores impacts on the cost of non-residential real estate with the results analysed in Chapter 5.

It is worth remembering that as originally conceived the process of town and country planning was intended to decant people from the high density slum conditions of large industrial cities and allow greener and lower density development in new towns and city extensions. Originally 'density controls' were designed to reduce densities and allow people more space in greener environments. Early plans earmarked land to accommodate then expected population growth. Unfortunately – and it is very unfortunate as is explained below – no account was taken of the effect of increasing incomes on the demand for space, and 'urban containment boundaries' (such as the original boundaries of Greenbelts or Areas of Outstanding Natural Beauty) largely reflected the transport realities, the incomes, the distribution of population and the ways of life as they existed in 1947 – more than two generations ago.

---

[2] Following Barker (2004) Planning Policy Strategy 3 (PPS3) was published requiring planners to take account of the impact of their decisions with respect to proposed housing numbers on 'housing affordability'.

These boundaries tended to become ossified with the result that our landscape has become a palimpsest of overdrawn lines freezing the status quo. Great swathes of land at the edge of cities are impossible to develop because they are Greenbelt: for example 77.8 per cent of the area of East Surrey – effectively a dormitory suburb of London – is Greenbelt land.[3] When today's planners look on maps to search out some potential areas they could designate for housing they find that almost everywhere is blocked from development for some reason or another. To this has been added the urgings of the 'densification' lobby (Urban Task Force 1999). While the explicit policy target for 60 per cent of all new housing to be on so-called 'brownfield' sites[4] was dropped in the 2012 NPPF, nevertheless, policy is officially to build on brownfield sites so far as possible and local authorities are free to set their own 'brownfield targets'.

The net result is that we now have a planning system directed to achieve precisely the opposite of what was originally conceived in 1947 – that is to allow the mass of the urban population more space and a greener environment in which to live. Since policy intentionally and very firmly restricts the land for housing or any other urban development it is no surprise that the supply of housing has become progressively more inelastic. Houses that provide more space and a greener environment cannot be built without the land on which to build them; and our system both explicitly and implicitly (by reason of how it is controlled and as a result of the incentives it has thrown up), drastically rations such space.

2. ELASTICITY OF SUPPLY AND PRICE VOLATILITY

Not only does restrictive planning increase the price of housing, as predicted by the basic laws of supply and demand, but it also increases price volatility. Price volatility is damaging for a number of reasons. It transfers asset values between groups. It creates financial instability, especially since house purchases are largely financed on credit – the origin of the current crisis in the financial system. It also makes monetary policy more difficult even for independent central bankers since it becomes increasingly difficult

---

[3] A third of the resident working population in East Surrey work in London.

[4] Like other concepts in the British planning system 'brownfield land' is a legal rather than a functional definition. Any land previously developed is in effect 'brownfield'. Although the term suggests polluted former industrial sites much of such land as is discussed below in fact has high environmental value, for example important wildlife habitats in former quarries or Ministry of Defence land, or amenity value because of informal access such as the park-like grounds of some 19th-century hospitals.

Table 4.1 *Price volatility in English housing and housing land markets in real terms*

Trough–Peak	Real price: 1975 = 100		% Change trough–peak		Peak–trough market house Completions 1975 = 100	
	Housing Land	Houses	Housing Land	Houses	Index	% Change
1982	114.8	95.1			75.2[a]	
1989	345.7	170.4	+208.0	+79.2	133.9[a]	+78.1
1993/95[b]	125.4	106.5	−63.7	−37.6	88.7	−33.8
2007	480.7	262.7	+283.33	+146.7	110.0	+24.0

[a] Completions bottomed in 1981 and peaked in 1988
[b] Real land prices and completions bottomed out in 1993: house prices in 1995

Sources: As Figure 4.1 and house completions, Table 2.6 DCLG/National Statistics (2008).

to ignore housing-market pressures rather than just inflation targeting in setting monetary policy. Also booms and busts in house prices create oscillating wealth effects feeding through to consumption spending.[5]

It is straightforward to argue that the less elastic is the supply of housing the higher are prices and the more price volatility one should expect for a given change in demand. This, after all, is the basis of any definition of elasticity. As discussed in this section, however, this simple link from restrictive supply to price volatility has profound implications for the highly restricted British housing market.

As Table 4.1 and Figure 4.1 show, the British housing market has been particularly subject to price volatility for the past generation. Glaeser et al. (2008) analysed price volatility and its relationship to the elasticity of supply across 79 US metropolitan areas. During the cycle of the 1980s and early 1990s the most volatile of the 79 markets was Los Angeles, where real prices rose 67 per cent from 1984 to the peak of 1989 and declined by 33 per cent in the following five years. This was substantially less than the average for England of a 79.2 per cent increase followed by a 37.6 per cent fall. The boom in Britain from the 1995 trough to the peak in 2007 was getting on for twice that of the previous cycle – an increase of 146.7 per

[5] Volume volatility also has its disadvantages since it will be associated with larger changes in employment. However, as the discussion of Glaeser et al. (2008) suggests, there may be offsetting effects if expectations of future prices (damped in more supply elastic markets) influence current demand since demand swings would be damped, too, in the more supply elastic markets.

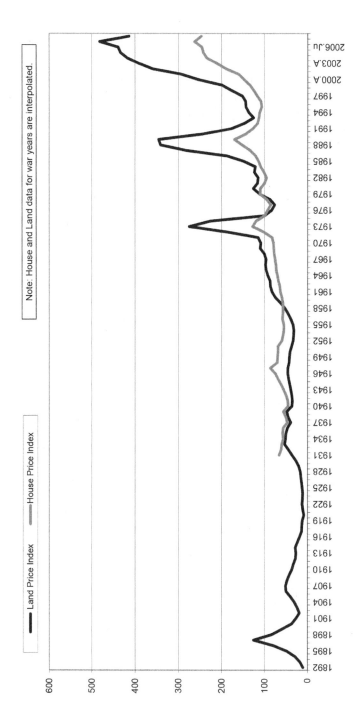

Sources: Land prices: Vallis (1972a, b, c), DOE Housing and Construction Statistics and VOA; house prices:DCLG/National Statistics (2008, Table 502).

Figure 4.1 Real land and house price indices (1975 = 100)

cent in real terms. We do not yet know how large in proportionate terms the subsequent fall will turn out to be, but at the time of writing (in 2013) it seemed already to be over with demand recklessly boosted in the Budget of March 2013 with the Help to Buy scheme. Worryingly, house building in England, measured by completions, has responded ever more reluctantly to price booms reflecting the ever increasing inelasticity of supply. We might note that the latest figures of house completions in England – for 2012/13 (Table 209 CLG/ONS (2008)) – albeit on a slightly different basis, suggest a fall to an indexed value of 57.9 compared to 1975 = 100: almost certainly the lowest in 100 years except for times of war – and below the level of the Edwardian era.

In reality, the simple link between housing supply and volatility predicted by basic demand and supply analysis is complicated by the dynamic nature of housing markets and the fact that expectations about future prices can influence both supply and demand. Glaeser et al. (2008) provide a plausible model of housing market cycles in which expectations about future house prices in the local market influence both demand and supply. Developers in their decisions to build may be most interested in expected future prices, rather than current prices. Buyers, when deciding to buy and when to buy, may also take account of future expected rates of house price change. This model suggests price and quantity volatility in response to conditions of supply may not be as clear-cut as the simple theory of markets outlined in the introduction suggests. If expected future house prices influence the behaviour of both buyers and sellers there are opposing forces generated by rising prices and in principle these could offset each other. If supply is less elastic then prices will rise proportionally more for any increase in demand which will feed back to expectations about future prices and so to current demand but also to the response of developers. Two clear-cut propositions emerge, however. In any 'bubble' that might arise,[6] price increases will be greater in markets where supply is less elastic; and any bubbles will be shorter in duration and occur less often in markets in which supply is more elastic. So even allowing for expectations about future prices influencing both demand and supply the outcome is likely not that different from that predicted by a more basic model. More inelastic supply will be associated with more price volatility and longer periods of what might be thought of as 'disequilibrium' – prices above the costs of production.

Glaeser et al. (2008) then test these propositions against the evidence for

---

[6] Glaeser et al. (2008) suggest a reasonable definition of a housing market 'bubble' would be when house prices rise significantly above the costs of constructing new houses including the costs of land, although they avoid a judgement as to whether recent housing cycles in the US have contained elements of a 'bubble'.

the 79 US metropolitan region markets using purely topographical indicators (to avoid any possibility of endogeneity[7]) as measures of the elasticity of supply and find that the evidence is consistent with their model. To investigate the first proposition they divide the 79 markets into two at the median of their measure of supply elasticity. They find that in the 1984–89 boom house prices increased in real terms an average of 23.2 per cent in the less supply-elastic markets but only 5 per cent in the more supply-elastic markets. They then investigate the second proposition by looking at the length of booms in the more and less inelastic markets. Here they divided the markets into three groups according to the estimated elasticity of supply in each. In the post-1996 boom period the ratio of the real house price to the full cost of construction rose at least 20 per cent above its 1996 level for an average of only 1.7 years in the most supply-elastic one-third of metropolitan areas, but for an average of 4.1 years in the least elastic one-third.

This evidence does not prove whether there was a bubble in some US housing market areas but does show that price volatility is closely related to the elasticity of supply of new housing. The evidence is also consistent with a model in which expectations about future house prices influence current demand and in which the supply side of the housing market is endogenised. When we compare this to the English housing market we find not only is the average price volatility in England greater than in the most extreme urban area market in the US but it has increased very substantially over time while the supply of new housing – as the last columns of Table 4.1 show – has become even more inelastic. A price increase in real terms between 1993 and 2007, 1.85 times as large in percentage terms as in the previous boom, produced an increase in building of only 31 per cent of the previous increase. The peak of market construction in 2007 was only 83 per cent of the level of construction of market housing averaged in each year of the 1960s. And the trough of construction (assuming the trough was in 2012–13) was well below all previous troughs. One of the main findings of Barker (2003) was how inelastic the supply response of house construction was in England and Wales. The evidence of Table 4.1 is simply further support for that view.

To summarise: the more inelastic is the supply response to price changes, the higher will be the real price level and the more volatile will be prices. In England, but increasingly in other countries, policy has been

---

[7] This purely physical measure of the supply of buildable land – that is excluding land with a slope of more than 15 degrees and excluding ocean or large bodies of water – within a 50 km radius of a metro area turns out to be quite closely correlated with measures of regulatory restrictiveness.

severely if indirectly restricting the responsiveness of supply to price. Not only that but output of houses in each successive boom has responded less, and in each trough has fallen to new lows since the 1960s. Although the restrictions on land availability have been in place since 1947 because the annual rate of new construction is small relative to the total stock of houses, these restrictions were slow to kick in but have been cumulative. In each cycle the situation becomes worse. Any attempt to fix this problem requires us to understand exactly how planning policies restrict supply. It is to this issue that we now turn.

3.   HOW DOES LAND USE PLANNING RESTRICT SUPPLY?

Let us turn to examine more closely the role of land use planning in restricting supply. The British system was identified by Barker (2003) as the primary source of Britain's housing supply inelasticity. But to understand the route by which our land use planning system or other systems of regulating land markets in use around the world, may constrain housing supply it is essential to understand the specifics of the system and the institutional and fiscal context within which it operates. As in many cases the British system of land use regulation and how it interacts with our fiscal system seems on close examination to be something of an international outlier.

Planning addresses other issues as well, but some system of land use planning or regulation is essential if for no other reason than the endemic problems of market failure associated with land markets. As noted in the introduction, and discussed further in Chapter 6, problems of market failure are endemic to land markets as a result of the particular characteristics of land. Because every parcel of land has a fixed location and significant transaction costs associated with it, owners or occupiers are locked into individual plots and their investments are illiquid. Moreover enjoyment of their rights of occupation is inevitably tied up with the actions of neighbouring plot occupants and all parcels are different from all other parcels because of their particular location. As explained in Chapter 3, a parcel's location determines consumption of a wide range of (local) public goods (such as less crime or cleaner air) and amenities (such as better views) available at specific locations; and of course, it is a plot's location with respect to accessibility to jobs that is central to modern theories of urban land prices. There are, moreover, issues related to the supply of public goods, such as open space which also generate problems of market failure in land markets.

Because of the very large number of owners and interested parties involved, transaction costs for individual plot owners are typically too large for owners to combine or co-ordinate actions to offset for these problems of market failure. This makes it costly for individuals to club together to purchase legal property rights to stop development on land where the wider social interest might be to conserve it as open space. This can happen – the National Trust is in effect an example – but is unlikely to provide a socially optimal solution to the problems of market failure.[8] Other types of economically based policy interventions in the form of fiscal measures and incentives have perhaps been under-explored, one suspects partly because of the relative lack of attention mainstream economics and the education of economists have given to land.

As argued in Chapter 3, not only does the fixed location of land lead to particular types of market failure but it also generates important distributional effects, normally ignored. Consumption of a wide range of important goods and amenities, often thought to be provided free, actually is conditioned on individual incomes and wealth because the value of these attributes is capitalised into house prices. Thus, the ability to benefit from better schools or the amenities generated by land use planning is determined by household income. For example, any amenity values generated by Greenbelts (see Box 4.1 on the social value of Greenbelts) differentially benefits richer house owners because the value of Greenbelt access is fully reflected in house prices. As a result only richer households can afford to purchase the flow of benefits that are associated with preserving the Greenbelt. The outcome – perhaps paradoxical to planners who are culturally egalitarian – is that the net effect seems to be that Greenbelts (or growth boundaries) produce an even more unequal distribution of welfare (measured as equivalent income) than the incomes of home owners themselves (Cheshire and Sheppard 2002). Our planning system allocates a scarce resource – land for urban development – but without any regard for prices or other market information. In analysing the effects of this allocative mechanism on housing supply (or, indeed, the supply of space for any given use) we need to think carefully about what exactly it is that a particular planning system allocates and whether, in the allocative process, it constrains the supply of what it is allocating.

The important point to stress is that the English[9] system of land use

---

[8] In the jargon of welfare economics Coasian solutions are unlikely to provide an optimal mechanism for resolving the problems of market failure.

[9] These comments and most of the data specifically relate to the English system but apply generally to the British system – exported to many of the ex-colonies of the British Empire. The adoption of a largely unmodified British system of planning, for example, explains both the lack of skyscrapers in Mumbai's skyline and why Mumbai competes with London in offering the most expensive office space in the world.

BOX 4.1   THE SOCIAL VALUE OF GREENBELTS

The value of Greenbelt land to society at large is an interesting question. The evidence suggests that its value has been falling over time. Methodologies have differed but the earliest study – Willis and Whitby (1985) – concluded that not only did Greenbelt land generate significant benefits but these benefits outweighed costs so there was a positive social value to retaining Greenbelt land – at least in the case studied – around Tyneside. A later study, using a similar 'contingent valuation' methodology for the Chester area (Hanley and Knight 1992), produced a substantially lower estimate of value but did conclude that the amenity value of Greenbelt land was 'significantly different from zero'. This was consistent with Cheshire and Sheppard's hedonic-based estimate for the Reading area in the mid-1980s (Cheshire and Sheppard 1995) but the same authors using hedonic techniques for the same housing market but with data for 1999/2000 were unable to find any significant value of Greenbelt land for households not located within the Greenbelt itself (Cheshire and Sheppard 2004). The most recent and comprehensive evidence (Gibbons et al. 2011) using hedonic techniques but for a very large sample of transactions covering the whole of England, confirms this. They concluded that Greenbelt land had no measurable value except for the owners of houses within it. Since that value was capitalised in the price of houses it did not represent a social value over and above the private value paid in the price of houses.

---

planning intentionally constrains the supply of land (not houses directly) and so only indirectly constrains the supply of housing. In this it differs from most other systems of land use control. Understanding this is critical to understanding the different economic impact of different systems of land market regulation (planning). In the next section this is illustrated with a brief comparison of four different planning systems.

4.   THE SUPPLY OF HOUSING AND ALTERNATIVE SYSTEMS OF LAND USE PLANNING

The planning systems of Germany, the Netherlands and the US provide informative comparisons and illustrate how the economic impacts of any system depend both on the fiscal, institutional and legal context in which it operates as well as its *de facto* goals (even if these are not always explicitly articulated). As previously discussed the fundamental structure of England's planning system was set by the 1947 Act. Not only did this act nationalise development rights, but it set certain policy objectives, particularly that of 'urban containment' (Hall et al. 1973). It established a system for allocating not numbers or square feet of housing or offices, but of allocating the area of developable land. The aim was to deliberately restrict (for perceived social and environmental purposes) the spread of existing urban areas. But as originally conceived the goal of urban containment would be combined with planning for freestanding new towns – so people could live with more space in greener environments. Land is separately allocated for each statutorily defined class of use. By far the most important urban land use was and is housing, and land for housing was calculated from projected numbers of households, assuming fixed densities of development. As you would expect with a regulatory/planning system coming from the engineering and design intellectual traditions that it did, the system worked in physical units and measures such as numbers of households and densities and it explicitly excluded any consideration of market signals or measures of market demand or supply. For commercial uses projections of job growth or area of shopping space per household were the indicators used to allocate land. Even following the introduction of the National Planning Policy Framework in 2012 this continues to be the case.

Not just the British but governments in all OECD countries have systems of land use regulation. Here we will look at how in outline German, Dutch and US systems operate and argue that the details of operation produce critically different effects on the supply (and quality) of housing. The Dutch and German systems, although superficially more rigid, are charged with supplying land sufficient to meet housing demand. In the US the federal government empowers each incorporated community to draw up and impose 'zoning' plans. This zoning system makes it very difficult to subdivide existing built lots and in many areas – as determined by the local community – imposes minimum lot sizes which to European eyes are extravagant: indeed even to US eyes where 10-acre minimum lot sizes are not uncommon such 'restrictions' seem extravagant. The result is that in those regions of the US where all suitable or available land has been zoned for development ('built-out'), because of the extreme difficulty of redeveloping at higher densities, their zoning system is restricting the supply not of land as such but of 'house plus land bundles'.

The Netherlands and Germany operate within a rather different planning tradition to the British – the Master Plan. In this system there is very close control of what can be built on any site, but the developer can just get on and build it without seeking 'development permission' – so long as what they build conforms to the requirements set down for the particular site. In Britain any change from the status quo, legally defined as 'development' – which would include not just construction but changing the use of a shop from selling holidays to selling houses[10] – is subject to 'development control' and needs individual planning permission. These systems are not so radically different as this description sounds since there is, in a British context, a local plan and what is planned for a given area of land will usually influence where and what is applied for and the outcome of the development control process. But the structure of decision making is different and recent research shows (see Ball et al. 2008, Ball 2011) the British system is slower, more subject to delay and more expensive to operate than a Master Plan system. It is arguably more open to political influence as well. But above all it means all development is subject to regulation induced uncertainty. The local planning committee may say no. This – as was shown in Mayo and Sheppard (2001) of itself renders housing supply more inelastic.

A second more fundamental difference between planning in England compared to Germany or the Netherlands is the obligation on local governments in those countries to provide sufficient land for development. Historically this has probably been most marked in the Netherlands where one of the most important traditional functions of local governments was land drainage (see Needham 1992) – 'producing land'.[11] This has continued to the present to influence attitudes to land so that in the Netherlands land supply is treated more as a utility, a necessary feature of life which it is the job of government to ensure is adequately supplied. Although the highest density country of any size in Europe, and a rich country too, housing in the Netherlands (and in Germany) is both of high quality and significantly cheaper relative to incomes than is the case in England.

The most recent data, provided in a comparison by Statistics Sweden (2005) show new build houses were 40 per cent larger in the Netherlands

---

[10] It is important to understand this legal definition of development does not coincide with economic concepts of development. Land uses are legally separated into 'use categories' and any change – whether from agricultural to housing or housing to office use as well as a significant increase in a building's size, constitutes in a legal sense, 'development'. It is the distinction between categories of use and the allocation of land for specific categories which produces the extraordinary price discontinuities in land values analysed in Cheshire and Sheppard (2005) and discussed in Chapter 6.

[11] There have been increasing signs of change in the Netherlands since about 1990 with growing pressure to constrain development and establish urban containment policies – see Rouwendal and Van der Straaten (2008).

and 38 per cent larger in Germany than in the UK. But British household sizes were larger than in either the Netherlands or Germany. A recent study by the Commission for Architecture and the Built Environment (CABE) concluded that the average floor area in a new build British home was 76 m^2 compared to 113 m^2 in France, 137 m^2 in Denmark or 214 m^2 in the US. However house prices in both the Netherlands and in Germany were lower than in Britain. In the Netherlands the price per square metre was 45 per cent less than in the UK. No directly comparable price information is available for Germany but there (OECD 2004) the real price of houses fell in both the decades of the 1980s and 1990s and was completely stable over the whole period 1971 to 2002, compared to an annual percentage rate of increase in the UK of 3.6 – the highest for any OECD country. Over the same 30-year period German real household disposable incomes increased at 2.6 per cent a year compared to 2.3 per cent in the Netherlands and 2.9 per cent in the UK (OECD 2004). In the Netherlands real house prices rose during the 1970s, fell at an average rate of 2.2 per cent a year during the 1980s but then rose sharply in the 1990s.

In England the overriding objective of planning policy has been 'urban containment' and more recently 'densification'. Although, as noted above, the target that 60 per cent of all land for housing should be 'brownfield' has been nominally dropped from the 2012 NPPF, its spirit lives on. Moreover, the aim of densification in the name of 'sustainability' or the new urbanism is gaining traction elsewhere. Phillips and Goodstein (2000) document this for the Portland, Oregon area of the US and the OECD seems to have adopted it as a component of their 'Green Cities' agenda (OECD 2012). Densification necessarily entails the restriction of the supply of urban land. Moreover, with our centralised fiscal system, local authorities who are the primary decision makers on development control have an effective fiscal disincentive to permit urban development. They have statutory obligations to provide services for new residents but almost no direct return to their tax revenues. Despite the introduction of a modest 'new homes bonus' local authorities raise very little – typically around 20 per cent – of their revenues from local property taxes. Most revenues come from central government for whom local authorities in effect act as agents in delivering services. The structure of fiscal incentives has been even more negative with respect to commercial property since all revenues from commercial property taxes go to national coffers. The provision to allow some retention of business rates does not promise to provide sufficient resources to offset this 'tax on development' levied on local communities (Larkin et al. 2011).

In the US the planning system is institutionally somewhat different again, since it is a zoning system. This gives it something in common with the Master Planning system but control of individual sites is substantially less detailed. There is a facet, however, which is something like the British system since it is possible, in principle, to get zoning waivers by applying to the local zoning board but such waivers are frequently politically impossible and are always expensive to obtain. If development conforms to the general requirements of the rules operating for a particular zone (and conforms to local building codes) it can go ahead. The decentralised US fiscal system which lets local communities retain all local property tax revenues provides a strong incentive to allow commercial development but some disincentive to allow denser residential development. Poorer households (who can only afford to live at higher densities) tend to be seen as consuming relatively more local government services compared to their property tax contribution. Having larger minimum lot sizes is in effect a way of keeping poorer households out of the community. Not only have high minimum lot sizes been used to restrict development for lower income households but zoning has made subdivision of existing structures and of built lots very expensive or impossible for similar reasons. New residential development, even in a high housing cost region such as the Boston, Massachusetts metropolitan area, is with a mean lot size of an acre. The California Bay Area is judged to be built-out (Glaeser et al. 2005) but there are communities in Marin County where there are 60-acre minimum lot sizes.[12] It is clearly not a lack of land that restricts housing supply in the Bay Area.

The real difference in economic terms between the US and British (and Dutch or German) systems, therefore, is that, with just some few exceptions such as Portland, OR, the US system does not control the supply of land, it controls the number of house plus land 'bundles' by means of either minimum lot size requirements or making subdivision of lots too expensive to occur. In the past, given the extensive supply of land and the ability to develop new subdivisions on the edge of existing urban areas which then got their own zoning powers, this did not have significant effects on supply elasticity or prices. It produced low density leapfrogging development but it did not restrict the total supply of houses. As Glaeser et al. (2005) have shown, however, it has recently been increasingly constraining the supply of housing particularly in the North East and West coasts as whole regions get 'built out' and existing communities become more restrictive. This seems to be happening, however, because of regionally differing combinations of minimum lot sizes and the high costs – pecuniary and political – of getting zoning ordinance waivers to permit the subdivision of existing built lots. Housing land is there but in large

---

[12] Introduced in the early 1970s ostensibly to maintain dairy farming, although, effectively preventing low income – even moderate income – residential development.

gardens and protected areas so it cannot be built on or developed at higher densities. Indeed a striking finding of Glaeser and Gyourko (2003) is that the implicit price of additional garden space in parts of New England appeared to be negative, implying, if true, that house owners were being constrained to consume more land than they would have chosen to if left free to choose optimal 'house-land bundles'.

What do these comparisons tell us? Perhaps most significantly that efficient planning does not necessarily entail a restriction on supply but inefficient planning systems can both encourage urban sprawl and effectively restrict the supply of house plus land bundles driving up the price of housing just as we achieve in Britain. Here, even though land use planning policies in combination with fiscal incentives restrict the supply of land relative to demand, it is only an indirect restriction on the supply of (new) houses. It does not directly restrict the supply of dwellings, just of the land on which they could be built and the height to which they can be built.

5. DOING IT THE BRITISH WAY: RESTRICTING THE SUPPLY OF LAND

As discussed above, restricting the supply of housing has profound implications for prices and volatility. But restricting the supply of land for housing does not directly restrict the supply of housing except in the most extreme circumstances – for example if combined with binding density and/or height restrictions on building. This section analyses what happens when – as in Britain – the supply of land is restricted and what this does to the elasticity of supply, price and price volatility of the different attributes of houses.

Analysing the effects of directly restricting the supply of housing land is the central point of this chapter. Housing is a complex – indeed a very complex – good consisting of many attributes bundled into one composite good. This, of course, is the central insight of hedonic approaches to analysing house prices and housing markets, in wide application since the theoretical developments of Rosen (1974) and discussed in Chapter 3. There must now have been thousands of hedonic studies of housing markets and over time there has been a striking improvement in their sophistication and the insights one can find in them. Data sets, statistical techniques, experience and computing power have all progressed so that the state of the art studies are increasingly good, detailed and believable. They seem to show that housing market search processes and price determination are really very sophisticated and consistent with there being pretty good information and well-functioning markets.

Of the physical attributes of housing the most important in terms of prices is the amount of space a house provides: and space not just internal to the house but also externally in the form of garden size. Indeed all credible hedonic studies find that space internal to a house is highly influential in determining the overall price of a house.

There are fewer studies which include garden or plot size as an attribute. Until the development of GIS software and digitised maps, measuring the dimensions of gardens included with structures was a very labour-intensive task. Of the few studies before 2000 to include plot size that by Jackson et al. (1984) was one of the earliest. This found a significant price being paid for more garden space – a finding common to the great majority of studies which have included this attribute.[13]

Another difficulty with including garden size as an attribute is that underlying urban economic theory predicts there will not be a single price but that the price of residential space will vary systematically with accessibility to jobs (commonly assumed to be concentrated in the centre of the city). Consistent with this, Cheshire and Sheppard (2004) show a statistically significant price being paid for (more) land with the price varying with both distance and direction from the city centre. In addition, for a given size of garden, a higher price was paid if it was squarer rather than long and narrow. These results provide strong evidence people get welfare from, and care about, space, in both houses and gardens. They pay more to consume more private space and so, implicitly, prefer to live at lower densities, all else equal. This result is consistent with Song and Knaap (2003) who again find a positive and significant price paid for houses built at lower density, all else equal. The 'compact city' may be a planner's dream but for ordinary people it is more like a nightmare.

The logic of a hedonic approach to analysing house prices is that, since housing is a composite good, the total price of which is the aggregate of the prices of each individual attribute, we must think of separate demand and supply characteristics for each attribute. Furthermore, even if we cannot presently identify these individual attribute supply curves, it is useful to think about them in order to see what can be concluded about their likely form. The supply of some attributes, such as frontage on the River Thames, or a view over Hampstead Heath in London or the River Seine in Paris, may be naturally in fixed supply. There are a fixed number of houses that provide such frontage or views. The supply of other attributes may

---

[13] The study of Glaeser and Gyourko (2003) was a form of hedonic analysis. This found a positive price paid for gardens but, as discussed above, a negative price paid for additional garden space over the mean garden size. In Britain, Day et al. (2006) find evidence that garden size is important.

also be highly inelastic. If, for example, parents looking for educational quality in fact seek to get access to not just a good state school but to the best state school in their housing market area, then the supply of educational quality will be highly inelastic. There can only be one best local school. Yet other attributes may be produced by a quasi-industrial process and so be elastic in supply. Examples might be central heating, fitted kitchens or the number of rooms in a given total space.

In the absence of any land market regulation or binding topographical constraints, one would assume that the supply of urban land would be more or less perfectly elastic. There would be a significant mark-up over agricultural land at the edge of the urban area because of the costs of providing transport and other infrastructure but such costs would be relatively constant in real terms, so more urban land could always be provided at a given price. This is consistent with the findings of Glaeser et al. (2008) that in elastically supplied markets house prices seldom deviated significantly from the estimated minimum profitable production costs. These were defined as building costs, land and land assembly costs and a normal profit. Land costs were assumed to be a constant 20 per cent of the total cost of a house: that is land prices were invariant with numbers of houses built except in so far as building cost might increase with output in a market.

This is also consistent with the evidence from Figure 4.1 which shows an index of real housing land prices for England and Wales from 1892 to 2008 (updated in Aldred 2010). From 1892 to about 1955 there was no systematic trend in real housing land prices. Between 1892 and the last pre-World War II population census in 1931, there was a 61 per cent increase in household numbers and a 25 per cent increase in real household incomes, but no increase in the real price of housing land. The construction of transport systems – suburban railways and roads – and other infrastructure, expanded usable urban land supply at a more or less constant real cost. Between 1955 and 2008 the real price of housing land increased by a factor of 12.3. Real house prices increased by a factor of only 4.5 over the same period with nearly all that increase being since 1971. As argued above, the distinctive difference between the English planning system and those of Germany, the Netherlands and the US in economic terms is that the English system explicitly constrains the supply of land, and has done so over a long period. The German and Dutch systems, although they impose a strong regulatory framework, have imposed only a modest constraint on land supply (although as noted above the Dutch seem to have become more restrictive since about 1990). And as noted above, in the US the system, where it restricts supply, mainly restricts the supply of land plus housing bundles and compared to Britain has done so only for a comparatively short time. The length of time a restriction is imposed is critical in the housing market because of the durability of buildings and the small size of the flow of new build relative to total supply or stock. Figure 4.1 is just a vivid realisation of this underlying economic reality.

Given the composite character of housing we should in principle think not just of the characteristics of the supply of individual attributes but also the structure of demand. Here there is some evidence (for example Cheshire and Sheppard 1998; Cheshire et al. 1999), and this suggests that the demand for space in houses, and externally in gardens, is highly income-elastic: evaluated at mean incomes, estimates of income elasticity for three different housing markets over three dates were typically around 1.6 for internal space and 1.75 for garden space.

To summarise: (1) the British planning system restricts the area of land for housing; (2) people prefer bigger houses and bigger gardens; and (3) as people get richer they spend an increasing share of their incomes trying to buy more space. The next section considers the implication for real house prices and welfare.

6.   PEOPLE LIKE MORE SPACE: POLICY IMPLICATIONS

The demand for housing land is a 'derived' demand – that is the land is demanded not for its own sake but because there is a demand for the houses (and gardens) that developers can put on it so they can make a profit from buying and developing it. It follows from this that our planning system only indirectly affects housing supply and the price of houses through its policies of containment and more recently densification by rationing the amount of land available to build on. Planners decide on how much land to release for development on the basis of projections of future growth in household numbers in their localities and assumed densities. Growth in household numbers – apart from projections being notoriously unreliable and so a poor tool for forecasting how many houses to build – would, even if known with perfect foresight, be only one factor in the relevant determinants of growth in demand for houses and housing space. Demand is determined by not just the number of households and their tastes with respect to housing, but by incomes. If we are to provide stable prices for a given quality of housing and are to do so via a 'planning' system rather than just by a regulated market (normally with some government provision for low income housing), then what we need to predict is the growth in effective demand for housing and garden space. Then the planning system would have to provide enough land to satisfy the forecast increase in demand. Indeed, since in a free society planners do not determine whether land allocated is actually sold to developers to build houses on, nor, when it is sold, whether houses are actually built by the developers, we would have to allocate not just that quantity of land predicted as being compatible with price stability but more. Not all the land allocated as available for development will actually be developed. One rule of thumb suggested (Evans and Hartwich 2006) is that this implies allocating 40 per cent more land than the estimated growth in demand indicates is needed.

To decide how much land would be needed to satisfy changing demand while maintaining constant real prices we would have to understand the structure of demand: that is how demand for different attributes of housing – in this case housing land and space in houses – varied as the price of these attributes changed and as incomes changed. As the British planning system does not do this, what are the implications for house prices and thus for welfare?

Cheshire et al. (1999) provide a partial answer using results of a 'micro-simulation' model for the English housing market.[14] From this it was possible to estimate both the price and income elasticities of demand for a range of housing attributes including internal and garden space. What the model implied was that the overwhelmingly more important driver of the demand for 'housing' was not household numbers but rising real incomes. This suggests that focusing on household numbers and ignoring changing real incomes will mean that the British planning system significantly and consistently underestimates increasing demand over time.

Aside from providing a stark warning about the dangers of ignoring income when predicting demand, the model made it possible to simulate the impact of changes in land supply on house prices because the demand for land was explicitly estimated and modelled. Land supply was assumed to be determined by the planning system. Since it was an equilibrium model, the short-term effects of interest rate changes and so on were not accounted for. The impact on house prices of any set of assumptions about changes in land supply, household numbers or real incomes could be simulated for England as a whole or disaggregated by region with

---

[14] The model is microsimulation in that it was built up from individual data on observed house prices, the full attributes of those houses and the incomes of occupants. The model was crude in that it involved grossing up from estimates of just three sub-regional housing markets (Darlington, Nottingham and Reading) but against that the stability of estimates of the structure of demand over time and across these markets was reassuring. All the estimates of the structure of demand told effectively the same story: there was a strong and stable income elasticity of demand that varied very little between the three markets or over time.

different assumed values for different regions. Two such simulation results are worth reporting. Both of these were for the period 1996–2016 and applied the then recently announced planning policy of providing 60 per cent of new housing on 'Brownfield' land. For modelling purposes this was implemented by assuming 60 per cent of any additional land designated for housing was within existing urban areas, with consequent increases in overall urban densities. Both simulations applied the then projected increase in household numbers of 4.4 million by 2016 (HMSO 1996). Simulation 1, however, assumed no growth in real incomes over the period while Simulation 2 assumed real incomes grew by 25 per cent – consistent with the observed trend growth between 1986 and 1993. Household and income growth were assumed to be at the same rate in all regions. These two simulations, although they embodied the same assumption about the brownfield/greenfield mix and about the growth in household numbers, produced remarkably different forecasts of real house price increases. If real incomes were set to be constant, the 4.4 million increase in household numbers produced an increase in real (quality-constant) house prices across England of 4.4 per cent over the whole 20-year period. But if we added to growth in household numbers real income growth over the 20-year period at past trend rates then the model forecast an increase in quality constant house prices of 131.9 per cent.[15] Thus in a world in which the supply of land is restricted, and holding assumed population growth constant, real income growth leads to highly significant real house price inflation. This stems from the strong income elasticity of demand for space.

Hilber and Vermeulen (2012) approach the issue from a slightly different perspective. They are interested in tightly pinning down the causal role of English planning policies in raising the price of housing. They measure restrictiveness by the refusal rate of major planning applications – employing an instrumental variables approach to deal with endogeneity – thus identifying the causal impact on house prices of the variations in the restrictiveness with which supply is constrained across all LAs in England. As well as the impact of planning they also estimate the effects of physical restrictions on land supply such as areas of water and the fact that land is already developed or is unbuildable for other reasons such as its steepness. These factors are significant but their contribution to variations in house prices is small relative to variations in planning restrictiveness across LAs. Their central estimate suggests house prices would be around 35 per cent lower if all regulatory constraints were removed. But as they say 'more

---

[15] This compares to the outturn of 120 per cent between 1996 and 2013 (using the Dallas Fed index for the UK) or 127.8 per cent from 1996 to 2008 for England and Wales using the series graphed in Figure 4.1.

pragmatically: had the South East, the most regulated English region, the regulatory restrictiveness of the North East, still highly regulated in an international context, house prices in the South East would be roughly 25 per cent lower.'

Even then, this is a substantial underestimate. Since their data on how restrictive LAs are is only available from 1979 their analysis starts, so to speak, with a baseline of 1979. Implicitly until then planning policy had had no effect on house prices although as the evidence of Figure 4.1 strongly suggests it had probably been having significant effects since the late 1960s. Indeed Peter Hall was already drawing attention to the likely effects of urban containment policies in 1973 (Hall et al. 1973). To adapt Philip Larkin, effective restrictions on land supply really started in 1964. So 25 per cent is certainly an underestimate for the total cumulative increase in real house prices attributable to our policies of urban containment.

7. CONCLUSIONS

The conclusion with respect to the impact of the present planning system on housing affordability and price stability is, therefore, extremely pessimistic. So long as we constrict the supply of land, and the demand for space is as income-elastic as it appears to be, projections of household numbers – even were they accurate – would be little help in guiding our system to improve housing affordability, maintain the quality of housing or dampen price volatility. Houses are not simple goods and if incomes are growing – which in the long term they have and are likely to continue to do – demand is not just for quality-constant houses (something quite imperfectly measured in current house price indicators) but for improving house quality. A central component in 'improving quality' is more space. As people get richer they do not want more beds: they want bigger beds and bigger bedrooms to put them and their extra clothes in. As people have got historically richer the bothy has given way to the two-up–two-down terrace and – if income and price permits – to a nice detached house with some garden. It is not difficult to understand. Such improvements in turn imply more land for housing and, in the absence of such an increase in land supply but rising incomes, average real house prices will continue to trend upwards. It is unpopular and difficult to confront the dilemma posed in this chapter but the irreconcilable conflict between current planning policies and underlying economic forces – the fundamentals – means we are faced with politically unpalatable policy choices. We discuss them in Chapter 6 after we have considered the impact of the current planning system on economic performance.

REFERENCES

Aldred, T. 2010. 'Arrested Development: Are We Building Houses in the Right Places?' London: Centre for Cities.

Ball, M. 2011. 'Planning delay and the responsiveness of English housing supply'. *Urban Studies* 48(2), 349–362.

Ball, M., P. Allmendinger, and C. Hughes. 2008. 'Housing Supply and Planning Delay in the South of England'. Working Papers in Real Estate and Planning, WP 04/08, University of Reading.

Barker, K. 2003. 'Review of Housing Supply: Securing our Future Housing Needs: Interim Report – Analysis'. London: HMSO.

Barker, Kate. 2004. 'Review of Housing Supply: Delivering Stability'. London: HM Treasury.

Cheshire, P.C. and S. Sheppard. 1995. 'On the price of land and the value of amenities'. *Economica* 62, 247–267.

Cheshire, P.C. and S. Sheppard. 1998. 'Estimating the demand for housing, land and neighbourhood characteristics'. *Oxford Bulletin of Economics and Statistics* 60, 357–382.

Cheshire, P.C. and S. Sheppard. 2002. 'Welfare economics of land use regulation'. *Journal of Urban Economics* 52, 242–269.

Cheshire, P.C. and S. Sheppard. 2004. 'Land markets and land market regulation: progress towards understanding'. *Regional Science and Urban Economics* 34, 619–637.

Cheshire, P.C. and S. Sheppard. 2005. 'The introduction of price signals into land use planning decision-making: a proposal'. *Urban Studies* 42, 647–663.

Cheshire, P.C., I. Marlee and S. Sheppard. 1999. 'Development of a Microsimulation Model for Analysing the Effects of the Planning System Housing Choices: Final Report'. Department of Geography and Environment, London School of Economics.

Day, B., I. Bateman and I. Lake. 2006. 'Estimating the Demand for Peace and Quiet Using Property Market Data', CSERGE Working Paper EDM 06-03, UEA.

DCLG/National Statistics. 2008. 'Housing Statistics 2008'. London: DCLG.

DOE (Department of the Environment). Various 1963–1987. *Housing and Construction Statistics*.

Evans, A.W. and O.M. Hartwich. 2006. *Better Homes, Greener Cities*. London: Policy Exchange.

Gibbons, S., S. Mourato and G. Resende. 2011. 'The Amenity Value of English Nature: A Hedonic Price Approach', SERC Discussion Paper 0074. London: SERC.

Glaeser, E.L. and J. Gyourko. 2003. 'The impact of building restrictions on housing affordability'. *Federal Reserve Bank of New York Economic Policy Review* June, 21–39.

Glaeser, E.L., J. Gyourko and A. Saiz. 2008. 'Housing Supply and Housing Bubbles', NBER Working Paper No. 14193, Cambridge, MA: NBER.

Glaeser, E.L., J. Gyourko and R.E. Saks. 2005. 'Why is Manhattan so expensive? Regulation and the rise in housing prices'. *Journal of Law and Economic* 428, 331–369.

Hall, P.G., H. Gracey, R. Drewett and R. Thomas. 1973. *The Containment of Urban England*. London: Allen and Unwin.

Hanley, N. and J. Knight. 1992. 'Valuing the environment: recent UK experience and an application to Greenbelt land'. *Journal of Environmental Planning and Management* 35, 145–160.

Hilber, C.A.H. and W. Vermeulen. 2012. 'The Impact of Supply Constraints on House Prices in England', SERC Discussion Paper 119. London: SERC.

HMSO. 1996. 'Household Growth: Where Shall We Live?' Cmd. 3471. London: HMSO.

Jackson, J.R., R.C. Johnson and D.L. Kaserman. 1984. 'The measurement of land prices and the elasticity of substitution in housing production'. *Journal of Urban Economics* 16, 1–12.

Larkin, Kieran, Zach Wilcox and Christiana Gailey. 2011. 'Room for Improvement: Creating the Financial Incentives Needed for Economic Growth'. London: Centre for Cities.

Mayo, Stephen and Stephen Sheppard. 2001. 'Housing supply and the effects of stochastic development control'. *Journal of Housing Economics* 10, 109–128.

Needham, B. 1992. 'A theory of land prices when land is supplied publicly: the case of the Netherlands'. *Urban Studies* 29, 669–686.

OECD. 2004. 'Chapter 2, Housing Policies', in *OECD Economic Surveys: Netherlands 2004*. Paris: Organisation for Economic Co-operation and Development.

OECD. 2012. 'Compact City Policies: A Comparative Assessment', *OECD Green Growth Studies*. Paris: OECD Publishing.

Phillips, J. and E. Goodstein. 2000. 'Growth management and housing prices: the case of Portland'. *Contemporary Economic Policy* 18, 334–344.

Rosen, Sherwin. 1974. 'Hedonic prices and implicit markets: product differentiation in pure competition'. *Journal of Political Economy* 82, 34–55.

Rouwendal, J. and J.W. Van der Straaten. 2008. 'The Costs and Benefits of Providing Open Space in Cities', Tinbergen Discussion Paper, 2008 – 001/3.

Song, Y. and G. Knaap. 2003. 'New urbanism and housing values: a disaggregate assessment'. *Journal of Urban Economics* 54, 218–238.

Statistics Sweden. 2005. 'Housing Statistics in the European Union 2004'. Karlskrona, Boverket, Publikationsservice.

Urban Task Force. 1999. *Towards An Urban Renaissance*. London: Urban Task Force.

Vallis, E.A. 1972. 'Urban land and building prices 1892–1969: I'. *Estates Gazette*.

Vallis, E.A. 1972. 'Urban land and building prices 1892–1969: II'. *Estates Gazette*.

Vallis, E.A. 1972. 'Urban land and building prices 1892–1969: III'. *Estates Gazette*.

VOA (Valuation Office Agency). Various years. *Property Market Report*.

Willis, K. and M. Whitby. 1985. 'The value of Greenbelt land'. *Journal of Rural Studies* 1, 147–162.

5. Planning and economic performance

1. INTRODUCTION

We showed in the last chapter how the UK planning system, as in many other countries, restricts the supply of land for housing and how this increases the real price of housing and also the volatility of housing markets. But of course since planning systems allocate land not just for housing but for all other types of land use, they have an economic impact not just in the housing market. In this chapter we look at the evidence as it relates to these wider economic impacts of land use regulation.

Planning systems set rules and guidelines that control the supply and location of land usable for a full set of legally defined purposes and so influence the level, location and pattern of activity. As shown in Chapter 4 this allocation is almost everywhere done independently of prices. That is true in Britain but also in most other countries including many in the EU, the US, Australia and New Zealand. The ultimate role of planning is to help promote a balance of environmental, social and economic welfare that meets the needs of current and future generations and offsets the endemic problems of market failure in the use of land. Doing so inevitably involves trade-offs, so any planning system has both benefits and costs. The benefits claimed for the British system have been well-discussed in recent popular debate.[1] Internationally and in other countries there have been equally strong assertions of the value of planning to combat, for example, 'urban sprawl', and to promote sustainable cities and the 'new urbanism'.[2] We do not rehearse these arguments in detail, although we return to them briefly in our conclusions. Rather, we focus on whether the current system, especially the British system, imposes costs that future reforms could mitigate or avoid.

The costs fall into two categories: direct and indirect. The direct costs arise from three sources: (1) simply from foregone incomes and employment in construction; (2) from the application of a highly and increasingly complex system of regulation; but most importantly perhaps from (3) the

---

[1] See for example CPRE (2011), Monbiot (2011), National Trust (2011) and Strong (2011).
[2] See OECD (2013), the American Planners' Association (1998) or the Congress of New Urbanism http://www.cnu.org/).

costs falling on the private sector in order to comply with the system. The indirect costs arise from the higher costs of space brought about by the constraint on its supply, and the controls imposed on the choice of location. These force activity to locate on sites that are often non-optimal from the point of view of operating costs or revenue generation. Household choices are similarly constrained.

The available evidence suggests that both these categories of costs are substantial, although the indirect costs are greater than the direct ones. In particular, the evidence we discuss below demonstrates that in Britain – particularly in England – the planning system substantially increases the costs of office space and also very significantly reduces output in the retail sector. Averaged over the period 1999–2005 in the most restricted (relative to demand) market – London's West End – planning constraints imposed a cost equivalent to an 800 per cent tax on the cost of building an additional m^2: even in a depressed provincial city such as Birmingham the equivalent cost was 250 per cent. The same cost measured for Brussels was 68 per cent, and in Manhattan it never exceeded 50 per cent in any year between 1996 and 2000 (Cheshire and Hilber 2008). In the supermarket sector the constraints imposed by Town Centre First Policy (fully) imposed in 1996 seem to have reduced output in a representative English store by some 32 per cent (Cheshire et al. 2012). This is equivalent to more than a lost decade's output growth in an industry which, in terms of employment, is the second largest in Britain. Moreover, the specific policy of Town Centre First – explained below – lowers employment in small independent retailers compared to national chains. And finally when we look objectively at the evidence, planning policies seem to considerably overvalue the wider environmental and welfare costs arising from greenfield as compared to brownfield development and especially overvalue the prevention of development on all Greenbelt land regardless of that land's actual environmental or amenity value.

These are strong claims that fly in the face of received policy wisdom. We think the evidence, however, warrants careful and critical evaluation. It is perfectly possible to argue that the costs we identify are worth paying to achieve other policy objectives. However, it is not helpful to pretend these costs do not exist. There are multiple links from planning to the economy, and any sensible and balanced debate on urban planning (in general) and on planning reform (in particular) must recognise this. In our next chapter, Chapter 6, we try systematically to evaluate possible ways in which planning systems in general but particularly the British planning system could be reformed. Any reforms to be effective should, so far as possible, retain planning's capacity to offset for market failures, protect the environment and co-ordinate different uses of land and the provision of infrastructure while eliminating the wider economic and social – even environmental – cost the system currently imposes.

2.   CONTEXT

Fully understanding the economic impacts of any system of land use regulation entails a clear and analytical understanding of its institutional details and context. As was argued in Chapter 4, it is essential to understand the institutions – and instruments – and how these interact with incentives generated either by the operation of the system itself or by the local and national tax system. This section spells out some of these details for the UK system to provide context for the evidence that is described below. Many of the most significant impacts of the planning system will apply in other contexts, so the reader who is interested in those general affects can safely skip ahead subject to the caveats about the need for institutional context to establish a full understanding of impacts.

In the UK each country's planning system has variations, although Wales tends to follow England quite closely and the English system is the dominant one. The current planning system in England involves:

- A hierarchy of planning policies: national planning policy (now unified as the National Planning Policy Framework), until recently regional strategies, and local development frameworks;
- Development control as the main mechanism for regulating local development: that is each change legally constituting 'development' requires application to and specific permission of the local planning authority – this is a committee of the local authority (LA) of jurisdiction;
- Section 106 Agreements (S106)[3] – sometimes called 'planning obligations' – as the main means of local community value capture from permitting development, complemented in 2010 by the Community Infrastructure Levy.
- Some national policies or restrictions (for example Town Centre First, Greenbelts, Sites of Special Scientific Interest (SSSIs) and Areas of Outstanding Natural Beauty (AONBs)).

---

[3] S106 Agreements were introduced in 1992 and allow Local Planning Authorities (LPAs) to give permission to develop in return for some specified 'community gain'. They thus involve a process of negotiation between would be developers and LPAs. The evidence suggests that they entail high transactions costs and so are only employed for major developments. Indeed only a minority of LPAs have ever negotiated a S106 Agreement.

The Coalition Government's National Planning Policy Framework (NPPF) was published in March 2012.[4] The main elements of the NPPF and associated reforms were:

- Significantly simplified national planning guidance.
- Devolved decision-making, with local authorities drawing up local plans via community consultation, subject to consistency with the NPPF.
- The introduction of new fiscal incentives to encourage development.
- A presumption in favour of sustainable development, where this accords with local Plans. If no up-to-date plan exists, the default answer to sustainable development should be 'yes'.
- The introduction of 'Neighbourhood Plans': these were to be for far smaller geographic units than LAs but had to be consistent with the LA's Local Plan.
- Maintain – even slightly extend – all existing protected status (Greenbelt, SSSIs and AONBs) and retain Town Centre First restrictions for retail development.
- The specific national target of 60 per cent of all new development being on brownfield sites was dropped but still brownfield was favoured and there was provision for local communities to set their own targets.

In parallel with the NPPF, the government has also introduced:

- A reformed Community Infrastructure Levy (CIL) as the main means of value capture, while limiting use of S106.
- Financial incentives for new housing through the New Homes Bonus, and for commercial development via the Business Increase Bonus.
- A Localism Bill and wider proposals for reforming local government finance.[5]

The explicit rationale for these reforms was that together they would localise the planning system at the same time as increasing rates of commercial and residential development.

As we discuss below there are tensions between these two objectives. In addition, in our judgement (see Chapter 6) the combined effect of

---

[4] DCLG (2012). A draft document (DCLG 2011a) was published in July 2011, with a public consultation from July – October 2011.

[5] See DCLG (2011b).

these reforms will not effectively increase – and may even decrease – the supply of the most productive developable land. At the time of writing – in September 2013 – the evidence was certainly not encouraging: house building was close to a historic low, house prices, especially in London and Southern England were rising more rapidly than at any time since 2007 and a study (Tetlow King 2012) showed that since the abolition of the Regional Spatial Strategies in 2010 there had been a reduction of some 8 per cent of land previously allocated for housing with the largest reductions tending to be in the highest demand regions. Given the apparent ineffectiveness of the post-2010 reforms to improve the rate of development or change any of the fundamentals – including Town Centre First policies – it seems sadly too appropriate to turn to look at the wider costs of Britain's current planning system. Our focus is Britain but we will also try to indicate some of the evidence from elsewhere in the world.

3. EVIDENCE ON ECONOMIC AND SOCIAL COSTS OF THE CURRENT PLANNING SYSTEM: DIRECT COSTS

As mentioned in the introduction, the planning system imposes both direct costs (reduced construction output, transactions and administrative costs of the present system) and indirect costs (impacts on housing and other real estate markets and prices, city size, development costs, and sustainability, as well as some specific sectoral effects). There may also be dynamic effects which we briefly consider in section 6. First let us consider the direct costs.

The most obvious is the foregone construction output with the loss of employment and direct and indirect income generation this entails. The construction sector is not only a substantial contributor to economic activity overall – some 6.2 per cent of the UK labour force worked in construction in 2013 (7.8 per cent if real estate activities were added) – but it has a high labour content and uses a higher proportion of locally and nationally produced inputs than most production industries. As a result construction contributes very strongly to both the wider economy and to employment.

Restricting the supply of land on which to build and forcing up its price reduces the supply response in the construction industry to a change in house (or other property) prices. From 1954 until 1978 annual house building in England and Wales only fell below 250,000 in one year, and for five successive years during the 1960s more than 300,000 houses were built. House building in England was around 100,000 a year from 2008 (see Table 5.1); that is, output in a major industry has fallen by two-thirds in the past 30 years. Following 2007 the British economy was, of course, in a major recession. But the contrast between the post-2007 period of economic crisis and the previous one – the Great Depression of the 1930s – only brings home the point more forcibly. From 1929 to 1937 a major component of the recovery was house building. According to Richardson (1962, p. 137) 'the housing boom of the thirties has been widely accepted as either the cause, or at least the symbol of economic recovery'. From 1928 to 1935 private annual house building in England and Wales increased from 64,426 per year to 285,759 – an increase of 340 per cent. By 1934 employment in construction was 789,940 (Stolper 1941). Houses were in seriously short supply in Britain in 2012 but since the peak of the economic cycle in 2007/08 house building collapsed – down by 40 per cent. Nevertheless, prices relative to incomes were near their all-time high of 2007. The median house price to income ratio for England in 2012 was 6.74 – a third higher than ten years previously and nearly twice as high as in 1997. Clearly the recession following 2007 explains only a small part of the loss of activity in construction. At its pre-crisis peak (2007/08 – see Table 5.1) annual house building was less than half that of the 1960s and only 55 per cent of its 1935 level.

So the first direct cost is just the straightforward but substantial lost output and jobs from building fewer houses. According to the CEBR (2011) increasing annual house construction from the then 94,000 to 300,000 would increase permanent jobs by 201,000 and add £75 billion to GDP.

On the second class of direct cost – the costs of running the system

Table 5.1   Building out of recession? The 1930s compared to the 2010s

	Private sector houses built in England and Wales		
Year	No. of houses[1]	Year	No. of houses[2]
1928	64,626	2003/04	137,960
1929	71,083	2004/05	147,120
1930	110,375	2005/06	152,820
1931	132,909	2006/07	154,670
1932	132,886	2007/08	155,490
1933	167,880	2008/09	120,230
1934	261,409	2009/10	98,320
1935	285,759	2010/11	87,710
1936	275,473	2011/12	93,880

Sources: [1] (Stolper 1941); [2] DCLG Housing Statistics.

– there is surprisingly little systematic evidence although plenty of 'anec-data' exists. There are, of course, direct administrative costs in the public sector partly paid by would-be developers in the way of fees. There are also compliance costs falling on developers in making applications and negotiating their way through a complex system of regulation. Barker (2006) in Chapter 3 estimated these costs as some £700m per year in the public sector plus £200m paid by would-be developers in fees with com-pliance costs amounting to at least a further £700m in 2005 prices. But reading Barker (2006) reveals how uncertain even these comparatively easy to estimate figures are and how much more difficult it is to credibly estimate the wider costs of compliance and delay imposed by the system.

These more indirect costs of delay and uncertainty are almost certainly much more significant. Notorious cases such as the M6 Toll road or Terminal 5 at Heathrow may take years to resolve. Appeal hearings on the latter took eight years and legal, consultants', premises or public service costs alone accounted for more than £100m (Barker 2006, Table 2). In the same report two separate estimates of the direct costs of delay are cited: one, for housing development only, was £700m per annum in 2005/06 prices; the other, which included infrastructure as well, was £2.7 billion in 2005/06 prices. Both estimates, however, were dated (from 1982 and 1992 respectively) and assumed only published elapsed times from appli-cation to decision as the measure of 'delay'. Ball and colleagues (Ball and Allmendinger 2008; Ball et al. 2008; Ball 2011), however, have shown that if delays are measured at the site level from when the first planning appli-cation is made to when permission is finally given then the mean delay is not 13 weeks as officially reported but 43 weeks because what happens is that there are refusals followed by negotiations followed by new applica-tions. Ball (2011) also showed that more urban, smaller and brownfield sites systematically had longer delays associated with them. We return to this point later.

There are three other types of cost, however, even more difficult to quan-tify. Mayo and Sheppard (2001) provide some evidence that the process of development control, because it injects uncertainty into the decision-making process, means developers require a higher expected revenue flow from any completed development (if they get permission, that is) to make it viable in financial terms. In contrast, a Master Plan or Zoning system means that if what a developer wants to construct on a site is allowed by the zoning rules and by building regulations then the development can just go ahead. There is no additional uncertainty or risk attached to the decision-making process. For any development to be financially viable the expected flow of revenues it will generate – obviously subject to risk and uncertainty – have to be discounted back to the present to see if they outweigh the more or less certain costs which occur in the present. Adding more risk or uncertainty by the mechanism of development control necessarily makes the supply of new development more inelastic – otherwise viable projects get pushed into the void. Developers make decisions in terms of their target rates of return and expected costs and revenues. Revenues occur in the future and only after planning permission has been obtained. Since the development control process is not rule-bound, developers will in effect add a risk premium to their target rate of return. The more uncertain is the outcome of the planning process (and of the costs in terms, say, of delays it imposes) then the higher will be the target rate of return and the less will get built for any ex-post revenue generation.

Obviously important, but even more difficult to put a realistic number on, is the cost of uncertainty in terms of complementary investment. This is likely to be more or less trivial with small projects, such as house extensions, but rise systematically with project size and with major infrastructure projects perhaps outweigh all other costs combined. If one thinks of a case such as Heathrow Terminal 5 or airport capacity in South East England, it is not just costs that might be imposed on businesses in the absence of an efficient major hub airport. It is the complementary investment decisions that are dependent on airport capacity. A multinational considering the locations of its European operations or an airfreight firm considering its needs for capacity, requires information with respect to the availability and location of future airport capacity. Such firms may either postpone their own investments or take them outside the UK in the presence of uncertainty generated by a planning system that imposes long delays and uncertainty on major infrastructure decisions. Equally, closing a long established piece of major infrastructure – say moving Heathrow to the Thames estuary – would impose devastating but impossible to quantify costs on all those firms and their labour forces who have located where they are because of the contribution to their competitiveness the infrastructure – Heathrow – generated.

There is finally the accumulated effects of all these aspects of Britain's planning system: its complexity; development control and the uncertainty it injects into development decisions; the full gamut of 'planning obligations' (Section 106 Agreement and so on, now supplemented with the Community Infrastructure Levy); the possibility that at a late stage in the development process other bodies will step in or politicians will respond to lobbying and retrospectively in effect change the rules of the game; and the limitation on the quantity of developable land set by the planning process. In combination it is possible they engender monopoly and restrict entry into the development process. As the Office of Fair Trading (2008) reports, large developers do control a significant proportion of new construction.

In 2006 the top ten house builders built 44 per cent of new homes. The industry in the UK is more concentrated than in, say, the US. But the UK is a much smaller country and, as the OFT further argues, because housing markets are geographically local what matters is concentration of output in local markets. On average in about ten LAs between 1998 and 2006 a single builder accounted for 50 per cent of construction. Even here they are reassuring: 'The evidence presented above does not indicate that the homebuilding industry has a significant problem with high levels of market concentration on either a local or national level' (Office of Fair Trading 2008).Where there was such a degree of local monopoly it was almost always because a single developer controlled one or several large sites with permission. That is, in so far as there was a problem it was because the planning process concentrated developable land in single ownership. But even here, because almost all housing markets extend beyond the administrative boundaries of one LA, there would be more competition than a 50 per cent share of output in an LA might suggest. In summary, in so far as there is a problem it is much more one of imposed but difficult to measure costs on the development process and higher rates of expected rates of return being sought to offset for uncertainty and risk than it is monopoly power given to developers.

4. EVIDENCE ON THE ECONOMIC AND SOCIAL COSTS OF THE CURRENT PLANNING SYSTEM: INDIRECT COSTS

Housing Markets and House Prices

As was discussed in Chapter 4, the UK suffers from a problem of housing affordability. Given the previous discussion the evidence is only very briefly summarised here. The problem of affordability is particularly acute for families with low to modest incomes, although in many parts of the UK high house prices are a problem more generally (Barker 2004). Looking at less well-off households in England the ratio of lower quartile house prices to lower quartile earnings peaked at 7.2 in 2007 and had only fallen to 6.5 in 2011 – still 80 per cent higher than in 1997. In London, at a ratio of 9.0–130 per cent higher than 1997 – the recession produced hardly any improvement in housing affordability at all for lower quartile earners (Keep 2012).

Research in the Spatial Economics Research Centre (SERC) suggests that planning restrictions substantially raise house prices, especially in popular areas. They also make both houses and gardens smaller. House prices react much more strongly to increased demand in communities where supply is more restricted by planning policy. Specifically, the research of Hilber and Vermeulen (2012) discussed in Chapter 4 suggests that an area moving from an average level of restrictiveness to having the lowest level of housing restrictiveness would see house prices fall by around 35 per cent. This represents a considerable underestimate of the true costs because it assumes planning restrictiveness had no impact on house prices prior to 1979. Apart from the evidence offered in Chapter 4 that price effects began to be apparent by the mid-1960s, Cheshire and Sheppard (2002) found a really substantial effect which must have taken years to build up even by 1983. In the more restrictive areas of south eastern England, there was by 1983 a net welfare cost of planning restrictiveness equivalent to a tax of nearly four pence in the pound on incomes. This was a net cost in that it allowed for the value of benefits generated. This net cost partly arose from higher house prices and partly from the effects on the composition or quality of housing (for example restricting the supply of land meant that houses were smaller, see Cheshire (2009)).

Of course, physical constraints on land availability – scarcity of land, the presence of steep slopes or flood plains – have an effect on house prices, but in England the effect is generally very small. Land scarcity does raise prices in the most urbanised places, particularly Greater London. Even in London's case, however, the evidence suggests that planning plays a much larger role (for example through height restrictions). Outside London, very few English communities actually face physical constraints on land supply (Hilber and Vermeulen 2012).

Again, as was discussed in the previous chapter, research also shows that planning restrictions increase housing market volatility. At least until the 2008 recession, average house price volatility in the UK was higher than the most volatile single market in the US (Los Angeles). When demand for houses falls, supply is fixed in both the UK and US by the existing stock (unless you destroy houses) so prices fall in all markets. However when, as in the UK, housing supply is very unresponsive to increased demand, booms drive up prices rather than leading to more building. That means the UK sees more volatility on the up-side of the market and this leads to more volatility overall (Cheshire 2009; Hilber and Vermeulen 2011).

Reduced Productivity Benefits of Larger Cities

Planning policies explicitly try to restrict the growth of cities by 'containment' policy. This bites hardest in the most productive cities where pressure for growth is greatest: most obviously in cities like London, Cambridge or Oxford. City size and diversity, however, provide an economic payoff:

a critical mass of people, resources and ideas help produce agglomeration economies (Glaeser 2011). Increasing that critical mass helps raise productivity: the consensus from recent studies is that doubling employment in a city raises average labour productivity by around 5 to 6 per cent (De La Roca and Puga 2011), although as discussed in Chapter 2, these effects are much more important for some types of economic activity (Melo et al. 2009; Combes et al. 2011). They are much more important in precisely those sectors of economic activity in which the British economy is specialised and our most prosperous cities are particularly specialised: skill-intensive traded services. Although urban density is strongly correlated with the effective or functional size of a city there is no evidence that density itself is a cause of these observed agglomeration economies.[6] It seems most likely that density is the outcome of agglomeration economies as both households and firms bid up the price of land to benefit from them thus causing development to be at higher density. Indeed Cheshire and Magrini (2009) find that once all other factors – including city size – are controlled for, higher density is associated with slower urban economic growth.

Given that current planning rules constrain the size of our more prosperous cities it is crucial to understand the economic costs of those constraints. On the basis of current evidence a complete assessment is not possible. But we can get first pass estimates of the effects by looking at the nominal gains on wages. Gibbons et al. (2013) use Mincerian wage regressions applied to ASHE data to estimate the 'area effects' on wages, holding worker characteristics constant. These regressions control for individual effects plus age and occupation (measured for one-digit classes). Area effects are identified from movers. This may not resolve all identification problems, but provides the best available evidence in the absence of random household assignment. If we use the results to compare a place ranked at the 75th percentile in terms of size to one ranked at the 25th percentile (for example Bristol compared to Huddersfield) we see an 'area wage effect' of 3.8 per cent. That is, an 'identical' worker gets paid a wage

---

[6] Two examples illustrate the difficulty of separating out density effects in causing agglomeration economies. (1) Building Crossrail, for example, will likely reduce the density of the London region as a whole as people take advantage of quicker travel to move out to cheaper land. But it will still increase the effective size of London since with easier travel the costs of productive interactions between economic agents will fall and their potential number will increase. It is estimated that it will bring an additional 1.5 million people within a commuting time of 45 minutes to central London (Crossrail 2013) – the same as adding both Zurich and Basel to London: not far short of adding Frankfurt. (2) Take two cities with identical populations and borders: building more houses will increase density. But it is then hard to attribute any subsequent economic changes to higher density, since population size has also gone up.

that is 3.8 per cent higher in Bristol (the bigger city). To a first approximation, this provides an estimate of the productivity benefits foregone when we constrain the supply of housing in bigger and more productive cities. As the evidence discussed in Chapter 2 suggests this constraint on growth, while significant for London, may be even more significant for second-tier British cities – such as Birmingham, Leeds, Manchester or Newcastle – or for highly productive medium-sized cities that should be growing to be in that second tier – such as Cambridge or Oxford. Or perhaps it is just that agglomeration economies in the London area are so great because of the activity and skill mix that London grows anyway despite the constraints.

Much more important is the feedback from city size to innovation and growth. Here the literature suggests that these effects are likely to be important, although we are a long way from being able to benchmark magnitudes in the way that we did above for wages. One piece of quantitative evidence is available from the analysis of differential rates of urban economic growth across Western Europe in Cheshire and Magrini (2009). They found after controlling for other factors including urban density that larger cities had grown faster. Their sample was confined to urban regions of more than one-third of a million population but if their results can be generalised then a one standard deviation increase in population size would be associated with a 1.8 per cent increase in annual growth rate.

Impact on Development Costs

There is more agreement that overly tight planning frameworks for cities have costs on development. For example, restrictions that have historically prevented sprawl and maintained urban sightlines deliberately place constraints on urban growth in popular cities – both outwards (via Greenbelts) and upwards (via height restrictions or floor area ratios). By raising development costs, especially in urban areas, planning restrictions lower levels of business investment in these areas. SERC evidence shows that these costs can be high in both the office and retail sectors.

Cheshire and Hilber (2008) carefully document how planning restrictions in England impose what can be thought of as a 'tax' on office developments that, averaged over the period 1999–2005, varied from around 250 per cent (of marginal construction costs) in Birmingham, to 400–800 per cent in London. In contrast, New York imposed a 'tax' of around 0–50 per cent, Brussels some 68 per cent, Amsterdam around 200 per cent and central Paris around 300 per cent. Such substantial implicit taxes on development and space costs should clearly affect investment in these cities. Koster et al. (2011) show that in Holland, height restrictions specifically act as constraints on agglomeration economies from tall buildings, echoing analysis by Glaeser (2011).

We do not know of comparable evidence for manufacturing or wholesale distribution, but to the extent that factories and logistics centres tend to use more land than offices, one could speculate that the effects might be larger for these sectors. Offset against this is the fact that Local Planning Authorities may continue to relatively oversupply manufacturing land (if it delays changing designation for sites no longer in use or demanded). One should stress this may only be a relative oversupply. Growth in relative prices over time certainly show that relative and absolute land shortages are much more pronounced for housing and office developments than they are for industrial land (Cheshire and Sheppard 2005). Evidence from the Netherlands moreover shows municipalities being much more willing to supply land for industrial than for residential or commercial uses on the grounds, it was thought, that local politicians assumed industrial land generated more and more 'useful' jobs for their communities and the system was historically and institutionally geared to providing land for industrial estates (Needham and Louw 2006).

Impact on Specific Sectors

There is strong evidence that current planning rules also negatively affect productivity in the retail sector. In recent SERC research, Cheshire et al. (2012) demonstrate that planning rules imposed in 1996 reduced output in a representative English store of a leading supermarket chain built after that date by some 32 per cent. There was also – like house prices – variation imposed by differences in restrictions across local authorities. Controlling for other factors influencing the number and size of stores in an area, the study found that there was a strong relationship between how restrictive an LA was in the application of planning policies and how many stores were located there; and those that were located in the more restrictive LAs tended to be smaller. Since more restrictive LAs had fewer and smaller stores, those that were there had a degree of monopoly power. This local monopoly power increased sales per m^2 of store space by 4.4 per cent. But the loss of stores and their smaller size meant that the loss of sales for the chain as a whole in more restrictive local authorities far exceeded the gain in sales per m^2 of floorspace. A one standard deviation reduction in local restrictiveness was estimated to increase the chain's sales in the area by – again – almost 32 per cent. This was not necessarily a net loss, however, since some sales were likely to be diverted from more to less restrictive areas.

The most important adverse effect on store productivity and output, however, was from Town Centre First policy, introduced in its final and most restrictive form in England in 1996.[7] Policies were more relaxed in Scotland and Northern Ireland allowing for the identification of the impact on retail sales in English stores by comparing them (all else equal) with stores of similar age in Scotland and Northern Ireland. This loss of productivity and output, detailed in the previous paragraph, seemed to arise partly from the fact that town centre sites were smaller but much more because they were less accessible for both deliveries and customers, tended to be awkward shapes and less convenient and so intrinsically less productive.

This is the result of one study, for a single operator (albeit a large retailer represented across the UK). But it does provide a measure of costs – and they are large. Given that real output increases on average by about 10 per cent every ten years the estimate of lost output growth is equivalent to well more than a 'lost' decade. Opponents of planning reform have suggested such evidence does not exist. This is incorrect. There is evidence that planning negatively affects retail productivity. All else equal, bigger supermarkets are more productive, and a supermarket's precise site configuration and location is important. Easy access for lorry deliveries and car-borne shoppers has substantial impact on productivity. More recent work (Cheshire et al. 2012) undertook a parallel study for a major clothing retailer. This had four years of data for 385 stores distributed throughout the UK. Again exploiting the difference in planning policy between England on the one hand and that in Scotland and Northern Ireland on the other, it was possible to estimate the loss of productivity imposed by Town Centre First policy; and again the estimated loss was more than 20 per cent.

Following the introduction of Town Centre First policy in the mid-1990s, the share of new retail development in urban areas rose from 14 per cent (in 1994) to 33 per cent in 2009 (British Council of Shopping Centres 2006). While the policy may have increased the quantum of retail activity in cities – thus raising high street 'vitality' – it also appears to have helped

---

[7] The two main instruments of Town Centre First policy are the so-called needs and sequential tests. The needs test requires the would-be developer to demonstrate that the local community 'needs' a new store. Need is legalistically defined in terms of square feet of retail space per person. The 'sequential' test requires the would-be developer to demonstrate that there is no designated 'suitable' site closer to the town centre than the one on which permission is requested. 'Suitable' means identified in local planning documents as suitable for retail use. That the actual site in question might be owned by a competing store group does not render it 'unsuitable'. Together these tests, introduced in England in 1996, gave substantial advantage to incumbents and store extensions and made it all but impossible to develop large floor plan out of town retail (see Barker 2006 or Cheshire et al. 2012).

change high street character. Specifically, evidence demonstrates that small and independent shops have been hurt by Town Centre First policies. Sadun (2008) and Haskel and Sadun (2009) find that Town Centre First rules have directly caused a reduction in smaller shops' employment – mainly because big supermarkets developed smaller formats and moved into high streets. Thus, by restricting space and raising rents, Town Centre First rules may also have contributed to high street 'cloning' and empty shops. Planning has both benefits and costs but again, despite claims to the contrary, there is evidence available demonstrating significant costs of planning policies on independent retailers.

5.   BENEFITS AND COSTS OF BROWNFIELD DEVELOPMENT

Many opponents of planning reforms think that development should be heavily focused on brownfield – that is, previously developed – land. This policy protects previously undeveloped land, but again it is far from costless.

There are three types of problem. The supply of brownfield land does not geographically match the demand for productive, developable land. A hectare in Liverpool is not a close substitute for another in Cambridge. The costs of developing brownfield sites are considerably higher than those of greenfield sites and, moreover, the supply of the easier-to-develop brownfield sites has been differentially used up. Developers go for the cheaper-to-develop site first. The extra costs arise not just from costs of clearing and cleaning brownfield sites but because they are typically smaller and more difficult to access. Ball et al. (2008) and Ball (2011) show also that – perhaps surprisingly – brownfield sites typically involve longer delay in getting planning permission. Finally sites which are legally defined as brownfield often have high amenity value and usually have greater environmental and social value than does high-intensity agricultural land (UK National Ecosystem Assessment 2010).

This can have extraordinary unintended consequences. To take one recent example, it can potentially destroy one of the most important breeding sites for an increasingly uncommon but iconic songbird – the nightingale.[8] While the development of 5,000 houses on the 'brownfield' site in question – former Ministry of Defence land on the Hoo Peninsula in Kent – was put on hold by Natural England's provisional designation

[8] See   www.http://spatial-economics.blogspot.co.uk/2013/04/to-kill-nightingale-and-not-build-houses.html.

of the site as a Site of Special Scientific Interest in 2013, still the general lessons apply. Those are not only that much land which is legally classified as brownfield has very high amenity value but the process of trying to develop it imposes very high costs. While the nightingales' nesting sites may have been preserved, both the planning authority who had spent years identifying it and negotiating with potential developers and the developers themselves have had to bear very significant costs. The aims of the system were wrong – build not on low amenity value land but build on legally brownfield land – and the rules were not clear and retrospectively changed adding both immediate costs and future uncertainty to the development process.

During the 1990s and mid-2000s, the combination of a national brownfield land target and a minimum density floor for development helped concentrate new development in urban areas – particularly core cities such as Manchester and Birmingham. As discussed in Chapter 2, these cities also benefited from a number of other important supporting factors – a benign macro environment, rising public spending, an expanding higher education sector, a growing consumer interest in city living, and readily available finance for building and buying (Nathan and Urwin 2006).

The national target ensured these trends played out more broadly. In 1998, approximately 50 per cent of development occurred on brownfield land (a figure that had been remarkably stable for long periods of time). The Labour government committed itself to a target of 60 per cent of new development on brownfield land by 2008. The target was met by the early 2000s. In 2005, 70 per cent of new development was on brownfield land (Urban Task Force 2005).

From the point of view of supporters of the policy, meeting the national target sounds like success. Qualitative research suggests that in cities like Manchester, brownfield policies that targeted the urban core helped repopulate city centres, and encouraged commercial activity to return. These policies also appeared to help local leaders reposition their cities' public image (Nathan and Urwin 2006; Unsworth and Nathan 2006).

However, somewhat surprisingly, we know of no evidence that rigorously assesses the causal impact of the brownfield target on the pattern of development within cities, or on the overall effects for the city as a whole. It is possible that in cities like Manchester, the brownfield target may have led to more development across the city than previously. However, an alternative strategy of focusing on higher-demand areas such as (say) neighbourhoods in the south of Manchester might have brought even higher overall development to the city, but with a different spatial pattern (and more limited house price gains for South Manchester homeowners).

In terms of the spatial pattern of development, large pieces of land that become available (for example, former defence land or hospital sites) are often some way from existing settlements (working against other stated objectives on densification). Worse, as highlighted by the post-2010 Coalition government, a small but increasing share of building on 'brownfield' land has been building on private residential gardens – the share of new homes built on previously residential land rose from 11 per cent to 23 per cent between 1997 and 2008.[9]

In short, apart from the extra cost imposed and often the loss of high amenity value land, targets for brownfield land tend not to deliver the kind of development people want in the places where they want it. The combination of brownfield targets and density standards has tended to produce large numbers of small flats in urban areas – although there is a clear need for larger, family homes in these places (Silverman et al. 2006; Unsworth and Nathan 2006).

These costs need to be offset against the possible benefits of preserving undeveloped land. Undeveloped land does deliver benefits, but, as noted above, SERC research suggests that for the type of land that accounts for 52.1 per cent[10] of open land in England – intensively farmed agricultural land – these are far less than usually claimed (Gibbons et al. 2011). While urban parks and high amenity land accessible to the public yield substantial social benefits, Gibbons et al. (2011) found that Greenbelt land as such – most of which is in high-intensity agricultural use with limited public access – was of measurable value only to those owning houses within it. Town dwellers near its borders were willing to pay no premium to live near it. This finding matches that of Cheshire and Sheppard (2004) although their result was specific to the area around Reading, Berkshire, and is consistent with a decline in estimated social values of Greenbelt land noted in the previous chapter.

Paradoxically, the restrictiveness of the current system also results in some clearly unsustainable development. In popular areas of the country, demand for land is high but supply is highly restricted. This means large financial gains to landowners in popular areas when land is made available for development. Often, it is local authorities or other public agencies who realise these gains by selling off their own land – in particular allotments, parks and school playing fields. According to the *Guardian*, the waiting list for allotments stood at 86,000 people in 2011.[11] The then National Playing Fields Association reported that no less than 40 per cent of all

---

[9] DCLG (2010) accessed 5 October 2011.

[10] UK National Ecosystem Assessment, (2010) Chapter 7 page 200.

[11] 'Garden sharing: growing your own vegetables on someone else's patch', *Guardian*, 2 September, http://bit.ly/n9dsBp (accessed 5 October 2011).

school and community playing fields in England were lost to development between 1992 and 2005. According to the *Daily Telegraph*, the number of grass cricket pitches in London fell from 1,126 to 681 between 1990 and 2010 while the number of football pitches fell by 20 per cent. By one of the ironies of the law of unintended consequences these figures were quoted in an article by the Chief Executive of the London Playing Fields Foundation extolling the *Daily Telegraph*'s lobby to defeat the Government's mildly reforming draft National Planning Policy Framework on the grounds that allowing any relaxation in land release would cause more playing fields to be lost: when it was exactly the lack of land and the consequent incentive for Local Planning Authorities (LPAs) to sell it for development that had been causing the loss.[12]

As Cheshire and Sheppard (2005) argue, the social and environmental case for not building on school playing fields or allotments is very strong. Even 'classic' brownfield land such as disused quarries, railway land or industrial sites is often used for informal recreation and is increasingly cited as providing important habitats for rare wildlife; not rare just in towns, but rare in Britain as a whole.[13] One of the primary functions of the planning system should be to protect such areas from development. But by causing land in desirable locations to be in such short supply the system has created strong incentives – sadly often too alluring to resist – which result in development going onto exactly the most socially and environmentally valuable land.

As discussed above, there is good evidence that Greenbelt policies impose a development 'tax' on urban businesses (Cheshire and Hilber 2008) and would-be house buyers alike. These costs might well be an acceptable part of a planning trade-off if the environmental gains were substantial. However, as Barker (2006) pointed out, in fast-growing cities like Oxford and Cambridge, development has leap-frogged Greenbelts into the countryside proper. The result is more commuting, congestion and pollution than relaxing restrictions might have achieved (Barker Review of Land Use Planning 2006). A recent study by GLA Economics showed that expressed as a proportion of the locally resident highly qualified working population whose jobs were in central London, there were important daily commuting flows from as far away as Norwich and the New Forest – let alone the expected places such as Oxford, Brighton or Winchester (Ennis and Theseira 2009).

---

[12] *Daily Telegraph*, 6 October 2011. The same logic applies to the development of MoD land – such as the nightingale habitat on the Hoo Peninsula.

[13] See for example: http://www.buglife.org.uk/conservation/currentprojects/Habitats+Action/ Brownfields, or http://www.butterfly-conservation.org/article/9/292/return_of_the_ ranunculus_the_moth_that_came_back.htm.

6.   DYNAMIC EFFECTS

The least well-understood aspects of the current planning system are its dynamic impacts – for example, the impact on patterns of saving and investment; the impact of regional house price differentials on spatial labour market adjustment; or how long-run trends in property prices affect the cost of living and doing business in London versus other 'competitor' cities. What are the implications of this for innovation and growth?

Empirical estimates (see Rosenthal and Strange 2004) are inconclusive on whether size of cities or specialisation matter more for growth. Duranton and Puga (2001) suggest that larger cities might act as incubators – creating more firms that then move out to more specialised cities once they are established. Glaeser (2011) strongly argues that there is a link from size to innovation and growth. He argues that this works through density, rather than size per se – although, as discussed in section 4.2, it would be fair to say that the correlations available to support this assertion are suggestive at best and surely simplistic. As mentioned above, Cheshire and Magrini (2009) find in Western Europe that larger cities – all else controlled for – have experienced higher rates of economic growth and that, for a given size, lower density cities grew faster. While this evidence is not conclusive it supports the idea that density per se is not conducive to agglomeration economies.

Claims have been made that restrictions on land supply in the most dynamic cities and resulting house price differentials are barriers to local labour market adjustment, which means that, all else equal, unemployment is higher in the economically less successful parts of Britain (Evans 1990). While it is tempting to believe that liberalising supply in more productive areas would indirectly benefit struggling areas, clear-cut evidence is lacking. However the case that such a liberalisation would improve both national economic performance and real incomes for many families across Britain is pretty compelling as we outlined in some detail in Chapter 2.

6.   CONCLUSIONS

To summarise, there is evidence that planning or zoning systems that restrict the supply of land or built space have significant economic costs which need to be balanced against any environmental or social benefits. This is a problem recognised in an increasing number of countries. But the UK system is at an extreme in terms of costs it imposes. This is partly because it has been in place so long – effectively since 1947 – but also because it is particularly dirigiste. It reduces the supply of new construction while increasing house prices and reducing housing quality (with a regressive impact on low to middle income families and younger compared to older people) and also increases housing market volatility. In addition there is strong evidence that planning restrictiveness, interacting with a lack of fiscal incentives to local communities to allow commercial development, increases office rents and also lowers retail productivity and employment in small independent retailers. Finally there is strong if not wholly conclusive evidence that the British planning system does not properly assess the true social costs of brownfield versus greenfield development.

Other possible costs of the system are not well documented (for example the negative impact on land-intensive manufacturing and wholesale distribution, the direct compliance costs, full costs of delays or the effects on investment of uncertainty, dynamic effects on economic growth) but they appear to be significant. Successive British governments have attempted to address these problems by reforming the system. But as yet all government reforms have been restricted to relatively modest reforms of process and procedure. They have not addressed the fundamental problem of the restriction on the supply of space. The most recent set of reforms introduced in 2012 were hotly contested but did attempt to address the issue of incentives (or the lack of them) to local communities to permit development.

It is perfectly valid to question the extent to which these reforms will be successful. Campaigners are also perfectly entitled to argue that the costs imposed by the planning system are prices worth paying to 'protect the countryside' or achieve other policy objectives. However, it is not helpful for public debate to pretend that the costs we have documented do not exist; or even that they are negligible. Existing research shows that this is simply not the case; indeed research shows the costs are very substantial even if some are difficult to measure exactly. There are multiple links from planning to the economy and any sensible debate on planning reform must recognise this. Furthermore any useful and rational debate should attempt to rigorously quantify the benefits conferred by the system rather than just assert them as 'fact'. There may be great social and environmental benefits associated with beautiful and unspoilt countryside, but recent evidence suggests the environmental benefits associated with intensive agricultural land without public access are negative (Firbank et al. 2011).

A final point: despite alarmist claims about 'concreting over England', recent research shows a surprisingly small proportion of England – even the South East of England including Greater London – is actually developed. The Foresight Land Use Futures research (2010) showed that only 9.95 per cent of England was in urban development and of this almost half was in parks or gardens. Domestic and industrial and commercial buildings together accounted for just 1.8 per cent of England's surface. The evidence equally shows that Greenbelt land is of very little amenity or environmental value to anyone except those who have houses within its bounds.[14]

REFERENCES

American Planners' Association. 1998. 'The Principles of Smart Development', PAS report #479. Chicago, IL, APA.

Ball, M. 2011. 'Planning delay and the responsiveness of English housing supply'. *Urban Studies* 48, 349–362.

Ball, M. and P. Allmendinger. 2008. 'Change, Rigidity and Delay in the UK System of Land-Use Development Control', Working Papers in Real Estate & Planning. Reading: Department of Real Estate and Planning, Reading University.

Ball, M., P. Allmendinger and C. Hughes. 2008. 'Housing Supply and Planning Delay in the South of England', Working Papers in Real Estate and Planning 04/08. Reading: Department of Real Estate and Planning, Reading University.

Barker, Kate. 2004. 'Review of Housing Supply: Delivering Stability'. London: HM Treasury.

Barker, Kate. 2006. 'Barker Review of Land Use Planning; Interim Report – Analysis'. London: HMSO.

Barker Review of Land Use Planning. 2006. 'Final Report – Recommendations'. London: HM Government.

British Council of Shopping Centres. 2006. 'In Town or Out of Town: Where Will New Retail Development Go?' London: BCSC.

Centre for Economics and Business Research. 2011. 'Forecasting Eye: Analysis and Interpretation of Key Data Releases'. London: CEBR.

Cheshire, Paul. 2009. 'Urban Containment, Housing Affordability and Price Stability – Irreconcilable Goals', SERC Policy Paper 04. London: SERC.

Cheshire, P.C. and C. Hilber. 2008. 'Office space supply restrictions in Britain: The political economy of market revenge'. *Economic Journal* 118, F185–F221.

Cheshire, Paul and Stefano Magrini. 2009. 'Urban growth drivers in a Europe of sticky people and implicit boundaries'. *Journal of Economic Geography* 9, 85–115.

Cheshire, Paul and Stephen Sheppard. 2002. 'Welfare economics of land use regulation'. *Journal of Urban Economics* 52, 242–269.

Cheshire, Paul and Stephen Sheppard. 2004. 'Land markets and land market regulation: progress towards understanding'. *Regional Science and Urban Economics* 34, 619–637.

---

[14] The work done to value Britain's natural resources (Firbank et al. 2011) concluded that intensively farmed agricultural land had a negative environmental value. Most Greenbelt land is in intensive agriculture. The work of SERC researchers associated with this assessment valuing Greenbelt land (Gibbons et al. 2011) was discussed in the text above.

Cheshire, Paul and Stephen Sheppard. 2005. 'The introduction of price signals into land use planning decision-making: A proposal'. *Urban Studies* 42, 647–663.

Cheshire, Paul, Christian Hilber and Ioannis Kaplanis. 2012. 'Land Use Regulation and Productivity – Land Matters: Evidence from a UK Supermarket Chain', Department of Economics Working Paper 12. Catalonia: University of Rovira i Virgili.

Combes, Pierre-Philippe, Gilles Duranton and Laurent Gobillon. 2011. 'The identification of agglomeration economies'. *Journal of Economic Geography* 11, 253–266.

Council for the Protection of Rural England. 2011. 'What We Want to See in the National Planning Policy Framework'. London: CPRE.

Crossrail. 2013. http://www.crossrail.co.uk.

DCLG. 2010. 'Clark – new powers to prevent unwanted "garden grabbing"'. London: DCLG.

DCLG———. 2011a. 'Draft National Planning Policy Framework'. London: DCLG.

DCLG———. 2011b. 'A Plain English Guide to the Localism Bill'. London: DCLG.

DCLG. 2012. 'National Planning Policy Framework'. London: DCLG.

De La Roca, Jorge and Diego Puga. 2011. 'Learning by Working in Big Cities', CEPR Discussion Paper No. 9243, London: CEPR.

Duranton, Gilles and Diego Puga. 2001. 'Nursery cities: urban diversity, process innovation and the life cycle of products'. *American Economic Review* 91, 1454–1477.

Ennis, N., and M. Theseira. 2009. 'Commuting Patterns in London by Qualification Level and Employment Location'. London: Greater London Authority.

Evans, A.W. 1990. 'A house price based regional policy'. *Regional Studies* 24, 559–567.

Firbank, L., R. Bradbury, D. McCracken, C. Stoate, K. Goulding, R. Harmer and P. Williams. 2011. 'Enclosed Farmland. In: The UK National Ecosystem Assessment Technical Report. UK National Ecosystem Assessment'. Cambridge: UNEP-WCMC.

Foresight Land Use Futures Project. 2010. 'Final Project Report'. London: The Government Office for Science.

Gibbons, Steve, Susana Mourato and Guilherme Resende. 2011. 'The Amenity Value of English Nature: A Hedonic Price Approach', SERC Discussion Paper 0074. London: SERC.

Gibbons, S., H.G. Overman and P. Pelkonen. 2013. 'Area disparities in Britain: Understanding the contribution of people vs, place through variance decompositions'. *Oxford Bulletin of Economics and Statistics*. doi:10.1111/obes.12043.

Glaeser, Edward. 2011. *The Triumph of the City*. London: Pan Macmillan.

Haskel, Jonathan and Raffaella Sadun. 2009. 'Regulation and UK Retailing Productivity: Evidence from Micro Data', CEPR Discussion Papers 7140. London: Centre for Economic Policy Research.

Hilber, C.A.H. and W. Vermeulen. 2012. 'The Impact of Supply Constraints on House Prices in England', SERC Discussion Paper 119. London: SERC.

Hilber, Christian A.L. and Wouter Vermeulen. 2011. 'The Impact of Restricting Housing Supply on House Prices and Affordability: Report for NHPAU'. London: DCLG.

Keep, Matthew. 2012. 'Regional House Prices: Affordability and Income Ratios', Standard Note SN/SG/1922. London: House of Commons.

Koster, Hans R.A., Piet Rietveld and Jos N. van Ommerren. 2011. 'Is the Sky the Limit? An Analysis of High-Rise Office Buildings', SERC Discussion Paper 0086. London: SERC.

Mayo, Stephen and Stephen Sheppard. 2001. 'Housing supply and the effects of stochastic development control'. *Journal of Housing Economics* 10, 109–128.

Melo, Patricia, Daniel Graham and Robert Noland. 2009. 'A meta-analysis of estimates of urban agglomeration economies'. *Regional Science and Urban Economics* 39, 332–342.

Monbiot, George. 2011. 'This wrecking ball is Osborne's version of sustainable development', *The Guardian*, 5 September. London: GMG.

Nathan, Max and Chris Urwin. 2006. 'City People: City Centre Living in the UK'. London: Centre for Cities.

National Trust. 2011. *Planning for People*. Swindon: National Trust, http://www.nationaltrust.org.uk/article-1356392050474/.

Needham, B. and E. Louw. 2006. 'Institutional economics and policies for changing land markets: the case of industrial estates'. *The Netherlands Journal of Property Research* 23, 75–90.

OECD. 2013. *Green Growth in Cities*. Paris: OECD.

Office of Fair Trading. 2008. 'Homebuilding in the UK: A Market Study'.

Richardson, H.W. 1962. 'The basis of economic recovery in the nineteen-thirties: a review and a new interpretation'. *The Economic History Review* 15, 344–363.

Rosenthal, Stuart and William Strange. 2004. 'Evidence on the Nature and Sources of Agglomeration Economies', in V. Henderson and J.-F. Thisse (eds), *Handbook of Urban and Regional Economics Volume 4*. Amsterdam: Elsevier.

Sadun, Raffaella. 2008. 'Does Planning Regulation Protect Independent Retailers?' Centre for Economic Performance Discussion Paper 0888. London: CEP.

Silverman, Emily, Ruth Lupton and A. Fenton. 2006. 'A Good Place for Children? Attracting and Retaining Families in Inner Urban Mixed Communities'. London: Chartered Institute of Housing/Joseph Rowntree Foundation.

Stolper, W.F. 1941. 'British monetary policy and the housing boom'. *The Quarterly Journal of Economics* 56, 1(Part 2), 1–170.

Strong, R. 2011. 'Hands Off Our Land: The Eden that is England's Countryside', *Daily Telegraph*, 2 September.

Tetlow King. 2012. 'Planning for Less', in: http://www.policyexchange.org.uk/images/publications/planning-for-less-full-figures.pdf.

UK National Ecosystem Assessment. 2010. 'The UK National Ecosystem Assessment: Synthesis of the Key Findings'. Cambridge: UNEP-WCMC.

Unsworth, Rachael and Max Nathan. 2006. 'Beyond city living: remaking the inner suburbs'. *Built Environment* 32, 235–249.

Urban Task Force. 2005. 'Towards a Strong Urban Renaissance'. London: Urban Task Force.

6. Planning: reforms that might work and ones that won't[1]

1. INTRODUCTION

The authors of this book represent three generations. The oldest is 72 and bought his first house in 1972. The house cost £2,500. He now lives in a large house – though smaller than the one he lived in when raising his children – in an attractive part of central London with no mortgage. The increase in the price of his house(s) over 41 years is equal to about twice the total salary (at historic values) he has earned from all his academic employment. One of us is in the middle of their working life and has two young children. He and his family live in a not-so-large house in a pleasant outer area of London. To buy this house required him and his partner to take on a mortgage that was an uncomfortable multiplier of their (then) joint salaries. The youngest of us is an early career academic who lives in a flat in London's 'inner suburbs' with his partner. Their outstanding mortgage is a similarly uncomfortable multiplier of their joint incomes. Not all this inflation in house prices relative to incomes and prices is due to our system of land use planning.[2] But the evidence suggests most of it is and it is both grossly inequitable and highly inefficient. It also means hiring skilled people to work in London is increasingly problematic especially if, like academics, their salary does not vary much with location.

This is a human illustration of some of the inequities and costs identified in Chapters 4 and 5, resulting from the planning system operated

---

[1] The authors are indebted to many colleagues and friends with whom they have over many years discussed how to radically reform land use regulation while retaining its essential functions. Thanks, too, to many planners, notably including Christopher Glaister. Most agree reform is badly needed but only the authors are responsible for the proposals in this chapter!

[2] An argument often heard is that the development industry is monopolistic. But as discussed in Chapter 5, official enquiries into this have never concluded that this specifically was a problem. At least at a national level the output of no producer approaches that conventionally associated with a degree of monopoly, and of course all new houses are competing with existing houses being sold. There might possibly be some problem in about 10 per cent of local markets mainly because a particular developer controlled the one or very few large sites where development was permitted. But even these problems seemed minor.

in Britain. Similar, if not such dramatic stories could be told for cities elsewhere in the world. We are not the first to have identified the major cost: more expensive and lower quality housing. Probably the first serious concerns on this score were raised in Hall et al. (1973). This was a work by a team seriously sympathetic to the ideals of planning but who saw that the rigid policy of urban containment and the specific way in which the boundaries of the Greenbelts had been determined during the 1950s was perverting what they saw as the underlying purpose of town planning. These were in their view to improve the quality of people's lives by improving the quality of their environment – the urban environment – in which the overwhelming majority of people spend the overwhelming majority of our lives. Far from providing people with greener environments and garden cities, the planning system had developed in a way which produced higher densities and made housing space more difficult to acquire.

Serious research by urban economists did not emerge until the 1980s and this still focused on the dominant urban use of land – housing (Cheshire and Sheppard 1989). That work in the UK sharply focused on the costs of planning came before that in the US is maybe not surprising. The UK had introduced effective and highly restrictive controls on the supply of urban land in the 1947 Town and Country Planning Act – well ahead of other countries.[3] In the US, Fischel (1985), although he had discussed the possibility that zoning might increase the price of housing, took this mainly as a sign that, if house prices rose following the introduction of zoning, then that showed that zoning was improving welfare.

In Britain the specific effects of restrictions on land supply attracted increasing attention from scholars from about 1990. Bramley (1993, 1998), Pennington (2000) or in somewhat more polemical vein, Evans (1990) and Evans and Hartwich (2005), made significant contributions. Government, however, did not publically show interest in the economic implications of planning until the Barker Review was set up in 2003 (Barker 2003, 2004). This, too, concentrated on housing supply but in 2006 Kate Barker was commissioned with a second review with a wider remit to investigate the effects of the British land use planning system on the economy more generally.

So, as we showed in Chapters 4 and 5, over the past 25 years in Britain increasing evidence has accumulated showing that not only does the

---

[3] Other countries had, of course, introduced forms of urban planning and land use regulation even in the late 19th century; or depending on how formally you defined it, even in Imperial Rome. In the US there had been some interest by economists in zoning and particularly the role of minimum lot sizes in excluding poor households from richer communities. But here we mean planning when it has the specific effect of constraining either urban land supply or the supply of particular types of real estate.

British system of land use planning have substantial costs but these costs do not appear to be compensated by benefits on anything like the same scale. Since about 2000, scholars in other countries have also taken up research in this area. In the US there has been the work first of Fischel but later of Glaeser, Gyourko, Quigley and others. Some of these works have been referenced in Chapters 4 and 5.

Here, however, we turn to how systems of land use regulation could be reformed in ways which would continue to moderate those endemic problems of market failure that exist in land markets but do so at substantially less economic cost. We are not supporters of that school of economic thought which argues no regulation of land markets is necessary. Some have argued that just by reforming property rights one could eliminate problems of market failure in land markets. We do not think this would work, primarily because there are so many actors affected by decisions about development. Although there are what economists would call 'clubs' providing conservation – the British National Trusts are examples of such a private initiative – they are not enough. There are public goods that need to be provided, such as urban parks, open spaces, national parks, habitats or important historic cityscapes or buildings where it is very hard indeed to imagine that private initiatives alone would ensure an outcome that was best from a social point of view.

Equally there are important external costs associated with development. People who experience development of nearby land which was previously open, people who have a new road, airport or railway built close by, or enjoy the proximity of a beautiful building, are open to real and sometimes significant loss, not just of amenities but often of financial assets too. There are simply too many people potentially affected by some types of development for them effectively to be able to exercise any property rights that they might be offered. For example, it has been suggested rights to develop should have to be put up for public auction on the grounds that those who might lose from the development could get together and buy the development rights (see, for example, Papworth 2012). But the losses are often thinly spread over many people while the profits of development go just to the developer. Transactions costs are far too high for individuals to be able effectively to outbid developers in the great majority of cases. So there needs to be a legally enforceable and state-operated system of land use regulation. What is not obvious is that such a system should restrict the supply of urban development of any type overall. But it will need to restrict development in many locations (to protect amenities or habitats, for example) and so far as possible ensure that losers from development are compensated.

Of course we could try to live with housing markets becoming ever more volatile and housing of a given quality becoming ever more unaffordable with the very undesirable macroeconomic and distributional consequences this would have. In the short term this is undoubtedly the most attractive 'solution'. The problem is it is utterly unviable in the long term. With every passing decade the problems would get worse, the wider economic costs would become more penalising, the economy and monetary policy more unmanageable and the outcomes – the divide between the property haves and the property have-nots – more unacceptable. In our judgement there is no doubt that if things go on as they are then at some point there will be a system breakdown and perhaps serious social unrest. Reform is unavoidable and only radical reform will work.

What forms of reform, then, would be effective given that there is a strong welfare case for state operated land use regulation? It seems to us possible reforms fall into three main generic types:

1.   dirigisme or state directives
2.   incentive-based
3.   price signals

and within each of these types there are particular solutions or tools.

This chapter considers each approach in turn, and highlights the pros and cons of each. Some approaches would work better or be more appropriate in the context of some national systems than others. Our emphasis here is on reforms applicable to the British context but we consider implications for other systems and institutional history as well. As it turns out, the UK's history and context suggests that a reformed planning system should be based on a combination of better-designed incentives and greater use of price signals.

2.   DIRIGISTE APPROACHES

The most rational dirigiste approach might be rigorously to follow the logic of 1947 state planning. If we are intent on allocating land (or, in the US, structure plus land 'bundles') for each use without regard to price then logically we need to introduce space rationing. If price does not determine the supply of land then the logic is that price should not determine its consumption. Each adult could, for example, have a ration of, say, 40 m^2 with dependent children having, say, another 20 m^2 each, but use their income to bid for where they wanted to live. We could, if we wanted, even introduce a trading system so young adults or those willing to live in more cramped conditions could sell some of their space ration, perhaps buying back space in later life. This would be in some sense inequitable but very much less inequitable than the outcome of the present system.

Such a 'solution' would be taking concerns about older people 'under-occupying' their houses to a logical conclusion. But since we have already shown in Chapter 5 that land is not actually in short supply in Britain (let alone in countries such as the US, Australia or New Zealand, also tightening up their controls on land supply for housing) and we do not think it is remotely possible to devise a system of officially deciding how much housing space people were entitled to, we reject this extreme – if logical – dirigiste solution.

A second version of the dirigiste approach to reform has in fact already been tried. This was the attempt to impose minimum land allocations on local authorities (LAs) implemented together with other 'top-down' changes in the 2007 Planning Act. Since these changes were implemented they must have been less barmy. Yet the whole tranche of changes accepted the irrationality of controlling supply by fiat while using the price mechanism to allocate the resulting housing and other development. In a sense it was within the logical and ideological framework set by the 1947 act. The 2007 reforms were the then government's response to the Barker Reports. They were designed to get more housing built and to ease the path of major infrastructure developments. Their logic was of centralised state planning. They introduced top-down institutional changes and land allocation 'targets' for LAs with a regional tier in the planning process and Regional Spatial Strategies informed by an expert assessment of housing demand supplied by a new body, the National Housing and Planning Advice Unit. They also centralised decisions on major infrastructure with the creation of an Infrastructure Planning Commission.[4] They did not significantly change the incentive structures faced by local planners (the Community Infrastructure Levy being the main exception here), change the underlying assumptions of the system, introduce price information into decision making (except that housing affordability became one of the targets for setting land availability) or change the fundamentals of policy.

The results were predictable. Local planning authorities (LPAs) had targets for delays and met them – mainly by increasing their refusal rates (see Hilber and Vermeulen 2012). Housing targets communicated by the

---

[4] This was a joint recommendation of two government reviews into transport (Eddington 2006) and planning (Barker 2006). The problem this new body was expected to solve was that arising from the very large geographical scale – sometimes national – of major infrastructure development, but the very localised scale of planning decision making. So major infrastructure provided an extreme case of the asymmetry of the spatial scale of costs compared to benefits and the consequent desirability of reflecting the benefits in a more balanced way in decisions.

new Regional Spatial Strategies continued to be couched in terms of physical units – land allocated for housing at presumed densities and with an assumption that land allocated constituted the 'supply of land' in an economic sense. Land allocations were provided by LAs on the basis of forecast household numbers and locations chosen by where the LPA wanted to put houses, not where people wanted to live; and the target of 60 per cent of all building being on brownfield sites was retained.

In our judgement, although the Regional Spatial Strategies did increase land allocation modestly, these reforms were doomed to failure since they did not tackle the underlying problem and targets could be met in ways which did little or nothing to satisfy demand. The case of targets to reduce delays was mentioned above but another problem was simply allocating land for high density flat development in town centres when the demand was for more space and more in suburban areas than in town centres. Both Manchester and Birmingham engaged in this policy. In the Examination in Public of the West Midlands Regional Spatial Strategy, the strategy was to allocate very little greenfield or suburban land on the basis that doing so would 'be very damaging to the environment and undermine the priority for urban renaissance as developers "cherry-pick" the most attractive sites' (Examination in Public 2009, paras 3.31 and 3.32). In other words, left to themselves, developers would build houses where people wanted to live.

The Infrastructure Planning Commission might have worked and the National Housing and Planning Advice Unit brought some evidence and economic analysis to bear on the housing market problems and their relationship to planning. On balance, however, we doubt the set of reforms introduced following the Barker Reviews would have made more than a minor dent in the problem of housing supply; they would have had no effect on the wider costs discussed in Chapter 5; and, in the long run, they would probably have proved politically unacceptable. In any case they were swept away by the new government elected in 2010 so it is not possible rigorously to evaluate them.

Overall our judgement is that reforms which accept the logic of centralised state planning and override individual preferences or attempt to significantly infringe individual rights will not work in an economy where the great majority of goods and services are produced and allocated by means of markets, or where successive governments – all governments in OECD countries – permit homeowner occupation and private land ownership. Such markets we would argue need regulating, but planning in the sense enshrined in the 1947 Act has failed and its failures will become progressively more serious. We need to find solutions through mechanisms other than state direction.

2.   INCENTIVE-BASED APPROACHES

All new development imposes costs – first, of course, the cost of resources necessary for construction. These are conventional private costs. But, as was argued in Chapters 4 and 5, there are genuine costs imposed by development in terms of short-term disruption to local residents but more importantly long-term loss of amenities and reduced asset values (from the fall in the capitalised value of those amenities embodied in the price of houses or other property) and increased congestion. There may also be longer-term costs in the form of more congested local facilities and infrastructure. Unless there is a system of regulation in place requiring compensation for such costs, then they are externalities – contributing to the endemic problems of market failure in land markets. A feature of all these costs is that they are usually very localised and often significant for those who bear them. The gains from new development, however, are widespread and go to all those who benefit from slightly cheaper or more conveniently located housing or additional employment opportunities. The benefits and costs of development are, therefore, spatially asymmetric – costs are very local and often substantial to individuals, while benefits tend to be widespread and, as far as individuals are concerned, are usually small and uncertain. This creates a problem similar to free trade – small gains for many against significant losses for the few – and so makes political decision making and the design of appropriate incentives difficult. We all want cheaper tee shirts imported from China or TVs from Korea unless, that is, we earn our livings making them in Manchester or Eindhoven.

Compensation

Some but not all of these costs can be offset by investment in new infrastructure or the provision of amenity land, schools or other local services; others, such as the loss of local amenities and their capitalised values, might be able to be compensated with direct money payments.

Three main methods have been suggested by which 'the community' could have necessary extra investment costs covered in order to maintain the quality of infrastructure and local public services. The first is by a system of 'betterment' levies; the second by negotiating with would-be developers some in kind recompense for permission to develop; and the third by impact fees. Both the first two of these methods are, in our judgement, complete failures. The history of betterment as a legal concept goes back to 1427 AD when the Crown demanded compensation from property owners whose property had been made more valuable by flood prevention and drainage works (Davies 1984). The concept in the context of real estate relates to an increase in value brought about by the actions of the state or the community rather than the owner. Of course normally, and certainly in Britain, granting permission to develop substantially increases the value of a parcel of land. It is not obvious, however, that it is the result of the state 'doing' anything: rather it arises because the state has expropriated the rights of owners to develop their land and then kept such development rights in short supply so that their value as developed parcels exceeds their value in their current use, even including development costs. This is rather different from, for example, the state funding the construction of a new metro system (such as London's CrossRail) and taxing land of those who have benefited from the improved access to help pay for it.

The real problem with taxes based on 'betterment' as applied to land values increased by granting permission to develop, however, is that each and every parcel has to be valued in its pre- and post-development state. Every case becomes a one-off with substantial costs absorbed by professional valuers/appraisers and the legal process. Three attempts have been made in the UK to impose a form of betterment tax, each more ambitious and complex than its predecessor: in 1947 (repealed in 1951); in 1967 (repealed 1970) and finally in 1975 with the Community Land Act (repealed 1979). This last act was designed to impose a tax of 100 per cent on the 'betterment' (increased value) resulting from planning permission and ultimately give local planning authorities a monopoly over all buying and selling of land for development. The fundamental reason all these attempts failed was the complexity and cost of their operation; a further problem was that since it was expected that they would subsequently be repealed (in each case the political opposition pledged to do this) they had the effect of at least in the medium term further restricting the supply of developable land.

Payment by developers 'in kind' for permission to develop was introduced in England and Wales in the 1991 Planning and Compensation Act. Section 106 of this, euphemistically entitled 'Planning Obligation' provided for LAs to impose conditions on granting permission such as the developer building a proportion of the houses as social or 'affordable' housing, providing a school or some other development required by the LA or even paying cash. The idea was to help the community capture some of the 'planning' gain so its underlying logic was 'betterment'. The problem with these Section 106 Agreements, as they came to be known, is that they inevitably had high transactions costs: each had to be separately negotiated. This meant they were *de facto* only applicable for larger developments. Crook and Monk (2011) estimated that while only 6 to 7 per cent of all non-householder permissions had S106 Agreements associated with them, when it came to large housing developments of 100 or more¹ it was more than 90 per cent. Moreover, big developers negotiated most of these agreements so built up (indeed invested in acquiring) great expertise in negotiating them – expensive, and from a social point of view a dead-weight loss. Local authorities typically do not have the skills successfully to negotiate favourable agreements, and in the outturn less than half all LAs have ever negotiated S106 Agreements. Nevertheless, because they are most likely to be negotiated in the case of big developments and in high demand areas, their value is considerable. In total they were estimated to be worth some £3.9 billion in 2007–08 with the biggest share (£2.6 billion) going to build affordable housing (see Crook and Monk 2011).

A final reason for judging that Section 106 Agreements generate very sub-optimal outcomes is that they act as a barrier to entry into the development industry. As noted most relate to large developments, and developers invest heavily in the expertise to negotiate favourable agreements. This is a fixed cost that new entrants and small firms have difficulty affording. Moreover it is yet another opaque element in the British planning system making it difficult for foreign firms to enter the market.

Impact fees rest on a different logic. Any commercial development imposes extra costs on the community: it generates additional road use, demand for water and drainage and local public services such as health care or education. Therefore, the argument goes, these costs should be thought of as a part of the costs of the development and paid by the developer. In the US, where they were developed, they legally have to satisfy a 'rational nexus' test: that is for them to be valid local government has to be able to show a clear connection between the development and the need for additional infrastructure and so on, and the level of fees has to be a function of these costs. In practice, where such fees are charged, it appears that they are 100 per cent capitalised into the price paid by developers for land (Ihlanfeldt and Shaughnessy 2004). The same is true of Section 106 Agreements in Britain, and so the ultimate incidence is on the owners of developable land. In the US they have been applied by many local jurisdictions and it has been shown that, where they are applied, they reduce planning restrictiveness (Burge and Ihlanfeldt 2006). Impact fees seem to have both a transparent logic and a transparent implementation and seem, on the basis of Burge and Ihlanfeldt's 2006 findings, to provide a worthwhile incentive to local communities to permit development.

In both the first and second Barker Reviews of planning in Britain

---

¹ To US ears, 100 or more houses does not sound like a large development. But the UK system, especially with its pressure to build on brownfield sites, means that any development of ten or more houses is classified as 'major'.

(Barker 2004a, b, 2006) there was a proposal to levy a 'planning gain supplement' related to the uplift in land values associated with getting planning permission in England. The justification for this relied on the concept of 'betterment'. Although government consulted on this in 2005 it was not introduced, perhaps for some of the reasons set out above explaining why all attempts at imposing betterment levies had failed. However, in 2008 government announced it would introduce a 'Community Infrastructure Levy' (CIL). The incoming government in 2010 confirmed this. Responsibility was legally passed to LAs both to set the level of CIL and decide when to introduce it. The result is it has been introduced in a piecemeal, apparently haphazard way. In the summer of 2012 the Greater London Authority had introduced its own CIL and four boroughs had introduced their own additional levy. Outside London ten LAs had introduced CIL in some shape or form. See Bracke and Cheshire (2013) for a description of the state of play as at mid-2013. Their very preliminary evaluation of the effects of CIL were that while it had had a major impact on the timing of development with a sharp peak in applications prior to its introduction outside London, there was no statistically significant effect on the volume of applications allowing for the post introduction recovery. Data is limited and results are very provisional but it seems possible that the very sharp post-introduction drop in applications has been confused with a permanent fall.

The logic underlying CIL is closer to that justifying an impact fee than a betterment levy, so it has the advantage that it can be calculated in advance and does not lead to expensive arguments about land values. It is too early to evaluate its impact and how it might change incentives and planning restrictiveness, but British CIL compared to the US impact fee has at least two obvious disadvantages. The first is the fact that it does not have to relate to actual costs imposed – there is no idea of a 'rational nexus' test; and related to this rates vary considerably even within the same LA. Wandsworth, for example, has four rates for residential development varying from £0 to £575 per m^2 of space to be constructed depending on location within the Borough and from £0 to £100 m^2 for commercial space (Wandsworth Borough Council, 2012). A second problem is that CIL did not replace S106 Agreements. These continued in parallel so instead of making the system of payments by developers/incentives to residents simpler, its introduction made the system more complex.

A fourth and final form of compensation is of course for developers directly to compensate local property owners for costs their development inflicts. In principle this is possible under the Planning and Compensation Act 1991 but the conditions under which compensation is payable are so complicated that in effect in England and Wales there is no system of direct compensation. It is difficult to see why developers should not directly pay local residents so that they feel they are compensated for development close to them. But in public debate such offers are usually dismissed as 'bribery'. For example the BBC, reported on developments in Petersfield (a rich town in the South East of England) as follows:

> A developer has denied offering bribes to residents to persuade them to support a proposed planning application in a Hampshire town. Residents claimed Morbaine (the would-be developer) sent letters offering them £20,000 each if they agreed not to object to plans to build a supermarket in Petersfield.[6]

Such payments would likely be closely targeted to those actually losing out from the development and if the residents had been willing to agree to the conditions attached – that they would not register an objection to the proposal – then by implication would provide (at least partial) compensation. But as the resident reported in the story said, 'she did not like supermarkets'.[7]

We do not advocate such one-off *ad hoc* payments as a solution although it is not obvious to us that they are morally repugnant. A far stronger case could be made for rule-governed payments: for example that all those who could make a reasonable case that they were adversely affected by any development should have the right to have their property bought by the developer at the current market price plus, say, 15 per cent. There would be difficulties because of the costs of valuation and resolving disputes but one could argue that it would still represent an improvement over the present situation. It would be important not to set the premium over current market value too high, but it would seem fair to allow some compensation for moving house for those who felt they really could not live with the proposed development and the disruption to their lives its construction would bring.

Fiscal Compensation

The second main form of incentive is via the tax system. An important reason why studies find little or no costs of regulatory restrictions on commercial property in the US (see Cheshire and Hilber, 2008) is that in the US commercial property taxes are a purely local tax. The widespread view in the US is that the tax revenues raised from commercial property

---

[6] http://www.bbc.co.uk/news/uk-england-hampshire-18802769.

[7] In passing one might note the resident would have known she had been compensated if she had been informed by recent research. A study by Pope and Pope (2012) concludes proximity to a Walmart increases house prices.

exceed the costs to the local community of providing additional services. So more commercial property in your locality not only increases jobs but reduces (or is supposed to reduce) your personal tax payments. Similarly the decentralised federal system in Switzerland means that local income taxes are significant so communities see a potential gain in attracting more – especially richer – residents. In strong contrast, in Britain local jurisdictions have almost no tax revenues other than those from residential property (the Council Tax) and that is subject to revenue equalisation administered by national government. As previously argued in Chapter 4 the result – the New Homes Bonus aside – is that local communities are effectively fined if they permit any development at all. They have a legal obligation to provide services for both business users and new residents but in the short run they get no fiscal compensation and while down the line they may on the basis of assessed needs and grants from central government, that prospect is distant and uncertain.

The post-2010 coalition government did recognise this issue and has tried to address it. They introduced a New Homes Bonus (NHB) and Business Rates Retention (BRR). The NHB came into force in 2011 and lasts for just six years. Over that period LAs will receive an annual grant equal to the residential property tax (Council Tax) associated with each new house built. This is certainly some incentive but authoritative analysis concludes that the impact on house building was seriously overestimated. The government department responsible (DCLG) announced that their modelling forecast the NHB would increase housing supply by some 140,000 over ten years. The National Audit Office (2013) report was unconvinced. Its judgement was that the assumptions underlying the modelling were unrealistic and that there was a serious arithmetic error leading them, even on those assumptions, to overestimate the impact of NHB by 25 per cent (paras 1.20 to 1.22). The NAO report concluded by saying that it had found little evidence that the NHB had yet had the intended effect of incentivising LAs to increase their planning approvals. It is of course early and it is difficult to estimate a counterfactual – a post-2010 world in which there had been no NHB – but given the evidence on the fall in the rate of new house construction summarised in both Chapters 4 and 5 and the evidence on the reduction in land allocated for housing post-2010 discussed below, then it is already evident that the NHB has not solved or even gone far towards solving the crisis of undersupply in the UK housing market. Modelling suggests a strong case to double or even triple the size of the incentive if it is to have a serious impact on the willingness of LAs to increase their land allocations for new housing (Larkin et al., 2011).

The BRR came into force in April 2013 and is expected to last until at least 2020. Its central provision is for LAs to keep (up to) half of the growth in business rates in their area although there are significant complications to even this benefit out. It should be remembered that, as discussed in Chapter 5, at present commercial property taxes in Britain are exclusively a national tax: a change introduced in 1990 which had a measurable effect on the supply of offices (Cheshire and Hilber 2008). There is therefore very good evidence of the fact that retention of commercial property taxes provides an incentive to LAs to permit commercial development, but the details of the BRR make it less transparent than say the City of London's ability to charge a 15 per cent levy on commercial property taxes or – more extreme – the situation in the US where commercial property taxes are purely local. Government DCLG modelling suggested the measure could add £10.1bn to GDP – although the range of estimates was very broad, from £1.7bn to £19.9bn (DCLG 2012a). Larkin et al. (2011) were more sceptical. Apart from concerns about the scheme's comparative opacity they thought that since it would be 'reset' every seven years, LAs might be incentivised to delay accepting proposals for commercial development until just after a 'reset'. It is certainly too soon to evaluate the impact of the BRR except to say it is at least providing some incentive in a world where none – even negative incentives – existed before.

Land Transactions

Financial rewards from land transactions can also provide an incentive for local communities to accept development. In the Netherlands historically local government had the function of land drainage: municipalities 'supplied' additional land to the community they served. While that function partially remains, it long since extended into a function of municipalities having sole legal rights to allocate and buy land for development. This land is then sold on (sometimes with the necessary improvements) to developers (Needham 1992). Although there have been increasing pressures to limit the supply of land for housing in recent years, this system of municipal land conversion continues to provide a substantial incentive for supplying industrial land (Needham and Louw 2006). The incentive may be stronger for commercial uses than for housing because there is no local income tax in the Netherlands so communities have to pay at least some share of the cost of additional local services or infrastructure. The incentive for commercial development remains stronger because that creates local jobs – popular with voters – as well as yielding profits to the local community from land sales.

This system of incentives works to increase the supply of development in the Netherlands because, of course, there is competition: municipalities compete with each other in land markets and in the 'market' for jobs.

This is in strong contrast to the situation in Korea, for example. There a national government agency determines the supply of land for each category of use and has sole rights to buy agricultural land at assessed market value in current use. This is then sold on to developers. Superficially, therefore, the system resembles that in the Netherlands but instead of all local governments competing and gaining, only the national government gains. The result is a highly monopolised land market with revenue maximisation as the objective rather than the affordability of housing (Hannah et al., 1993). This introduces an incentive to restrict supply.

There is strong evidence both from international comparisons and from changes such as the British decision to introduce the Uniform Business Rate (UBR) in 1990 that the willingness of local communities to accommodate development is influenced by the structure of fiscal systems and in particular property taxes. If national governments take all – or nearly all – revenues or ensure complete income equalisation across local communities there is a strong disincentive for LAs to permit development. Their costs of providing services increases but they do not get the revenues to pay for it so overall service quality is liable to get worse. At the polar extreme to Britain are countries like Germany or Switzerland with substantial income from local property taxes. That real house prices in Switzerland increased by a factor of only 1.3 between 1975 and 2012 and fell in Germany compared to increasing in real terms by a factor of over 3 in the UK[8] is likely to be at least partly explained by the difference in incentive a decentralised tax system provides. We cannot, however, put an exact figure on the difference tax incentives make to housing supply although our judgement is that changes in Britain since 2010 will not make a substantial difference.

3   PRICE SIGNALS

We have identified two fundamental economic problems with systems of land use regulation, especially as they operate in Britain. The first is an unnecessary and damaging restriction of the overall supply of space, for both living and working discussed in Chapter 4. The second is an economically inefficient use of land: for example, the SERC research on both offices and the impact of Town Centre First policy on office costs and retail productivity discussed in Chapter 5 is evidence of this. Unless these high costs are offset by at least equally large social or environmental benefits then there is a significant loss of economic efficiency and of welfare.

[8] http://www.dallasfed.org/institute/houseprice/index.cfm.

Introducing price signals into decisions about land allocation potentially solves both these problems while continuing to allow land use regulation to improve on market allocation and offset for market failure. The idea is simple. As we know, markets generate price signals on the basis of vast amounts of information reflecting both underlying conditions of supply and the preferences and incomes of millions of individuals or firms. Planners may allocate the supply of space for each category of use and determine its location, but markets allocate the supply made available to buyers. This process generates land prices such that available supply of each category of land in every location is allocated to buyers. In our judgement the evidence provided by hedonic studies of property markets (see Chapter 3) strongly implies that land markets work very much more effectively than might be thought. In general the assumption of equilibrium in land markets is a useful one.

Given this, we could use the difference in price of land at boundaries of type of use to indicate to planners whether they should allocate more of land for use (A) than use (B) – allow conversion, in other words. If we observe agricultural land has a market price of, say, £10,000 per ha when, if the parcel could be used for housing it would command £7.5 million per ha, then the market is signalling that there is a shortage of housing land in that location. The same would apply if we observed land for industrial use fetching £1 million per ha while just across the road housing land was fetching £7.5 million. Instead of land prices changing continuously across space between one use and another there are discontinuities in land prices. We should allow for both environmental costs and the costs of infrastructure – discussed below – but with these suitably incorporated we can measure the net discontinuities and use them as price signals to improve land allocation by planners.

The question is how should planners respond to such signals? Historically, both by training and, at least in Britain, by law, they have ignored them entirely. As economists who recognise the importance of market failure we would not claim that such land price discontinuities should be slavishly followed. It might be that there is great demand to build houses in beautiful coastal sites, national parks, heritage sites or important habitats. But clearly there is a public good involved in preserving such locations. Building on such land would impose costs to many others far beyond just the costs of development. These costs – loss of public amenities, for example – will not be reflected in the market without regulation to prevent development. It is because they are preserved that land prices are high: supply of development is intentionally restricted and there is a clear public benefit as a result.

This, in essence, was the argument of the Foresight Land Use Futures

Project (2010): that the use of any given parcel of land should be determined on the basis of both the market demand for it and its wider social, amenity and environmental value. Similarly the National Planning Policy Framework (DCLG 2012b) sets out as a core planning principle the need to 'take account of market signals, such as land prices and housing affordability'. The problem is to translate these general principles into workable solutions to guide decision making.

Cheshire and Sheppard (2005) attempt to do just that. Their suggestion is that observed price discontinuities – the difference in market prices across boundaries of use categories – should become a 'material consideration' leading to a presumption in favour of any proposed development unless (a very important 'unless') it could be shown that the observed monetary value of the discontinuity[9] reflected wider environmental, amenity or social values of the land in its current use. They recognise, of course, that in practical terms it is impossible to exactly value the 'wider environmental, amenity or social values of land in its current use'. As is explained below they argue, however, that in the UK (at least) this does not matter for practical purposes.

First, this is because there is a very large amount of land where the 'wider' values are negligible. This is partly because of the large amounts of land zoned for industry or retail use which have a substantially lower market price than nearby housing land. But much more it is because of the vast area of high-intensity farmland throughout Britain. If rigorous evidence was required it would seem difficult to sustain an argument that the higher price observed for housing compared to industrial land in a prosperous town like Oxford represented sufficient 'wider environmental, amenity or social value' to justify rejecting a proposal to develop the land for housing. At the start of January 2011 – the most recent data available at the time of writing – industrial land in Oxford had an estimated market price of £1m per ha, compared to £4m for residential land (VOA 2011). So where land had already been identified for development, conversion from one use to another – economically more efficient – use would surely become much easier and cheaper.

Much more significantly there is the substantial evidence that there is virtually no significant value of a 'wider environmental, amenity or social' type associated with intensively farmed land. Indeed two official government reports – Foresight Land Use Futures Project (2010) and Firbank

---

[9] They in fact suggested that to be on the conservative side and bias decision-making in favour of environmental and so on values, some arbitrary fixed amount should be included; that is development should not be allowed if the value of the discontinuity plus some fixed additional premium or threshold could not be justified on amenity grounds.

et al. (2011) – concluded that intensively farmed land had negative 'wider environmental, amenity or social value'. Since the market price of farmland is inflated by both relief from inheritance taxes and agricultural subsidies there could be no credible case that it should be protected from development on grounds of 'wider value' – even when in a Greenbelt. In Chapter 5 we showed there was good evidence that Greenbelt land has no value to people living near it: its only value is to those who own houses within it. The loss of such values would, it is true, represent a loss of 'wider social and amenity value' – that is it would represent an external cost of developing Greenbelt land – but the cost would be very small relative to the gains in welfare associated with cheaper and more spacious housing. Even if, to reflect this, a high fixed cost (as discussed in endnote 9) was added as a kind of tax on greenfield development, only a tiny proportion of available high intensity farmland would be needed fully to satisfy the demand for residential use as well as for economic demands for out of town locations.

Figure 6.1 helps make this point. It maps all the Greenbelt areas of England. Just taking three counties near London – Essex, Hertfordshire and Surrey – Greenbelt land covers 73.3 per cent of Surrey, 51.6 per cent of Hertfordshire but only 43.1 per cent of Essex since a good part of Essex is far away from London and is anyway protected agricultural land. Intensive farming covers[10] respectively 37 per cent of Surrey, 59 per cent of Hertfordshire and 67 per cent of Essex. Greenbelt land covered 580,730 ha in the combined East and South East (DCLG, 2013): the latest data from the Generalised Land Use data for 2005 show that in these combined regions a total of 66,980 ha was covered by all types of building added together.

Figure 6.1[11] also shows us what percentage of each Greenbelt area was devoted to intensive agriculture. This is defined very conservatively only to include arable land. Managed pastures which are also mainly highly intensive in their demands for fertiliser or the absence of wildlife are not included. We can see that in the three Greenbelts of southern England where pressure of demand for housing was highest, those of Cambridge, Oxford and London, intensive agricultural land accounted for respectively 74, 44 and 37 per cent of their areas. The most recent data available from the Valuations Office Agency, for 2007, show that had one been able to get permission to convert a hectare of agricultural land in Cambridge's Greenbelt the price would have increased from about £10,000 per ha to

[10] Data are from Defra County data and DCLG Local Planning Authority Greenbelt Statisics
[11] Thanks to Sevrin Waights for constructing this map.

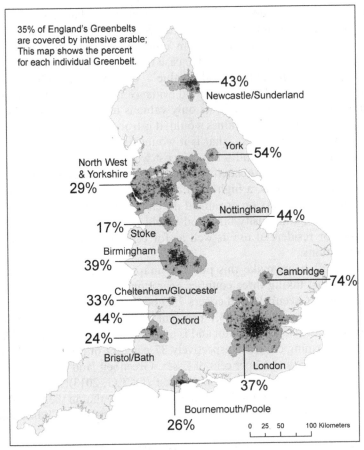

35% of England's Greenbelts
are covered by intensive arable;
This map shows the percent
for each individual Greenbelt.

43%
Newcastle/Sunderland

York ─ 54%

North West
& Yorkshire
29%

Nottingham ─ 44%

17% Stoke

Birmingham
39%

Cambridge ─ 74%

Cheltenham/Gloucester
33%

44%   Oxford

24%

Bristol/Bath

London
37%

Bournemouth/Poole
26%   0   25 50   100 Kilometers

This map was prepared by Sevrin Waights. Calculations are based on Land Cover Map 2000.
Intensive arable land was defined as use categories 4.1, 4.2 and 4.3 and so is a conservative
estimate of 'intesively farmed agricultural land'.

Figure 6.1   Intensive arable land in English Greenbelts (per cent)

about £3.5 million; around Oxford the price would have gone to between
£3.8 and £8 million. If one could have got permission to convert any of
the thousands of hectares of Greenbelt land in the London boroughs of
Barnet, Enfield, Hillingdon or Redbridge to housing, prices would have
increased to between £6.4 million (Redbridge) to £8.6 million (Barnet).
Prices may have come down a little since 2007 but they are doing more
than signalling a shortage, they are screaming a policy-induced famine
of housing land in southern England in exactly the locations it is most in

demand for housing. This famine could be entirely eliminated overnight by allowing building on just a tiny fraction of Greenbelt land of absolutely no environmental or amenity value whatsoever, and, to repeat: concerns about any social value of the land for food are entirely misplaced since there the market works well. All the value of agricultural land for food production is reflected in its market price. Indeed, as noted above, the market price of agricultural land is already inflated by agricultural subsidies and – even more – by its value for tax avoidance since it is exempt from inheritance tax.

So a major attraction of using price signals to resolve problems of land supply and the economically inefficient use of land is that it would never in practice be necessary to try exactly to measure the 'wider environmental, amenity and social value' of land in its current use. There would be a short learning process, but after one or two test cases developers would learn where it was profitable to apply to build and that would be where the wider values associated with the current use of the land were negligible. The initiative or proposal to build has to come from would-be developers – not from the planning side. So, despite appearing to involve similar practical problems to betterment levies, since costs of any legal arguing about the value of land in this use or that would be borne by would-be developers – they have to take the initiative to apply and when they lost costs would be awarded against them – there would be a very substantial incentive to apply only on sites with negligible 'wider environmental and so on' value. Similarly, planners, if they attempted to block applications on low environmental value land, would learn where the decision would go against them if they tried to prevent building and would learn not to refuse applications experience had shown they would certainly lose. This would generate a strong incentive for LAs to pro-actively allocate more low-amenity land for development. They would do that where they thought it was most advantageous (or perhaps least disadvantageous in a conventional planning perspective) for the community they served to allow development.

So by using the price signals generated by land markets to trigger permission to develop subject to the requirement that the differences in land prices did not reflect an environmental, amenity or social value associated with the current designation of land uses one would: (i) produce an incentive for developers to find low-amenity land where demand would be high for housing (or occasionally some other use) and (ii) an incentive for the local community to find low-amenity land on which development was most desirable. To reduce urban land take it would be possible to set some significant premium over and above the difference in land prices as a kind of tax on greenfield development if that was thought desirable. The point is that in reality, since there is such a large supply of low-amenity land around our cities presently frozen by Greenbelt designation, such a change would solve the crisis of land supply and housing affordability very quickly indeed. After a short learning process and a few test cases it would change expectations about future land supply and so discourage any land hoarding and substantially reduce prices. Such an adjustment, because of the way the financial system is tied into real estate values, would require careful management during the transition but, like giving the Bank of England freedom to set interest rates and target inflation, would settle down quite quickly. Finally it would not entail 'grabbing the Greenbelt' or 'concreting over England'. Those are scaremongering slogans. There is far more low-amenity Greenbelt land in intensive agriculture than would possibly be needed for housing for generations to come. At 50 houses per ha there is enough Greenbelt land just within the existing boundary of Greater London to double current rates of building within London – some 20,000 homes a year – for 84 years. Remember Greenbelts cover one and a half times as much land in England than all present urbanised areas. Urbanised areas in total account for less than 10 per cent of England and while gardens and parks cover some 5.7 per cent actual buildings cover only 1.8 per cent of England's land (Foresight, 2010). The gap between reality and perceptions is very great indeed.

4.   EFFECTIVE SOLUTIONS

The effective solution to what we see as a real crisis of policy failure requires a mix of measures. This crisis is faced not just by Britain but by several other countries – New Zealand, South Korea, the East and West coasts of the US and coastal China all spring to mind. The mix of measures which is appropriate will vary according to the national tax structures, institutions and legal systems. What would work in Britain with its very centralised fiscal and government systems and planning that tightly restricts land but is permissive in its attitude to redevelopment would not be appropriate, for example, in the decentralised US. There, property taxes are local and the zoning system tightly restricts the supply of land-plus-house bundles (the total number of parcels of land that can be developed) and their redevelopment at higher densities but is not restrictive with respect to the total area of urban development; and hardly restrictive at all when it comes to commercial development. What works in the Netherlands would not necessarily work in China, and so on.

In our judgement effective solutions will combine both sensible incentives with appropriate responses to price signals from land markets. In Britain, incentives could take either of two main forms. Local authorities could be empowered with a legal monopoly on land supply (or at least some extended legal powers for trading in land) so that a system similar to that which operates in the Netherlands is created: or the very highly centralised British tax system could be decentralised so that property taxes – at least – become a purely local tax as recommended, for example, by the London Finance Commission (2013). As was shown in Cheshire and Hilber (2008) the conversion of business property taxes to a purely national tax (with the introduction of the Uniform Business Rate in 1990) generated a transparent negative incentive for LAs to permit any commercial development. Since they were legally required to provide services but obtained no revenues from commercial properties they were in effect fined if they allowed any new commercial development. The negative effect of this, because it demonstrably further reduced the supply of commercial property, increased business costs more than any feasible commercial property tax could have done.

This also reveals a further aspect of incentives. To be effective they have to be transparent and people have to know they are there for the long term. It could be argued that really the Uniform Business Rate (UBR) changed little. Britain, like many other European countries, has a system of revenue equalisation across local jurisdictions so that approximately every local authority ends up with an income from taxes determined according to its assessed 'needs' not according to its local tax revenues. So local communities never benefited all that much from commercial (or residential) development even when commercial property taxes were determined locally. But of course the process of revenue equalisation was not necessarily complete, it was uncertain and it only occurred with a lag. UBRs made the absence of any tax revenue to the local community from commercial development fully transparent, complete and certain. And the change significantly changed the behaviour of local communities with respect to their willingness to allow development. The Business Rates Retention scheme introduced in April 2013 seems to be a recognition of the problem but it is still small (compared for example to the radical proposals of the London Finance Commission, 2013) and time limited. It is too early to evaluate its effects but while welcome our judgement is that it is neither generous enough nor permanent enough to make substantial improvement.

Nevertheless, what we know about the impact of the UBR provides a positive message: a tax incentive does not seem to need to be all that big to modify behaviour, but it does need to be fully transparent, certain and long term. This suggests that if all political parties could agree that local authorities should retain – without any revenue penalty from national revenue equalisation – a significant proportion of its property tax revenues (from both commercial and residential property) the planning system would become significantly less restrictive. The problem in implementing such a solution, however, seems to be an almost total unwillingness on the part of central government, especially the Treasury, to give up any power over taxes and revenues to local government. Britain is a highly centralised state and property taxes are the fourth largest source of tax revenue to the national government (IFS 2012). The very restricted size and limited life of the New Homes Bonus may well be witness to this problem. The evidence so far on the impact of the New Homes Bonus is certainly not encouraging.

Moreover while tax incentives might be able to reduce planning restrictions on supply, they would not resolve another important part of the costs of planning: that planning policies do not take into account people's preferences of where to live (the 'wrong houses in the wrong places') or economic efficiency. Planning systems – whether on the British or US model – that is, with strong local controls determining what can be built – are very effective mechanisms for preventing development local voters do not want; they empower NIMBYism ('not in my back yard'). What they lack is incentives to allow residential development where would-be house-buyers, nearly all of whom are not local voters, want it. If they follow the British model they also lack incentives to permit commercial development where potential users judge it to be most economically efficient. Special interests – whether those of local residents who would personally lose out from development, or existing owners of real estate such as local shop owners – are both empowered and incentivised to block development. They not only may have a lot individually to lose but they have votes or voices.

The other main mechanism for generating incentives for the local community – rights to land conversion – has also been suggested as a solution to the problems of restrictiveness in Britain. The most widely discussed is the 'Community Land Auctions' proposal (Leunig 2007, 2011). This has something in common with the system that operates in the Netherlands:

> Community Land Auctions are akin to competitive tendering. The local authority invites offers of land, and accepts those that are good value. Good value is a combination of price and appropriateness for development, where the latter incorporates both sustainability criteria, as well as desirability for the final purchaser. The council grants planning permission, and then re-auctions the land that it accepts, and keeps the difference in value. (Leunig 2011, p. 7)

This suggestion would seem to provide a possible solution to restrictions on land supply not only in the UK but in other countries or regions too where there is a regulation-induced shortage of land supply. It would potentially provide communities with a significant incentive to provide land for development and, because those incentives would increase directly in proportion with the market price of land, there would be an incentive to provide land where, and for what uses, restrictions were most economically damaging. At the same time, since where the land was and its characteristics, as well as the costs to the local community of it being developed, would be under the control of the local planning authority it would seem to protect wider community interests and retain the powers of local communities to 'plan' their patterns of development and co-ordinate development with infrastructure capacity.

Whether it would in fact provide a real solution to land supply, however, is open to doubt. The first concern relates to the asymmetry of costs and benefits of development. While the size of the revenues would, in principle, reflect the scale of the current scarcity imposed by restrictions on land supply, unless the revenues were used to fully compensate those who lost out, heavily concentrated in the immediate neighbourhood of the new development, opposition to development would significantly remain.

The second doubt is far more serious. The Dutch system works because it has evolved over hundreds of years out of the municipal function of land drainage and then selling drained land. Dutch local authorities have accumulated considerable commercial expertise and skills but even so are accused of 'over-supplying' industrial land for political reasons and even of over-supply of office space. At the same time they have come under increasing NIMBY pressure to supply less housing land. The price of land for housing has increased sharply in real terms as a result and, according to Vermeulen and Rouwendal (2013), the restriction-imposed extra cost of housing land now substantially exceeds the benefits from preserving farmland in the 'Green Heart' of the Randstad.

So even in the Netherlands community land conversion and trading does not appear to work all that effectively as an incentive to provide the appropriate quantity of land for the most economically efficient use and in the most appropriate locations. And the Dutch have had centuries to develop the necessary institutional and financial structures as well as the commercial skills. British local authorities work within very tightly regulated financial constraints and have no commercial skills at all in identifying, preparing and selling land in a way which both appropriately responds to market failure and earns a full return for the local community.

Commercial development is a highly specialised and skilled process despite the often expressed dislike for 'developers' or 'land speculators'. Left to themselves – witness the recent history of Ireland, Spain or Stockton (California) – developers often get it very wrong. Successful development also requires access to finance: there are substantial up-front costs whereas returns are uncertain and take a long time to realise. We can be almost certain that English LAs would have to set up a whole new commercial operation and most would get it wrong. That is if many of them did anything at all.

They would get it wrong not just because their tradition is planning which dances to a whole different rhythm to development, but they would not be allowed to borrow on commercial terms even if they had the skills to do so. The proposal for 'Community Land Auctions' does not just have something in common with the Dutch system, it also has something in common with the Community Land Act of 1975. This gave powers to Local Authorities to buy land, whether by agreement or by much simplified compulsory purchase, at current use value and sell the land on for development. These powers were hardly used. According to Prest (1981), in the two-and-a-half years of its operation only about 150 acres was bought in the whole of England and Wales. A major reason for this failure was the borrowing constraints imposed on local authorities by Treasury rules. To have any chance of working, community land auctions would have to be organised by quasi-commercial organisations operating to private sector financial rules, perhaps responsible to groups of local authorities representing spatial housing markets (or Travel to Work Areas). Not only would such a system take a lot of public resources and time to set up, it begins to sound more and more like the (failed) Land Commission established in 1967. This was designed to channel gains from development of land to the 'community' but operated at a national level. Planning powers stayed with local authorities. As the chairman of the Commission said when charged with failing to provide land to builders, the problem was that planning authorities were not willing to allocate land under the system (Blundal 1993).

We are highly sceptical, therefore, that community land auctions offer a practical solution for the problems of land allocation in Britain. It does not work that well in an institutional setting that has evolved around it – the Netherlands – and would not work in Britain given the skills available to, and constraints faced by, local government. The first requirement for successful reform is to have incentives via the tax system. Such incentives need to be transparent and they need to be significant. There also needs to be a way of directing compensations to those who actually lose out from development. One way of addressing that issue would be a more wholehearted adoption of impact fees. The Community Infrastructure Levy (CIL) is flawed but could be helpful if reformed and simplified. The requirement in the US that impact fees legally require a 'rational nexus' – that is the level at which they are set must reflect actual costs imposed on the community by the development – seems very sensible. It makes them politically easier to defend and more transparent. Certainly the English decision to impose CIL while retaining S106 Agreements and empowering LAs to set whatever rate they choose is very counterproductive. Our system, instead of becoming more transparent and simpler to negotiate, was made more opaque and more difficult to operate.

Second we would argue in favour of properly introducing price signals into the decisions planners make about land release along the lines discussed in the previous section. Not just listing land price differentials as a factor that needs to be taken into account as in the new Guidance issued following the introduction of the NPPF; but requiring that in the absence of evidence that such price differentials were justified by environmental, amenity or social values there should be a presumption in favour of allowing development.

Finally, in the longer term we would advocate that the existing process of making decisions used in the UK – development control – should be replaced by a rule-based system as used in most of continental Europe or the US. Development control injects uncertainty and confrontation into every decision, and the bigger and more important the proposed development the worse the uncertainty and delays become. More uncertainty in the ultimate decision, apart from imposing costs of arguing and hearing the case, means developers require higher expected returns for a project to be viable. This renders the supply of housing and other space more price inelastic (Mayo and Sheppard 2001). The British tend to view development control as uniquely democratic and 'British'. Plan-making can be democratic while development control (and the subsequent appeals and politicisation of decisions) triggers argument, confrontation and uncertainty.[12]

So the components of a solution to the problems created by the English system of land use regulation would require a mix of:

1. Incentives in the forms of (a) retention of a proportion of taxes on both business and residential property by local government which would be exempt from the national system of revenue equalisation; and (b) impact fees;
2. Make land price discontinuities a 'material consideration' with a presumption in favour of development being permitted unless (an important unless) the wider amenity values of the land in its current use justified the premium.

---

[12] One of us owns a house in rural France. Recently he wanted to renovate it and double its size. Employing professionals who knew what the local planning and building regulations allowed resulted in a positive decision with no local opposition in a total of 13 days.

3. Replace development control as a decision-making mechanism with local plans drawn up according to national guidelines and approved democratically by the local community; in short a rule-based system. Such a reform might be an excellent candidate for the recommendations in Chapter 8. That is the changes should be introduced in a randomly selected set of perhaps 50 or 60 LAs. These would be provided with adequate advice and resources to draw up local plans adequate to provide a proper basis for rule-based decision making, maybe drawing on expertise from German or Dutch planners used to working with such systems. After approval by national government and democratic local process by which they were adapted then the results in terms of the costs and quantity of development could be evaluated. They would have to have a guaranteed life of perhaps ten years but this would give a serious basis both to evaluate how they worked and perhaps, depending on the outcome, signpost future improvements.

As any observer of the British scene will understand, such proposals would meet fierce and bitter political resistance. We think the evidence of the economic and welfare – even environmental – damage done by Britain's current planning system is overwhelming, however, and that the impact will get progressively more damaging over time since supply of space is ossified but demand develops. The question is not will we reform it but when will we reform it and will that be before a catastrophic collapse? The political problem is that while we desperately need reform it is never now that we desperately need it. Moreover, as the experience of both the post-Barker reforms and the reforms of the post-2010 Coalition government have demonstrated, only radical reforms have any chance of working. The problem is that any radical reforms are politically unpalatable, but no alternative strategy will work.

REFERENCES

Barker, K. 2003. 'Securing our Future Housing Needs: Interim Report – Analysis'. *Review of Housing Supply*, London: HM Treasury.
Barker, K. 2004. 'Delivering Stability: Securing Our Future Housing Needs: Final Report – Recommendations', *Review of Housing Supply*. London: HM Treasury.
Barker, Kate. 2006a. 'Barker Review of Land Use Planning: Interim Report – Analysis'. London: HM Treasury.
Barker, Kate. 2006b. 'Barker Review of Land Use Planning: Final Report – Recommendations'. London: HMSO.

Blundal, V. 1993. *Labour's Flawed Land Acts 1947–1976*. London: Economic and Social Science Research Association.

Bracke, P. and P. Cheshire. 2013. 'A Preliminary Investigation of the Effects of the Community Infrastructure Levy (CIL)', SERC Discussion Paper No. XXX. London: SERC.

Bramley, G. 1998. 'Measuring planning: indicators of planning restraint and its impact on housing land supply'. *Environment and Planning B* 25, 31–57.

Bramley, Glen. 1993. 'The impact of land use planning and tax subsidies on the supply and price of housing in Britain'. *Urban Studies* 30, 5–30.

Burge, Gregory and Keith Ihlanfeldt. 2006. 'The effects of impact fees on multi-family housing construction'. *Journal of Regional Science* 46, 5–23.

Cheshire, Paul and Stephen Sheppard. 1989. 'British Planning Policy and Access to the Housing Market: some empirical estimates". *Urban Studies*, **26**, 469–85.

Cheshire, Paul and D.G. Hay. 1989. *Urban Problems in Western Europe: An Economic Analysis*. London: HarperCollins Academic/Routledge.

Cheshire, Paul and Stephen Sheppard. 2005. 'The introduction of price signals into land use planning decision-making: a proposal'. *Urban Studies* 42, 647–663.

Crook, A.D.H. and S. Monk. 2011. 'Planning gains, providing home'. *Housing Studies* 26, 997–1018.

Davies, K. 1984. *Law of Compulsory Purchase and Compensation*. London: Butterworths.

DCLG. 2012a. *Business Rates Retention Scheme: The Economic Benefits of Local Business Rates Retention*. London: DCLG.

DCLG. 2012b. 'National Planning Policy Framework'. London: DCLG.

DCLG. 2013. 'Local Authority Greenbelt Statistics: Annex 1, Table 1: Area of Designated Greenbelt Land by Local Planning Authority as at 31 March 2012'. London: DCLG. Available at: https://www.gov.uk/government/publications/local-authority-green-belt-statistics-for-england-2011-to-2012.

Eddington, R. 2006. 'The Eddington Transport Study: The Case for Action'. London: HM Treasury on behalf of HMSO.

Evans, A.W. 1990. 'A house price based regional policy'. *Regional Studies* 24, 559–567.

Evans, A.W. and O.M. Hartwich. 2005. *Bigger Better Faster More: Why Some Countries Plan Better than Others*. London: Policy Exchange.

Examination in Public. 2009. Report of the Panel, Vol. 1, West Midlands Spacial Strategy Phase Two: Revision.

Firbank, L., R. Bradbury, D. McCracken, C. Stoate, K. Goulding, R. Harmer and P. Williams. 2011. 'Enclosed Farmland', *The UK National Ecosystem Assessment Technical Report. UK National Ecosystem Assessment*. Cambridge: UNEP-WCMC.

Fischel, W.A. 1985. *The Economics of Zoning Laws: A Property Rights Approach to American Land Use Controls*. Baltimore, MD: Johns Hopkins University Press.

Foresight Land Use Futures Project. 2010. 'Final Project Report'. London: The Government Office for Science.

Hall, P.G., H. Gracey, R. Drewett and R. Thomas. 1973. *The Containment of Urban England*. London: Allen and Unwin.

Hannah, L., K.-H. Kim and E.S. Mills. 1993. 'Land use controls and housing prices in Korea'. *Urban Studies* 30, 147–156.

Hilber, C.A.H. and W. Vermeulen. 2012. 'The Impact of Supply Constraints on House Prices in England', SERC Discussion Paper 119. London: SERC.

IFS. 2012. 'A Survey of the UK Tax System', Briefing Note BN09. London: Institute of Fiscal Studies.

Ihlanfeldt, Keith R. and Timothy M. Shaughnessy. 2004. 'An empirical investigation of the effects of impact fees on housing and land markets'. *Regional Science and Urban Economics* 34, 639–661.

Larkin, Kieran, Zach Wilcox and Christiana Gailey. 2011. 'Room for Improvement: Creating the Financial Incentives Needed for Economic Growth'. London: Centre for Cities.

Leunig, Tim. 2007. 'In My Back Yard: Unlocking the Planning System'. London: Centre Forum.

Leunig, T. 2011. 'Community Land Auctions: Working towards Implementation'. London: Centre Forum.

London Finance Commission. 2013. 'Raising the Capital'. London: GLA.

Mayo, Stephen and Stephen Sheppard. 2001. 'Housing supply and the effects of stochastic development control'. *Journal of Housing Economics* 10, 109–128.

National Audit Office. 2013. 'The New Homes Bonus, Report for the DCLG'.

Needham, B. 1992. 'A theory of land prices when land is supplied publicly: the case of the Netherlands'. *Urban Studies* 29, 669–686.

Needham, B. and E. Louw. 2006. 'Institutional economics and policies for changing land markets: the case of industrial estates'. *The Netherlands Journal of Property Research* 23, 75–90.

Papworth, T. 2012. *Planning in a Free Society*. London: Adam Smith Institute.

Pennington, M. 2000. *Planning and the Political Market: Public Choice and the Politics of Government Failure*. London: Athlone/Continuum.

Pope, D.G. and J.C. Pope. 2012. 'When Walmart Comes to Town: Always Low Housing Prices? Always?' NBER Working Paper 18111. National Bureau of Economic Research.

Prest, A.R. 1981. *The Taxation of Urban Land*. Manchester: Manchester University Press.

Vermeulen, Wouter and Jan Rouwendal. 2013. 'On the value of foregone open space in sprawling cities'. *Journal of Regional Science*, online (July) http://onlinelibrary.wiley.com/doi/10.1111/jors.12033/.

VOA. 2011. 'Property Market Report 2011'. Valuation Office Agency.

Wandsworth Borough Council. 2012. 'Community Infrastructure Levy (CIL) Charging Schedule', November, http://www.wandsworth.gov.uk/cil.

PART III

Can governance make a difference and what can policy do?

7. Devolution, city governance and economic performance*

1. INTRODUCTION

There are several ways to structure thinking about what urban policy might do to improve economic performance. One way is to take a specific area of policy and to use available evidence and the analytical framework provided by urban economics to carefully analyse what we know about the impact of that policy on urban economic outcomes. This is what we have done in Chapters 4–6 with our focus on planning policy – an area where urban economics has much to say about the likely impact of policy and where we have argued that British policy, in particular, is in need of radical reform. A second way to think about what urban policy should do is to consider a range of specific policy instruments, using insights from urban economics to compare and contrast the likely impacts. This is the approach that we adopt in Chapter 8. A third possibility is to abstract from the details of specific policies, and ask instead whether the way in which policy decisions get made influences urban economic performance. That is the approach that we adopt in this chapter that looks at the link between devolution, governance and economic outcome.

By necessity, this is the most context-specific of the chapters of this book. While some of the discussion on the evidence on the link between devolution and improved urban economic performance might be of more general interest, some of the more detailed policy context might not. Readers interested in the general issues, but not the specific British context, can safely skip ahead to Section 4, which considers the theoretical and empirical evidence on the costs and benefits of devolution. Readers with no interest in these issues can skip ahead to Chapter 8 with no loss of continuity.

* This chapter draws on SERC Policy Paper No. 5, authored by Paul Steeples. His ideas and generosity are gratefully acknowledged.

2.   DEVOLUTION IN THE UK

Devolution of policy responsibilities and resources to lower tiers of government has been a strong theme in UK policymaking for the past decade and a half. For the first decade, those downward shifts of power have been to countries of the Union, and to English regions. In more recent years, the agenda has refocused on devolution towards cities and, more recently, to local communities.

Under the 1997–2010 Labour government, substantial powers were delegated to the Scottish Parliament and, to a lesser extent, to Wales, Northern Ireland and London. In the remainder of England, important elements of economic development policymaking and delivery were delegated to Regional Development Agencies (RDAs) and other non-departmental public bodies. Following a failed referendum on regional government (in the North East in 2004), Labour also took tentative steps towards devolution to cities setting up multi-area agreements (MAAs) covering groups of local authorities, and establishing two 'city-region' pilots in 2010, in Manchester and Leeds.[1]

The Coalition government formed in 2010 has also made devolutionary moves under the banner of 'localism' – with a much greater focus on cities and local communities, a greater role for the private sector, and some rowing back on previous policies.[2] RDAs have been abolished, and replaced with Local Enterprise Partnerships (LEPs), a number of cities have struck 'City Deals' with Ministers, and there has been significant financial devolution to local authorities. Less successfully, Ministers floated English executive city mayors in a series of referenda, with all but three of 12 cities rejecting the idea. At the time of writing, Ministers were also introducing a new initiative, the Single Local Growth Fund, worth around £2bn annually, which will further extend the city deals both in terms of depth and geographical coverage (HM Treasury (HMT) and Department for Business Innovation and Skills (BIS) 2013).

Devolution to cities has thus come to the fore of policy thinking in the UK over the past ten years or so, with a particular focus on city-regions – that is, urban cores and their economic hinterlands. The current debate has involved academics and think tanks, as well as politicians and officials[3]

---

[1] DCLG 2006, 2008b; Department for Business Enterprise and Regulatory Reform and Communities and Local Government 2008.
[2] HM Government 2010; Cabinet Office 2011; DCLG 2011a.
[3] Harding et al. 2004; Parkinson et al. 2004; Core Cities Group 2006; Marshall et al. 2006; Marvin et al. 2006; Parkinson et al. 2006; Jones et al. 2008; Lee 2008; Shakespeare 2008; Centre for Cities 2009; Conservative Party 2009; Dolphin 2009; Steeples 2010; Sims 2011; Swinney et al. 2011.

with advocates of city-regional devolution making three arguments in favour: first, cities and their hinterlands are engines of economic growth, and devolution will deliver an economic dividend; second, devolution allows policy innovation and can internalise spillovers, improving policy outcomes; third, introducing stronger elected local leaders will have a revitalising effect on local democracy. Versions of these arguments have been made in other similar debates taking place elsewhere (Rodríguez-Pose and Bwire 2004; Rodríguez-Pose and Gill 2005).

Economic arguments have been prominent in this debate, with strong linkages being made between the realisation of the economic potential of city-regions and their governance arrangements. For example, Parkinson et al. (2004, p. 6) argue: 'Continental cities have responsibilities for a wider range of functions . . . and their combination of powers and resources seems to make continental cities more proactive, more entrepreneurial and probably more competitive.' Similar arguments were used by Britain's Deputy Prime Minister in 2012 when making the case for the devolution process: '[T]o unlock [cities' full potential as engines of growth] we need a major shift in the powers available to local leaders and businesses to drive economic growth.'

This chapter takes a critical look at the case for greater devolution to cities, focusing on these economic arguments and drawing on international evidence. We begin by exploring the question of the appropriate spatial scale at which to think about cities and devolution. This is not a question that is unique to this issue or, indeed, to this particular debate: as we shall see in the next section, academic and policy debates about 'functional urban regions' (FURs) date back to at least the 1940s. Indeed, if this were a conventional textbook, we might have considered these definitional issues in Chapter 2 before talking about urban economics and city performance. Instead, we have postponed discussion to this chapter because both researchers and policymakers have typically deployed a confusing array of spatial units and proxies – which has tended to muddy debates about devolution, whether it is desirable and what it might mean in practice.

The third section of the chapter considers the evidence that devolved governance arrangements affect urban economic performance. To do this, we look at the comparisons drawn between English and European cities, as well as the international literature on governance more generally. It turns out that there is no consistent evidence directly linking aspects of devolution (control of policy, tax-raising powers, having a mayor and so on) and the economic success or failure of cities.

However, work by Cheshire and colleagues (Cheshire and Gordon 1996; Cheshire and Magrini 2005, 2009) does show a connection between the scale at which a city is governed and its economic performance. This is not an argument for devolution *per se*, but it does suggest alternative rationales which the third section of the chapter explores in more detail. Even if there are few direct links between devolution and urban economic outcomes, there may be indirect effects if economic development powers are devolved to appropriate levels: local leaders are free to develop innovative policies, and can have stronger incentives to do so. Devolution may thus also improve public service outcomes more generally. As we shall see, correctly matching powers to scales is critical: shifting development control powers to local authorities, for example, may have empowered NIMBYism rather than prevented it (as discussed extensively in Chapters 4–6).

Section 4 returns to the UK context, and considers the 'demand for devolution' in three policy areas – planning, transport and business support. Drawing on interviews with English policymakers at regional, city-regional and local level in 2008–09, we examine the extent to which the expected advantages of devolution – particularly the ability to vary policy to respond to regional and local circumstance – might be realised. We also identify a number of areas where further consideration of the appropriate spatial scale for policy-making might be desirable (particularly in policies involving employment, skills and business support).

Given the limitations of the economic case for devolution *per se*, we suggest that discussions around devolution should focus more on the impact of tailored, locally-variable policies and the extent to which more flexible local decision-making processes (complemented by central government support systems) are needed to deliver such policies. Some of the questions on policy effectiveness are taken up in Chapter 8. However, consistent with our approach in this chapter, we focus instead on the extent to which current 'localism' reforms actually allow for greater local flexibilities. The final part of the chapter reviews the current policy mix, covering the four main elements of localism as they relate to urban areas: city-regional partnerships (LEPs), financial devolution, City Deals and elected city Mayors. As we explain below, localism has a number of positive elements (city-regional focus, emphasis on process over structures) but also holds out a number of challenges for the future (weak incentives, variable capacity and experience across local areas, politically negotiated geographies, some 'over-devolution' in aspects of planning policy).

Understanding how the role of central government changes, as well as local government, is crucial to dealing with these challenges. Looking forward, localism also offers a good chance to improve the evidence base around devolution: City Deals, in particular, are effectively a series of policy experiments, and need to be accompanied by rigorous evaluation.

3.   DEFINING CITIES: CONCEPTS AND HISTORY

Defining Cities

Attempts to delineate the city for the purposes of collecting data and undertaking analysis typically distinguish between the 'administrative city', the area covered by a local administrative unit; the 'physical city', or contiguous built-up area; and the 'functional city', or economic system (HMT, Department for Trade and Industry (DTI), and Department for Communities and Local Government (DCLG) 2006; Marshall 2006). The functional city – or 'functional urban region' (FUR) – is the closest concept to the city that forms the basis of most urban economics, in that it captures both an urban core and its self-contained economic hinterland.

There is a surprisingly long history of thinking about cities as self-contained FURs. The US Census Bureau invented the Standard Metropolitan Statistical Area (SMSA) for the 1940 Census, as suburbanisation was already making administrative city boundaries inappropriate as ways of representing whole cities as economic and social systems. By the 1960s, a series of pieces by Fox and colleagues had set out the notion of 'functional economic areas' in the US (see Fox and Kumar (1965) for a review); Brian Berry and colleagues (Berry et al. 1968, Berry 1973) later developed the notion of a 'Daily Urban System' based on commuting patterns, and which in many urban areas aggregated SMSAs into much larger units. In the UK, academics at the London School of Economics and the Political and Economic Planning group constructed a series of Metropolitan Economic Labour Areas (MELAs) (Hall and Hay 1980). These were later formalised into a system of FURs (Hall and Hay 1980; Cheshire and Hay 1989).

For researchers and policymakers, there are clear attractions for thinking about cities in terms of such functional systems (Cheshire and Hay 1989; Cheshire 1995; Cheshire and Gordon 1996). First, it allows more straightforward comparisons across areas on measures of economic and social performance, and avoids arbitrary differences generated by administrative boundaries, or by morphological differences between economically similar systems. (As we shall see, boundary issues plague much of the current devolution debate.) Second, as self-contained units, the effects of both local economic shocks and policy interventions are largely contained within FUR boundaries. This explains why such functional definitions lie at the heart of urban economics. More practically, if used as the basic building blocks for urban policymaking it they align policymakers' economic 'reach' with the economic system. In turn, if aligned with the voting population, this creates further incentives to develop effective policy (Oates 1999). It turns out that there is good empirical evidence for both these channels (see Section 4).

However, the application of these concepts is hindered by a lack of clear, common definitions for functional urban units. On top of the variegated historical picture, recent studies of cities across Europe (see, for example, Cheshire and Gordon 1996; Bagnasco and Le Galès 2000; Cheshire and Magrini 2000, 2005, 2009; Herrschel and Newman 2002; Le Galès 2002; Buck et al. 2005; Salet 2006) each present different potential definitions and typologies of cities. As discussed below, this lack of definitional clarity creates problems for meaningful comparisons in the performance of cities and city-regions across Europe.

A second issue, arguably more politically than analytically challenging, is that functional definitions of the urban system will be, by definition, incomplete, with a number of rural communities missing. In the UK, Travel to Work Areas (TTWAs) offer a 'space-filling' alternative based on largely self-contained commuting zones.[4] In their standard form, TTWAs have been criticised for not including urban cores, and for not capturing commuting patterns of very high-skilled individuals (Robson et al. 2006). SERC researchers have developed an alternate system of 'primary urban' TTWAs that overcomes the first problem (Gibbons et al. 2011).

Recent UK government thinking about cities and urban economies has exhibited many of these conceptual tensions and confusions. For example, the 1997–2010 Labour government variously focused on 'Physical Urban Areas'[5] and TTWAs in the 2006 State of the Cities Report (Parkinson et al. 2006); 'city-regions', in its review of Devolved Decision-Making (HMT, DTI, and DCLG 2006), and both local authorities and 'sub-regions' in the HMT-led Review of Economic Development (HMT 2007) and in subsequent proposals for pan-local authority Economic Prosperity Boards and Metropolitan Area Agreements.[6] Reviewing this complexity, Pike and Tomaney (2008, 2009) are critical of the number of spatial levels in play in current policy and the lack of prioritisation between them.

---

[4] Travel to Work Areas (TTWAs) are functional measures based on commuting patterns. Specifically, of the resident economically active population in a TTWA, at least 75 per cent actually work in the area, and of everyone working in the area, at least 75 per cent actually live in the area.

[5] Physical Urban Areas (PUAs) are measures of the urban built-up area, constructed for 56 English cities with a minimum size cut-off of 125,000 in terms of their 2001 population.

[6] Department for Business Enterprise and Regulatory Reform and Communities and Local Government 2008; DCLG 2008a, b)

These issues remain for policies developed by the Coalition government elected in 2010. Coalition thinking on urban areas began with a general interest in 'cities and communities' in the 2010 Coalition Agreement, reflecting both the Liberal Democrats' local political base and work on decentralisation done by the Conservatives in opposition (Conservative Party 2009). Since then, the desire to find new sources of economic growth has resulted in a move towards greater decentralisation. Coalition Ministers have – in theory – signed up to the city-regional concept by replacing RDAs with LEPs, which are intended to reflect 'functional economic geographies' (BIS 2010a, b). Building on this, a series of 'City Deals' with major conurbations are designed to provide a basis for more effective economic strategy and policymaking (Cabinet Office (CO) 2011, 2012). However, Ministers have also pushed for single-authority elected mayors, and some LEPs reflect local political bargaining and coalitions rather than true economic geography (see Section 5.1).

The Politics of Urban Devolution in the UK

There is substantial policy and government interest in cities as potential layers for economic governance. As sketched out in Section 2, this interest is driven by three considerations: first, the belief that productivity and economic growth are driven by agglomeration economies, generally operating in England at a level larger than a typical local authority and smaller than regions; second, the belief that policy should be devolved to the lowest effective and appropriate level; third, and particularly since 2010, a renewed interest in local democracy and empowering local leadership.

The belief that cities are sources of economic dynamism has a long history, and draws on a large body of work in urban economics and economic geography (see Chapter 2). These arguments have only recently been marshalled by those in favour of devolution. Fothergill (2005) and Hildreth and Bailey (2013) both identify changes in emphasis in English regional policy, away from redistribution of economic activity between regions and towards the identification and correction of market failures which are seen as preventing places from fully realising their indigenous potential for growth. This change began under the last years of the Labour government: in 2004 the policy shift is put largely in a regional context (HMT, DTI, and Office of the Deputy Prime Minister (ODPM) 2004), but two years later policy documents show a much stronger emphasis on the city as an engine of growth and productivity, and as the key to achieving the government target of reducing the gap in growth rates between the English regions.

There has also been promotion of the city devolution agenda both by the cities themselves – for example by the revitalisation of the Core Cities lobby group from 2001 – by think-tanks such as the Centre for Cities, the Work Foundation and the New Local Government Network (New Local Government Network 2005, 2006; Marshall et al. 2006; Jones et al. 2008), and through reports prepared on behalf of the DCLG (Harding et al. 2004; Parkinson et al. 2004; ODPM 2006; Robson et al. 2006). At the time of writing the current administration has continued to make the economic case for devolution (see the quote from Nick Clegg in Section 2), but under 'localism' has also justified change based on the desirability of devolving functions as close to users as possible, 'bringing an end to the top-down initiatives that ignore the varying needs of different areas' (CO 2011, p. 3).

A third driving force for the city agenda has been the desire for greater democratic accountability at local level. In part, this stems from the failure of the referendum on an elected regional assembly in the North East in November 2004 (Turok 2008). For many policymakers, cities provide a potential answer to the perceived lack of democratic legitimacy at the regional level. While this line was not strongly pursued by the Labour administration, the Coalition has strongly argued for devolution as a means to democratic accountability, for example in 'Local Growth': 'By shifting power to the right levels we will increase democratic accountability and transparency, and ensure that public expenditure is more responsive to the needs of local business and people' (BIS 2010a, p. 5).

Here, shifting power to cities is justified both on the basis of democratic re-engagement, and via fiscal federalist arguments about optimal scales for public service delivery. Coalition ministers have also argued that new forms of elected local leadership are an integral element of the localism agenda: 'by creating more directly elected mayors we can foster growth by giving more power to local areas, making municipal decision-making more accountable and responsive to local economic conditions' (BIS 2010a, p. 3). Supportive think tanks, such as the Centre for Cities (2009) and the Institute for Government (Sims 2011; Swinney et al. 2011) have also made this connection, linking economic, public service and democratic rationales for devolution and arguing that new types of elected local leader can help deliver the expected gains.

In most cases, then, the devolution logic chain moves quickly from an acknowledgement of the economic importance of city-regions, to assertions about the economic, public service and democratic gains to devolution, to more technical discussions about governance arrangements. It is important to take a step back and examine each rationale for devolution in more detail.

4. THE COSTS AND BENEFITS OF DEVOLUTION: THEORY AND EVIDENCE

Within modern urban economics, devolution arguments have a long history. Tiebout (1956) sets out a welfare-optimising model for local public goods, where citizens' varying preferences are met by local governments offering different packages of public services and mobile 'consumer-voters' moving to the areas which match preferences best. Note that a key assumption of Tiebout is that the effects of public policies are confined within local area boundaries. In many cases, moving to a Tiebout solution involves devolving powers from the centre. But if local areas are administrative units, some policies – such as economic development interventions – may spill over those local boundaries. In this instance, there is a case for scaling up power to an appropriate level.

In a seminal paper, Oates (1972) outlines a parallel case for 'fiscal federalism' – the devolution of service delivery and the collection of taxes and charges. Oates (1999) suggests that 'understanding which functions and instruments are best centralized and which are best placed in the sphere of decentralized levels of government' will lead to improved public service outcomes. Again, a critical assumption in Oates is that powers and governance scales are matched appropriately. In some policy fields this will mean cities; in others, smaller local geographies will be first-best.

So how might devolution influence urban economic outcomes? In theory, devolution to cities has both pros and cons. Drawing on Oates' arguments, devolving powers towards urban areas may help their economic growth through first, allowing greater innovation and experimentation in policymaking; second, a better match of local programmes to local needs; and third, allowing a closer fit between the scale at which policy is made and the area over which it operates. In turn, optimal scales for economic policy may strengthen incentives for policymakers to develop effective programmes – since they will have a strong impact on local voters, rather than spilling over onto neighbouring areas (Cheshire and Gordon 1996).

On the other hand, there may be a loss of national efficiency through a loss of economies of scale and scope, if services are devolved to the wrong level. This problem can be overcome if local areas can buy in services from larger organisations (for example, parish councils buying in rubbish collection from a larger neighbouring authority). More seriously, when local government capacity is uneven, some areas may be better placed to take advantage of devolution than others – potentially widening economic disparities (Rodríguez-Pose and Bwire 2004; Rodríguez-Pose and Gill 2005).

This raises a third set of issues about the process of devolution, central–local relations and interactions (Hildreth and Bailey 2013). Most obviously, programmes to devolve power from the centre to local areas need to be sensitive to local differences and local capacity, so that central government may need to provide continued support to weaker local actors. Less obviously, the package of devolutionary measures needs to be well-designed, with an appropriate spread of policy fields and levers, including a suitable monitoring and evaluation framework. That is, the roles and responsibilities of central government also change. As we shall see in the English case, recent policies to devolve power to cities do not always meet these criteria.

Advocates of devolution naturally emphasise the upsides, and have not always addressed these process issues. For example, the Competitive English Cities report commissioned by DCLG (Parkinson et al. 2004) argues that: 'it is difficult to disagree with the view that their combination of powers and resources make continental cities more pro-active, more entrepreneurial and probably more competitive' (p. 25). Similarly, the Centre for Cities claim that 'intuitively, the state of affairs in continental Europe and the US suggests England needs to move towards greater power at the sub-national level to promote economic development' (Marshall et al. 2006, pp. 12–13). More modestly, The Work Foundation's Ideopolis programme claims that 'some evidence suggests that appropriate local governance arrangements can be an important driver of growth' (Jones et al. 2008, p. 25).

However, academics typically strike a more cautious tone. Gordon (2006, p. 156) believes that 'in a metropolitan situation . . . "Governance" is not so much the answer as the question . . . there is going to be no neat, one-off answer to [the question of governance]'. Le Galès (2002, p. 18) similarly states that 'Governance is not a matter of efficiency or a miracle problem-solver'. In the UK, Goodwin et al. (2002) and Hudson (2006) raise concerns about uneven political capacity, and uneven benefits from devolution.

Given these limitations, the literature on the economic effects of devolution has tended to take three main forms:

1. Descriptive, cross-country studies comparing economic performance and governance arrangements (on relevant functions such as transport, strategic planning and economic development);
2. Analytical studies testing for direct connections between devolution and urban economic performance;
3. Studies exploring indirect links, notably how governance scales shape urban economic outcomes.

We consider each of these in turn, and then consider some of the broader literature on devolution, public service outcomes and wellbeing.

Comparative Studies

League table comparisons of urban economic performance make attractive political stories, although they also show up politicians' tendencies to 'revert to easy football metaphors' (Nathan and Marshall 2006). Unfortunately, they turn out to be of very limited use in policymaking. The 1997–2010 Labour government (ODPM 2006) and the Conservative Party (2009) both talked about moving English cities up 'the European league table of economic performance'. In the UK, a 2002 Barclays Bank analysis ranking European cities by GDP per capita has been frequently cited as a definitive account of the competitive position of English and European cities (for example in Parkinson et al. 2004, 2006), and used to justify an increased focus on cities.

Nathan and Marshall (2006, p. 7) are highly critical of this data, commenting that 'several results are counterintuitive, to say the least. Can London really be the twenty-third most productive city in Europe? And how does the minor [sic] German city of Karlsruhe come out ahead of Paris?' They point to problems in the choice of GDP per head as a measure of competitiveness, and to serious difficulties in defining and comparing each functional city-region.[7] Practically, these issues make robust comparative analysis across countries very difficult to do: there is no standard methodology and results can differ wildly. Consistent with this, analysis by Clark (2006) collates 19 different indexes ranking cities internationally according to different environmental, social and economic indicators. Each index produces a radically different 'league table'.

Over and above questions of what to measure and at which scale, there are also problems in making comparisons caused by cities' history and place in the national framework as a whole, particularly if path dependency plays a role in shaping the current institutional mix. These factors lead to fragmentation in modes of governance – Le Galès (2002, pp. 230–31) comments that the elements of governance 'tend to vary in two dimensions (1) within nation states, which seem to be increasingly differentiated, and (2) over time, since reforms have been pursued almost

---

[7] The Barclays datasets combines 'city-regions' measured on both functional bases (core plus hinterland) and administrative bases (core only). This means that some urban economies will be significantly under-bounded. Worse, the data also uses a mix of workplace-based measures (GDP) and residence-based (population). Urban cores will have very high GDP but low resident numbers, so this will inflate the relative performance of under-bounded locations while deflating that of city-regions 'proper'.

uninterruptedly in search of new, non-fixed rules of the game between different levels of government. All this underlines the wide diversity of local government in Europe, including within nation-states themselves.'

Thus, factors relating to the comparability of cities themselves (in terms of size and composition); the factors used to measure and compare economic performance; and the widely varying historical, economic and institutional contexts in which each city is placed, all contribute to the difficulty of making meaningful cross-country urban comparisons, let alone drawing valid conclusions relating to governance. And in the small print, at least, UK government reports are now very cautious about this kind of analysis.[8]

Testing for Direct Links

A second set of studies attempts to directly test links between devolution and urban economic outcomes. Typically this is done by collecting data on cities' economic performance and government arrangements, then using regression analysis to look for systematic – and non-random – connections between the two. Ideally, researchers may be able to use a policy 'shock' to try and identify the causal effects of devolution.

As a recent review by Pike et al. (2010) makes clear, there is no clear relationship between devolution and economic outcomes. Cross-country studies variously find negative links between decentralisation and economic growth (Ezcurra and Rodríguez-Pose 2010); no relationship in developed countries (Davoodi and Zou 1998), and an inverse U-shaped relationship, with positive effects of devolution on productivity and growth in centralised countries, but negative effects from 'excessive' decentralisation (Thiessen 2003).

More detailed cross-area studies also give mixed results. Rodríguez-Pose and Bwire (2004) look at regional outcomes across six countries, finding that devolution is generally irrelevant to regional economic growth, and for Mexico and the US, linked to lower economic efficiency. Two studies for US states find in the first case, no economic rationale for further devolution (Xie et al. 1999), and in the second case, that decentralisation has had a positive effect on state-level growth (Akai and Sakata 2002). But working at the urban level, Stansel (2005) finds a positive link between decentralisation and income growth for a cross-section

---

[8] For example, the 2006 *Devolved Decision-Making Report* that 'given that United Kingdom GDP exceeds many of our European competitors, it is likely that some of the difference between English and European cities is driven by different definitions of city boundaries (HMT, DTI, and DCLG 2006).

of US Metro Areas. For China, Zhang and Zou (1998) find decentralisation is associated with lower provincial economic growth. In the UK, exploratory analysis by Pike and colleagues (2010) finds limited evidence of a 'devolution dividend' on economic outcomes, not least because any devolution effect is over-ridden by national economic growth.

As with the comparative literature, there are also substantial methodological challenges in undertaking these studies. Bruess and Eller (2004) highlight issues of omitted variables, accurate measurement of decentralisation, and identifying causal effects when a policy 'shock' is unavailable.

Testing for Indirect Effects

Given the limits of these approaches, other researchers have sought to identify some of the indirect effects of devolution on economic outcomes. One set of studies explores the quality of local political and institutional leadership. A series of mainly qualitative empirical studies suggest – perhaps not surprisingly – that the strength of urban leadership plays a role in securing urban economic outcomes (Deas and Giordano 2002; Kaufmann and Kraay 2003).

In a series of theoretical and quantitative empirical studies, Cheshire and colleagues (Cheshire and Hay 1989; Cheshire and Gordon 1996; Cheshire and Magrini 2005, 2009) find good evidence linking the scale of economic governance to urban economic performance. Cheshire and Magrini's 2009 paper tests 'whether there is a positive relationship between the degree of co-incidence of governmental boundaries with those of functionally defined city-regions and the growth performance of the city-region' (p. 2). Drawing on Oates and Tiebout (see Section 2), they suggest that if urban government can operate across the local spatial economy and the effects of its actions are contained within the area the government represents, it will be better able to design effective economic policies, and this should translate to positive urban growth.[9] As sketched out earlier, the structure of incentives will also be more appropriate to generate effective policies: policy impact will be more visible on voters, who will punish/reward policymakers appropriately at the ballot box. As with Tiebout, it is critical that specific powers are matched with the appropriate governance scale; for economic policy and economic development, the 'economic city' is intuitively the right one.

---

[9] The authors also suggest that if 'the size of the 'relevant' unit of government considerably exceeded the size of the FUR, then the capacity to generate local growth promoting policies would begin to weaken. This is because the interests of the FUR would begin to be lost in those of the larger unit which might pursue policies favouring rural areas or smaller centres' (p. 7).

To test this, Cheshire and Magrini deploy 122 FURs for European countries, then compare the size of local administrative units to get a measure of fit. It turns out that better-fitting local governance systems are strongly related to urban economic growth – suggesting that both the channels above are operating. As the only clear-cut evidence linking aspects of devolution to urban economic outcomes, this work has been highly influential in UK policy debates. Cheshire and Magrini's 2005 paper is extensively discussed in the pro-devolution literature (see Marshall et al. 2006; HMT, DTI, and DCLG 2006; HMT 2007; DCLG 2008; Morris and Williams 2008) – and was extensively quoted by the policymakers interviewed by Steeples (2010) in his overview of the UK city-regional agenda.

However, this is not a 'slam-dunk' economic case for shifting powers to cities. As the authors are careful to explain, 'the variable used in the present paper ... is an indirect measure, designed to reflect not the policies themselves but the capacity of an urban government to generate such policies' (Cheshire and Magrini 2005, p. 12). In their 2009 paper, Cheshire and Magrini go on to suggest that the devolution 'bonus' may not be symmetric: that is, the success of cities with a FUR tier of government may partly derive from the relative failure of those without. Thus, while this work is a significant contribution to the evidence base in the area of urban growth and governance, it certainly does not support all of the devolution agenda described earlier.

Devolution, Public Services and Wellbeing

Fiscal federalist arguments suggest that devolution may also improve public service outcomes, and thus local wellbeing. Under devolution (to the appropriate scale), the local policy mix will be better aligned with citizens' preferences; local people will have a greater say on decision-making; decisions on expenditure should be made at a level which can match them closely to real resource costs; and there may be greater benchmarking and competition between places, driving the efficient provision of public services (Tiebout 1956; Oates 1972, 1999).

The cross-country evidence base on devolution and public service outcomes generally points to net benefits of decentralisation. For example, Adam et al. (2008) look at fiscal decentralisation and public sector efficiency across 21 OECD countries, 1970–2000, finding a significant positive link between the two – whether decentralisation is proxied by local tax bases, budget shares or fiscal autonomy. Canaleta et al. (2004), comparing outcomes across 17 OECD countries, find a negative link between decentralisation and regional inequalities, and a positive link from devolution and regional convergence. In more recent work, Lessman (2009) and Ezcurra and Rodriguez-Pose (2009) also find no link between decentralisation and inequalities, with Lessman's research finding that poorer OECD regions benefit from decentralisation.

Frey and Stutzer (2000) studying Swiss cantons, find evidence that the increasing use of devolution – and direct democracy – increases citizen wellbeing, since 'political outcomes [are] closer to voters' preferences' (p. 918) and people benefit from political participation. More recently, analysis by Diaz-Serrano and Rodríguez-Pose (2012) uses European Social Survey data to test these links across 29 European countries. They find that fiscal and some forms of political decentralisation have a positive significant effect on wellbeing, although the size of the effect is influenced by the measure of devolution chosen. Importantly, they also uncover evidence that wellbeing is more strongly connected with local government capacity to deliver than devolution per se.

5. LOCALISM AND CITIES: AN EARLY ASSESSMENT

As we argued in the introduction, given the limitations of the economic case for devolution per se, discussions around devolution should focus more on the impact of tailored, locally-variable policies and the extent to which more flexible local decision-making processes are needed to deliver such policies. Questions on the effectiveness of local flexibilities are (partially) taken up in Chapter 8. In the remainder of this chapter we focus instead on the extent to which current 'localism' reforms actually allow for these greater local powers.

In the UK, there is increasing recognition of the relevance of fiscal federalist arguments. Under the last government, the independent Lyons Inquiry on local government discussed devolution and service outcomes as part of the overarching concept of 'place-shaping' (Lyons 2007). This gained significant purchase on government thinking, particularly in the DCLG, and as we saw in Section 2, is now an integral element in the Coalition's push for localism.

At the same time, similar considerations have come into play in recent discussions of Scottish devolution, which was originally largely driven by democratic and historical forces (Morgan 2007, p. 1239). For example, many of the responses to the consultation undertaken by the Commission for Scottish Devolution have commented on the increased scope the devolved settlement gives for the adoption of policies which are innovative and tailored to Scotland's specific circumstances, although not all agree that this has been realised in practice (Commission on Scottish Devolution 2008, evidence volume pp. 35–39).

The rise of the 'policy flexibility' agenda in England also, arguably, stems from frustration inside government at the limits of a heavily central-ised approach. Drawing on a series of interviews with central, regional and local policymakers in 2008 and 2009, a time when the UK city-regional agenda was gathering speed, Steeples (2010) highlights the potential for further devolution in three areas of policy, planning, transport and business support. Interviewees suggested, for example, that the lack of a formal role in the planning system means that cities were unable to introduce policy variation or meaningful prioritisation without the active consent of their constituent local authorities and needed to operate within the constraints of then-current regional spatial strategy. Although the role of cities had been recognised in transport policy, and bodies introduced at that spatial scale, practical scope for policy variation was limited by a lack of control over finance. There were also problems of legitimacy and robustness at the city level where controversial decisions were contem-plated (such as introducing road-charging schemes). On business support, there was clear potential for policy variation at all levels on business support, but there appeared to be no real attempts to assess what benefits variation does or could bring.

More broadly, Steeples also uncovers significant frustration with the then-piecemeal approach to devolution, the multiple justifications advanced by Ministers, emerging turf battles between city, local and regional agencies, and problems persuading certain Whitehall depart-ments of the merits of devolving power and/or budgets. However, the lack of clear-cut evidence for the benefits of devolution presents problems for developing a clear narrative, and on guiding policy detail. And experience from other countries suggests that in practice, delivering devolutionary change is a complex, long-term and essentially iterative process – involving multiple institutional transformations.

A recent, comprehensive overview of the European experience (Salet 2006) covers change in the Netherlands, France, Finland, Italy, Portugal and Germany – as well as the UK – and in each case the complexity of the issues involved, the number of actors and the fragility of the networks in which they operate and the vulnerability to setbacks, disputes and competing priorities are stressed.

Even Le Galès, an enthusiast for the city-regional agenda, is noticeably guarded on the extent to which it can successfully be put into practice: 'Institutional and political barriers are often hard to overcome, notably in terms of financial resources, expertise, legal autonomy, and political fragmentation' (Le Galès 2002, p. 272).

Given these constraints, then, how far has UK been able to advance? The remainder of this chapter reviews the key elements of the current devolution agenda for cities, and assesses future prospects. Under the coalition government elected in 2010, devolution is seen as a means to deliver 'localism'. At the time of writing, the localism agenda combines three rationales for devolution: economic growth, public service reform and democratic renewal. For cities, localism has four main policy strands:

- Institutional change – abolition of RDAs and the wider regional tier of government; introduction of public-private LEPs which are intended to operate across 'functional economic geographies', and are chaired by private sector representatives;
- New forms of political leadership – referenda for elected mayors in England's 12 biggest cities, which were held in April 2012; moves by other cities to 'combined authority' models; and most recently, endorsement of 'metro mayors' for wider city-regions;
- Incentives – to encourage local government to deliver against national objectives, particularly house-building (the New Homes Bonus) and 'pro-growth' economic development (the Business Increase Bonus and critically, Business Rates retention);
- New ways of working – a series of bespoke 'City Deals' struck between Whitehall Ministers, elected city leaders and LEP boards. Initially covering the eight major conurbations outside London, City Deals have now been extended to a number of smaller, 'second-tier' cities.[10]

The political and institutional configuration of localism within the Coalition is also substantially different from devolution under the last government. Devolution has historically 'belonged' to the DCLG and its predecessor incarnations, which as a single spending department has had limited success in persuading other central government players to cede control of power and/or budgets to local actors. By contrast, localism is one of few areas of shared agreement between the Coalition partners, and to date has been given high priority, with the appointment of Ministers for Decentralisation and Cities (as well as for Planning) and the establishment of a Cities Policy Unit, which is intended to drive forward the 'cities agenda' across government. In theory, shifting the cities agenda into the heart of UK government is a major step forward for devolution advocates.

[10] CO 2011, 2012; DCLG 2011b, c, 2012a.

Institutional Change

The regional tier developed under Labour has been removed entirely – it was seen by the Coalition as both inefficient and not close enough to local communities. New local partnerships and forms of elected leadership replace the old institutions. The development of LEPs – which replace RDAs – is a key part of this institutional shift. LEPs are (mostly) self-determined groups of local authorities operating over, in principle, 'real local economies', although in practice geographies are much more variable (see below).

The 39 LEPs now in place are tasked to take a 'strategic lead . . . to set out local economic priorities', with a portfolio of responsibilities including employment and skills; physical infrastructure and transport; housing and planning; innovation, including work with universities and colleges; support for SMEs and start-ups, and tourism (BIS 2010a). LEPs are constituted as public–private partnerships, with 50 per cent private sector representation on LEP boards, and private sector chairs. LEPs initially received no core funding from central government, but are now able to bid for a share of the Single Local Growth Fund, worth around £2bn a year, which devolves a small number of Whitehall programmes covering transport, adult skills and housing (HMT 2013). Some LEPs will be able to raise money through Enterprise Zones and Tax Increment Financing projects, as well as bidding for money through the Regional Growth Fund; some will also receive EU Structural Funds

The outlook for LEPs as a whole is mixed: individual partnerships' prospects are closely related to local policymaking capacity and experience, as well as their ability to raise their own funding. Because they have been negotiated by local elites, LEPs' coverage of functional economic areas is as dependent on local political bargaining as it is on true economic geographies: while some LEPs cover recognizable spatial economies, others are clearly political coalitions and are under-bounded (Hildreth and Bailey 2013). Given the importance of appropriate scale in securing economic gains from devolution, such political LEPs may find it harder to generate economic benefits – and may have weaker incentives to do so.

In addition, for many local authorities, LEPs represent a wholly new way of working, introduced at speed – and at the same time as major reductions in local government resources. A minority of authorities (mainly in large cities) has clear plans, good links to business and neighbouring councils. These LEPs are also most likely to be able to access Enterprise Zone, Tax Increment Funding and Regional Growth Fund funding streams. They arguably have the brightest prospects.

Political Leadership

Under Labour, RDAs were originally intended to be executive agencies of elected regional government (Pike and Tomaney 2009). Elected regional assemblies' chances were halted in 2004, when a referendum in the North East – the region considered most likely to vote for change – rejected the idea of elected regional government by a 78/22 margin.

The Coalition similarly planned to introduce elected mayors in the 12 largest English cities: the stated intention was to have 'London-style' mayors with a range of economic development powers, working alongside LEPs to advance urban economic performance. Think-tanks, notably the Centre for Cities (2009), had called for 'Metro Mayors' operating on a city-regional basis with clearly specified powers, using much of the evidence discussed above to support their case. However, this was rejected by Ministers who announced a series of confirmatory referenda in which only single-authority mayors would be offered, with an unspecified set of powers to be determined after the vote. Two of the 12 cities, Leicester and Salford, had already voted for a mayor, and council leaders in Liverpool moved to a mayoral model without a vote as part of the City Deal negotiation (see below). However, only one city of the remaining nine, Bristol, voted in favour of a mayor when polls were held in April 2012. Analysts suggested the lack of clarity on powers and low awareness from voters both played a role.

With the failure of the City Mayors initiative, at the time of writing major cities such as Manchester, Liverpool, Sheffield, Leeds and Newcastle have begun to move instead to formalise partnership arrangements, through combined authority models. The result is to leave elected leadership in major cities looking increasingly messy: Manchester now has a city-regional combined authority but also includes a council, Salford, which has an elected mayor; Liverpool has a city mayor but a city-regional LEP and City Deal (see below). Most recently, the Heseltine Review (Lord Heseltine 2012) recommended the government permit 'metro mayors' for city-regions, as a potential evolution of the combined authority model; Ministers have now accepted this recommendation (HMT and BIS 2013).

Incentives

Passing powers downwards to local leaders limits central government's ability to directly affect urban economic performance. The Coalition's response has been to combine decentralisation with incentives for local areas: notably to promote house-building and to encourage 'pro-growth' economic strategies.

If local incentives are to achieve the desired outcomes, the critical issues are their structures and size. As we discussed in Chapter 6 this is especially clear in the case of housebuilding in the UK, where the government would like more homes to be built in popular parts of the country. However, existing homeowners in a given local area have clear incentives to try and prevent additional building for reasons discussed extensively in Chapter 4. A scheme intended to incentivise house building – the New Homes Bonus – was introduced in 2011. As we have noted, the evidence so far is that the incentive design is far too weak for the programme to have any real impact on housing numbers.

In parallel with the New Homes Bonus, reforms to Business Rates were introduced in 2013 to encourage local authorities to accept proposals for commercial building. As set out in detail in Chapter 6, Business Rates retention allows councils to keep half of the additional property tax revenues arising from new commercial buildings. There are also doubts about whether this scheme will provide large enough and transparent enough incentives really to change local authorities' behaviour.

Both these proposals highlight the importance of getting the basic scale of governance right. The National Planning Policy Framework (DCLG 2012b) keeps development control at the local authority level, rather than moving it to the city-regional scale (although some LEPs have taken on aspects of strategic planning). However, the costs of physical development are very localised, while the benefits (such as additional jobs or slightly lower house prices) are spread over a larger area, and may accrue over many years. The forward risk is then that relatively weak incentives for housing and commercial development are outweighed by resistance to development. Rescaling aspects of planning and development control to the city-region level, and pooling incentives across boundaries, could help mitigate these difficulties.

City Deals

Of the four elements of localism, City Deals potentially represent the most profound devolutionary shift, by changing the way English urban areas and Central Government work together. The deals are individually brokered agreements between Whitehall and individual cities: local leaders negotiate bespoke fiscal and administrative shifts; Ministers have 'non-negotiable asks' from cities, including a clear economic rationale and evidence base, agreed outcomes and 'strong and transparent governance arrangements' (CO 2011).

In late 2012, eight deals had been concluded with each of the English Core Cities (CO 2012); at the time of writing another 20 were in the process of negotiation with smaller cities (Clark 2012). Despite the individual negotiation process, Smith and Sarling (2012) identify a number of common features in the 'wave one' deals: all eight cities have developed urban-level finance and investment vehicles, negotiated powers over employment and skills policies, and all but one has asked for strategic control over transport policy. Other key areas of deals are housing, trade promotion and sectoral support policies including – in many cases – low carbon sectors.

Smith and Sarling are broadly positive, praising deals for being tailored to individual city needs and capacities; matching new powers and resources; focusing on economic 'fundamentals' such as skills, and working on a city-regional footprint. Overman (2012) is more sceptical, highlighting instances of powers granted in one area in exchange for commitments in another. He questions how both sides will handle cases where 'agreed outcomes' are not met, and has some worries about the efficacy of sector-specific policies.

Nathan (2011) highlights some wider challenges for City Deals. The deal-making process needs to trigger fundamental institutional and cultural shifts in central and local governance, which typically will take many years to work through. Long-term commitment from central government is vital, but there are signs that buy-in across Whitehall is variable. Nathan also highlights the need for investment in local capacity-building: the deal-making process involves substantial transactions costs between local and central government, with some local players better able to bear these than others. There are also questions for central government about how many deals can be effectively managed at one time. In practice, it is clearly proving challenging for officials to implement a 'second wave' of deals with smaller (less experienced, lower-capacity) cities alongside the 'wave one' Core Cities. Smith and Sarling (2012) suggest that government should move towards a common base offer for future City Deals, with a set of clear and transparent rules covering outcomes, monitoring and targets.

6. CONCLUSION

Theory, evidence and experience suggest two continuing challenges for devolution advocates. First, there are good reasons to expect devolution to an authority with appropriate boundaries in relation to the spatial reach of economic interventions to deliver net economic benefits. But it is difficult to consistently identify positive or negative direct effects of devolution *per se* on outcomes we care about, especially economic outcomes. There is stronger evidence that the scale of economic governance matters, and in turn, rescaling economic policy functions have a series of important indirect effects on processes of decision-making and their quality. But this does not *per se* make the definitive case that many devolution advocates might like.

Conversely, there are also good grounds for thinking that devolving policies to an inappropriate local jurisdiction will negate any positive economic impact. As discussed above, because the costs of physical development are very local, while the benefits likely extend over a whole FUR, devolving development control and local plan construction to neighbourhoods and local authorities is essentially empowering NIMBYism.

Second, Ministers and senior policymakers typically express a desire for clear governance structures. However, as we have seen, the reality of urban governance is typically messy. This desire for clarity is, arguably, a continuation of a trend in Britain identified in Ashford (1982). This contrasted a formalised British system of national and local government, based on national policies with local delivery, with a French system based on 'institutional and organisational tension, not only among the various levels of government, but also within the administrative system' (p. 364). In Ashford's view, such a 'supple, adaptable relationship between local and national government' (p. 363), based on the accumulation of powers and responsibilities in a pragmatic, opportunist way at local level, represents a better response to policy problems which are complex and frequently changing.

As discussed above, the majority of studies of evolving forms of city governance throughout Europe have stressed the importance of networking, trust, and other soft relationship factors in developing a successful city-regional governance structure. When combined with the lack of clear evidence on devolution's impacts and effects, this presents challenges in making an objective case for devolution. The fact that a case for particular powers and responsibilities to be located at that level cannot be strongly made on the basis of current comparative evidence means that ambiguity and uncertainty is likely to continue.

The UK's experience of localism to date highlights many of these issues. Government has identified cities as key to economic development, but allowed the geography of administrative partnerships (for example LEPs) to be determined locally. City Deals should begin new ways of working with – potentially – profound shifts in central–local relations. Conversely, the city mayors experiment has – arguably – unhelpfully complicated the institutional landscape; local agencies and actors have variable resources and capacity; and central government's commitment to devolution varies across departments. This is not the 'supple' system Ashford calls for.

To keep their desired momentum, we believe that devolution advocates need to develop a more concrete, clearly-argued case based on the areas in which the content of policies and/or the ways in which they are delivered could be varied at city level, the economic benefits expected to result from this, and the constraints preventing variation under current circumstances. Policymakers also need to stop looking for a simple structural solution to the problem of city governance, and to emphasise that the city offers a potentially useful approach to the problem of managing policy formulation and delivery.

As the City Deals process is demonstrating, this needs to involve continuous negotiation of powers and responsibilities, based around pragmatic assessments of which policies could be better delivered at city-region or local level – a process rather than a structure. One of the most attractive features of City Deals is that they are essentially a series of policy experiments. The act of designing and implementing deals is, itself, a potentially rich source of evidence about 'what works'. Rigorous evaluation of City Deals and other devolution initiatives, and their possible effects of urban economic outcomes, will help build a much clearer picture about how devolution can help British cities move forward.

REFERENCES

Adam, Antonis, Manthos Delis and Panthelis Kammas. 2008. 'Fiscal Decentralization and Public Sector Efficiency: Evidence from OECD Countries', CESifo Working Paper Series No. 2364.

Akai, Nobuo and Masayo Sakata. 2002. 'Fiscal decentralization contributes to economic growth: evidence from state-level cross-section data for the United States'. *Journal of Urban Economics* 52, 93–108.

Ashford, D. 1982. *British Dogmatism and French Pragmatism: Central–Local Policymaking in the Welfare State*. London: George Allen and Unwin.

Bagnasco, A. and Patrick Le Galès. 2000. 'European Cities: Local Societies and Collective Actors?', in A. Bagnasco and P. Le Galès (eds), *Cities in Contemporary Europe*. Cambridge: Cambridge University Press.

Berry, Brian. 1973. *Growth Centers in the American Urban System: Community Development and Regional Growth in the Sixties and Seventies*. Cambridge, MA: Ballinger.

Berry, Brian, P.G. Goheen and Harvey Goldstein. 1968. 'US Bureau of the Census Metropolitan Area Definition: A Re-evaluation of Concept and Statistical Practice', Bureau of the Census Working Paper 28. Washington DC: Bureau of the Census.

BIS (Department for Business Innovation and Skills). 2010a. 'Local Growth: Realising Every Place's Potential', Cmd. 7961. London: HMSO.

BIS. 2010b. 'Understanding Local Growth'. London: BIS.

Bruess, Fritz and Markus Eller. 2004. 'Fiscal decentralisation and economic growth: is there really a link?' *Journal for Institutional Comparisons* 2, 3–9.

Buck, Nick, Ian Gordon, Alan Harding and Ivan Turok. 2005. 'Conclusion: Moving Beyond the Conventional Wisdom', in N. Buck, I. Gordon, A. Harding and I. Turok (eds), *Changing Cities: Rethinking Urban Competitiveness, Cohesion and Governance.* London: Palgrave Macmillan.

Canaleta, Carlos Gil, Pedro Pascual Arzoz and Manuel Rapun Garate. 2004. 'Regional economic disparities and decentralisation'. *Urban Studies* 41, 71–94.

Centre for Cities. 2009. 'Cities Manifesto'. London, Centre for Cities.

Cheshire, Paul. 1995. 'A new phase of urban development in Western Europe? The evidence for the 1980s'. *Urban Studies* 32, 1045–1063.

Cheshire, Paul C. and Ian R. Gordon. 1996. 'Territorial competition and the predictability of collective (in)action'. *International Journal of Urban and Regional Research* 20, 383–399.

Cheshire, Paul and D.G. Hay. 1989. *Urban Problems in Western Europe: An Economic Analysis.* London: HarperCollins Academic/Routledge.

Cheshire, Paul and Stefano Magrini. 2000. 'Endogenous processes in European regional growth: convergence and policy'. *Growth and Change* 31, 455–479.

Cheshire, Paul and Stefano Magrini. 2005. 'European Urban Growth: Throwing Some Economic Light into the Black Box', in 45th European Regional Science Congress, Amsterdam.

Cheshire, Paul and Stefano Magrini. 2009. 'Urban growth drivers in a Europe of sticky people and implicit boundaries'. *Journal of Economic Geography* 9, 85–115.

Clark, Greg. 2006. 'International City Benchmarking and Indexes: Towards Diagnosing Ingredients of Cities' Success and Failure'. Mimeo. London: ODPM.

Clark, Greg. 2012. Speech at City Deals Wave Two Launch, London, 29 October.

CO (Cabinet Office). 2011. 'Unlocking Growth in Cities'. London, Cabinet Office.

CO. 2012. 'Unlocking growth in Cities – City Deals: Wave 1'. London, Cabinet Office.

Commission on Scottish Devolution. 2008. 'The Future of Scottish Devolution Within the Union'. Edinburgh: Commission on Scottish Devolution.

Conservative Party. 2009. 'Control Shift: Returning Power to Local Communities', *Responsibility Agenda. Policy Green Paper No. 9.* London: The Conservative Party.

Core Cities Group. 2006. 'Our Cities Are Back. Competitive Cities Make Prosperous Regions and Sustainable Communities'. Third Report of the Core Cities Working Group. Sheffield: Core Cities Group.

Davoodi, Hamid and Heng-fu Zou. 1998. 'Fiscal decentralization and economic growth: a cross-country study'. *Journal of Urban Economics* 43, 244–257.

DCLG (Department for Communities and Local Government). 2006. 'Strong and Prosperous Communities: The Local Government White Paper'. London: DCLG.

DCLG. 2008a. 'Planning and Optimal Geographical Levels for Economic Decision Making: The Sub-Regional Role'. London: DCLG.

DCLG. 2008b. 'Why Place Matters and Implications for the Role of Central, Regional & Local Government', Department for Communities and Local Government Economics Paper 2. London: DCLG.

DCLG. 2011a. 'A Plain English Guide to the Localism Bill'. London: DCLG.

DCLG. 2011b. 'Local Government Resource Review: Proposals for Business Rates Retention – Consultation', London: DCLG.

DCLG. 2011c. 'New Homes Bonus: Final Scheme Design'. London: DCLG.

DCLG. 2012a. 'Business Rates Retention Scheme: The Economic Benefits of Local Business Rates Retention'. London: DCLG.

DCLG. 2012b. 'National Planning Policy Framework'. London: DCLG.

Deas, Iain and Benito Giordano. 2002. 'Locating the Competitive City in England', in I. Begg (ed.), *Urban Competitiveness: Policies for Dynamic Cities.* Bristol: Policy Press.

Department for Business Enterprise and Regulatory Reform, and Communities and Local Government. 2008. 'Prosperous Places: Taking Forward the Review of Sub-National EconomicDevelopment and Regeneration'. London: BERR and DCLG.

Diaz-Serrano, Luis and Andrés Rodríguez-Pose. 2012. 'Decentralization, subjective well-being, and the perception of institutions'. *Kyklos* 65, 179–193.

Dolphin, Tony. 2009. *The Impact of the Recession on Northern City-Regions.* Newcastle: IPPR North.

Ezcurra, Roberto and Andrés Rodríguez-Pose. 2009. 'Does Decentralization Matter for Regional Disparities? A Cross-Country Analysis', SERC Discussion Paper DP0025. London: SERC.

Ezcurra, Roberto and Andrés Rodríguez-Pose. 2010. 'Is Fiscal Decentralization Harmful for Economic Growth? Evidence from the OECD Countries', SERC Discussion Paper DP0051. London: SERC.

Fothergill, Steve. 2005. 'A new regional policy for Britain'. *Regional Studies* 39, 659–667.

Fox, K.A. and T.K. Kumar. 1965. 'The functional economic area: delineation and implications'. *Papers and Proceedings of the Regional Science Association* 13, 177–200.

Frey, Bruno S. and Alois Stutzer. 2000. 'Happiness, economy and institutions'. *The Economic Journal* 110, 918–938.

Gibbons, Stephen, Henry G. Overman and Guilherme Resende. 2011. 'Real Earnings Disparities in Britain', SERC Discussion Paper 0065. London: SERC.

Goodwin, Mark, Martin Jones, Rhys Jones, Kevin Pett and Glenn Simpson. 2002. 'Devolution and economic governance in the UK: uneven geographies, uneven capacities?' *Local Economy* 17, 200–215.

Gordon, Ian. 2006. Finding Institutional Leadership for Regional Networks: The Case of London and the South East' in W. Salet (ed.), *Synergy in Urban Networks? European Perspectives and Randstad.* The Hague: Sdu Publishers.

Hall, Peter and D. G. Hay. 1980. *Growth Centres in the European Urban System.* London: Heinemann Educational.

Harding, Alan, Simon Marvin and Nigel Sprigings. 2004. *Realising the National Economic Potential of Provincial City-Regions: The Rationale for and Implications of a 'Northern Way' Growth Strategy.* London: Office of the Deputy Prime Minister.

Herrschel, Timo and P. Newman. 2002. *Governance of Europe's City Regions: Planning, Policy & Politics.* London: Routledge.

Hildreth, Paul and David Bailey. 2013. 'The economics behind the move to "localism" in England'. *Cambridge Journal of Regions, Economy and Society* 6, 233–249.

HM Government. 2010. 'The Coalition: Our Programme for Government'. London: Cabinet Office.

HMT (HM Treasury). 2007. 'Sub-National Economic Development and Regeneration Review'. London: HMT.

HMT. 2013. 'Investing in Britain's Future', Cmd. 8669. London: HMT.

HMT and BIS. 2013. *Government's Response to the Heseltine Review*. London: HMT and BIS.

HMT, DTI (Department for Trade and Industry) and DCLG. 2006. 'Devolving Decision-Making 3: The Importance of Cities to Regional Growth'. London: HMT.

HMT, DTI and ODPM. 2004. 'Devolving Decision Making 2: Meeting the Regional Challenge: Increasing Regional and Local Flexibility'. London: HMT.

Hudson, Ray. 2006. 'Regional devolution and regional economic success: Myths and illusions about power'. *Geografiska Annaler: Series B, Human Geography* 88, 159–171.

Jones, Alexandra, Neil Lee, Laura Williams, Naomi Clayton and Katy Morris. 2008. 'How can Cities Thrive in the Changing Economy?: Ideopolis 2 Final Report'. London: The Work Foundation.

Kaufmann, D. and A Kraay. 2003. 'Governance and Growth: Causality Which Way? Evidence for the World'. Washington, DC: World Bank.

Le Galès, Patrick. 2002. *European Cities: Social Conflicts and Governance*. Oxford: Oxford University Press.

Lee, Neil. 2008. 'Building on What's There: What Cities and Policymakers can Learn from Endogenous Growth and the New Economic Geography'. London: The Work Foundation.

Lessmann, Christian. 2009. Fiscal decentralization and regional disparity: evidence from cross-section and panel data'. 7 October, SSRN.

Lord Heseltine. 2012. *No Stone Unturned in Search of Growth*. London: BIS.

Lyons, Michael. 2007. 'Lyons Inquiry into Local Government. Place-Shaping: A Shared Ambition for the Future of Local Government – Final Report'. London: HM Stationery Office.

Marshall, Adam. 2006. 'Linking Governance and City Performance: A Review of the Evidence Base'. City Leadership Web Annex 1. London: Centre for Cities.

Marshall, Adam, Dermot Finch and Chris Urwin. 2006. 'City Leadership: Giving Cities the Power to Grow'. London: Centre for Cities.

Marvin, Simon, Alan Harding and Brian Robson. 2006. 'A Framework for City-Regions: Final Report'. London: Office of the Deputy Prime Minister.

Morgan, Kevin. 2007. 'The polycentric state: new spaces of empowerment and engagement'. *Regional Studies* 41, 1237–1251.

Morris, Katy and Laura Williams. 2008. 'A Council of Perfection? Reviewing the Links Between Types of Governance and the Economic Success of Cities'. London: Work Foundation.

Nathan, Max. 2011. 'City Deals: What next?', in *Spatial Economics Research Centre Blog*.

Nathan, Max and Adam Marshall. 2006. 'Them and us: Britain and the European city'. *Public Policy Research* 13, 109–118.

New Local Government Network. 2005. 'Seeing the Light? Next Steps for City-Regions'. London: New Local Government Network City Regions Commission (NLGN).

New Local Government Network. 2006. 'Views of the City: Can City-Regions Find their Place?' London: NLGN.

Oates, Wallace. 1972. *Fiscal Federalism*. New York: Harcourt Brace Jovanovich.

Oates, Wallace E. 1999. 'An essay on fiscal federalism'. *Journal of Economic Literature* 37, 1120–1149.

ODPM (Office of the Deputy Prime Minister). 2006. 'State of the English Cities Report'. London: Office of the Deputy Prime Minister.

Overman, Henry. 2012. '(Core) City Deals', in *Spatial Economics Research Centre Blog*.

Parkinson, Michael, Tony Champion, Richard Evans, James Simmie, Ivan Turok, Martin Crookston, Alison Park, Alan Berube, Mike Coombes, Danny Dorling, Norman Glass, Mary Hutchins, Ade Kearns, Ron Martin and Peter Wood. 2006. 'The State of English Cities Report'. London: Office of the Deputy Prime Minister.

Parkinson, Michael, Mary Hutchins, James Simmie, Greg Clark and Hans Verdonk. 2004. 'Competitive European Cities: Where do the Core Cities Stand?', Report to the Office of the Deputy Prime Minister. London: Office of the Deputy Prime Minister.

Pike, Andy, Andrés Rodríguez-Pose, John Tomaney, Gianpiero Torrisi and Vassilis Tselios. 2010. 'In Search of the "Economic Dividend" of Devolution: Spatial Disparities, Spatial Economic Policy and Decentralisation in the UK', SERC Discussion Paper 0062. London: SERC.Pike, Andy and John Tomaney. 2008. 'The Government's Review of Sub-National Economic Development and Regeneration: Key Issues', SERC Discussion Paper 0008. London: SERC.

Pike, Andy and John Tomaney. 2009. 'The state and uneven development: the governance of economic development in England in the post-devolution UK'. *Cambridge Journal of Regions, Economy and Society* 2, 13–34.

Robson, Brian, Robert Barr, Kitty Lymperopoulou, James Rees and Mike Coombes. 2006. 'A framework for City-Regions: Working Paper 1: Mapping City-Regions'. London: Office of the Deputy Prime Minister.

Rodríguez-Pose, Andrès and A. Bwire. 2004. 'The economic (in)efficiency of devolution'. *Environment and Planning A* 36, 1907–1928.

Rodríguez-Pose, A. and Nicholas Gill. 2005. 'On the "economic dividend" of devolution'. *Regional Studies* 39, 405–420.

Salet, W. 2006. 'How to Cope with the Metamorphosis of the City-Region', in W. Salet (ed.), *Synergy in Urban Networks? European Perspectives and Randstad Holland*. Den Haag: Sdu Publishers.

Shakespeare, Tom. 2008. 'The Future for Regional Governance', Localis Research Paper No. 1. London: Localis.

Sims, Sam. 2011. *Making the Most of Mayors: Lessons Learnt from the Existing Mayoral Local Authorities*. London: Institute for Government.

Smith, Rachel and Joe Sarling. 2012. 'Here's the Deal: Overview of the Wave 1 City Deals'. London: Centre for Cities.

Stansel, Dean. 2005. 'Local decentralization and local economic growth: a cross-sectional examination of US metropolitan areas'. *Journal of Urban Economics* 57, 55–72.

Steeples, Paul. 2010. 'City-Region Governance, Policy Variation and Economic Performance', SERC Policy Paper 005. London: SERC.

Swinney, Paul, Kate Blatchford and Rachel Smith. 2011. 'Big Shot or Long Shot? How Elected Mayors can Help Drive Economic Growth in England's Cities'. London: Centre for Cities/Institute for Government.

Thiessen, Ulrich. 2003. 'Fiscal decentralisation and economic growth in high-income OECD countries'. *Fiscal Studies* 24, 237–274.

Tiebout, Charles M. 1956. 'A pure theory of local expenditures'. *Journal of Political Economy* 64, 416–424.

Turok, Ivan. 2008. 'A new policy for Britain's cities: choices, challenges, contradictions'. *Local Economy* 23.

Xie, Danyang, Heng-fu Zou and Hamid Davoodi. 1999. 'Fiscal decentralization and economic growth in the United States'. *Journal of Urban Economics* 45, 228–239.

Zhang, Tao and Heng-fu Zou. 1998. 'Fiscal decentralization, public spending, and economic growth in China'. *Journal of Public Economics* 67, 221–240.

8. Urban policies

1. INTRODUCTION

All governments are concerned with tackling the problems of areas that experience sustained economic decline and/or underperformance. In Britain, as elsewhere, several factors have combined to raise profound questions about future government policy in this area. First, as discussed in Chapter 2, it is clear that the most recent recession has impacted on different places in different ways and, unfortunately that most of the places that have suffered most were already struggling and are likely to be the least well placed to recover. Second, the recession has had a negative impact on government finances. Coupled with the credit crunch this has had serious implications for the viability of traditional funding models for local development and regeneration policy. Specifically, in Britain, this model relied on high levels of government expenditure leveraged with 'Section 106 agreements' extracted from private developers who were benefiting from relatively buoyant commercial and residential property markets (and as was explained in Chapter 6, such agreements are mostly reached for the biggest development applications so disproportionately benefiting richer and growing areas). Both national government cutbacks and a stagnated construction industry make the situation post-2007 far less favourable for local government finances (Parkinson 2009). The third significant factor is, as explained in Chapter 7, the change in government. The post-2010 coalition places greater emphasis on decentralised decision making across a range of policy areas, including those of regeneration and local economic development.

This chapter builds on Chapter 2 and argues that policy in Britain, as in many other countries, has been too focused on public expenditure to 'turn around' declining places. Unfortunately, as we have already seen from that chapter's analysis, in both the medium and longer run there has been remarkably little convergence across places in Britain – declining places continue to struggle despite considerable policy intervention, often over a period of 50 years. At best, this shows that those policies have not been able to counter market forces that continue to work against these declining places. At worst, it suggests that many policies may have been completely ineffective in terms of improving local economic performance.[1] As this chapter will show, the evidence suggests that the balance sits somewhere between these two extremes.

We draw on previous chapters, supplemented with findings from evaluations of existing interventions, to challenge a number of aspects of the 'place-based' approach, particularly when it is aimed at turning around declining places. Taken together, this evidence underpins the three main messages that have been the focus of this book: the need for realism in the face of strong market forces that create unevenness, the ineffectiveness of many popular government interventions to counter these forces and the need to judge interventions primarily on the extent to which they benefit people rather than places.

2.   THE CAUSES OF SPATIAL DISPARITIES AND THE OBJECTIVES OF URBAN POLICY

Before we start to consider the impact of specific interventions it is useful to take a step back to remind ourselves of some of the lessons learnt from previous chapters about the causes of spatial disparities. Places in Britain (as elsewhere) are certainly unequal in terms of population, earnings, employment and other socio-economic outcomes. Policy in many countries seeks to reduce these disparities by intervening in the poorest places. But when thinking about the impact of policy it is important to remember that these disparities are simply aggregates of the outcomes for people who live and work in different places. They do not, in themselves, measure the advantages or disadvantages that a place offers to people or the extent to which the balance of advantages and disadvantages may vary across people. One crucial element in assessing the impact of policy is, therefore, to understand what causes these area level disparities and the extent to which they affect different people.

As we discussed in Chapter 2, disparities between different cities arise because of the interaction between area effects (the extent to which some cities offer better outcomes for similar types of people) and composition effects (the extent to which the characteristics of people differ across cities). In Britain, to the extent that we are able to separate these effects out, area effects account for about 30 per cent of the difference across cities, while sorting accounts for around 70 per cent (Gibbons and Overman 2012). Note that the UK is a little unusual in that sorting

---

[1] Although in some circumstances they have evidently helped improve social outcomes, or provided important public goods. We discuss these points later in the chapter.

appears to play a bigger role than in some other countries. Comparisons with France, for example, would suggest area effects explain about 50 per cent of area disparities (Combes et al. 2008). The role for area effects in explaining differences across cities sems higher in the US than it is in Britain (Moretti 2012). We can only speculate on the reasons for these differences. It might be that personal inequality is lower in France (reducing the role for sorting), while in the US planning that does not place emphasis on 'urban containment' leads to more large cities (increasing the role for the agglomeration effects that partly underpin area effects). Regardless, these numbers suggest that tackling city level disparities – for example to achieve government objectives for spatial 'rebalancing' – would require policy interventions aimed at improving both area effects and improving city composition.

Let us set aside, for the moment, whether such interventions are feasible and instead consider the link between disparities between cities and individual inequalities. If we were able to completely eliminate area effects between cities, how much difference would this make to overall individual inequality? The answer, at least for Britain, is 'not very much'. Gibbons et al. (2013) show that only about 1 per cent of the variation in individual earnings inequality in Britain is explained by area effects. Another way of looking at this is to realise that in a developed country like Britain, within-city inequalities far exceed any between-city differences. In short, for understanding individual earnings inequality, who you are matters far more than where you live.

The link between city level disparities and individual inequalities is further complicated by the fact that earnings disparities between cities are uninformative about differences in overall wellbeing, unless we take account of costs of living and local amenities. As most people are free to choose where they live, cities with high wages should have high housing costs or low quality of life. In a country where housing markets are highly regulated (see Chapters 4 and 5) it should come as no surprise that Gibbons et al. (2011) show that there is a clear link between area level wages and house prices. In Britain, on average, higher area level wages are offset by higher housing costs so high nominal wage cities do not pay higher real wages (that is net of housing costs). Further, the evidence shows that cities with better amenities (measured on a range of dimensions) pay lower real wages. This is just what the spatial equilibrium framework outlined in Chapter 2 would predict.

In short, sorting by people in response to wage, price and amenity differences results in concentrations of low-skilled people in low-wage cities and high-skilled people in high-wage cities. As explained in detail in Chapter 3, within cities the role for sorting is even more pronounced and leads to marked residential segregation despite the absence of strong direct neighbourhood level effects on wages (or other socio-economic outcomes).

All of this has profound implications for thinking about urban policy. Most importantly, thinking about spatial disparities in this way suggests that while area averages (for either cities or neighbourhoods) are useful for scene-setting, they are not a very useful guide to policy. They do not tell us whether policy should be targeting people or places and they do not have a clear link to individual wellbeing. Differences in average incomes across cities reflect the interaction of area effects (in turn determined by a huge range of factors, including agglomeration economies and historical factors, as described in Chapter 2) and the sorting of people. More broadly, they also reflect public policy choices (such as pay-setting in the public sector). High wages tend to be offset by high house prices or low quality of life so income differences on their own are not very useful indicators of differences in wellbeing. It is for this reason that we argue that policy should be assessed by its impact on people not places. People trade off wages, cost of living and amenities and most can move in response to changes in any of these. As a result the impact on observed area differences offers a very poor guide to the overall effects of policy on individuals.

Of course, this does not mean that there is no case for policy to vary across places. As we discussed in Chapter 7, there are strong reasons to think that an area's governance may become more effective if policymakers can draw on local knowledge, and can develop bespoke, innovative solutions to challenges in that area. In addition, poorer places have concentrations of poorer families so some policy interventions will necessarily be focused on those places. At its simplest, for example, it makes sense to target policies aimed at helping poor people to the neighbourhoods where poor people are concentrated. Finally, as explained in Chapter 2, while tackling area effects might not matter so much in reducing individual inequalities it may play an important role in improving economic growth.

That said, in practice, British urban policy has in our collective judgement been too heavily focused on places. Because of the existence of area effects living in some places negatively affects individual outcomes. The usual response to this observation is to try to improve those 'bad' areas. An alternative would be to focus on improving outcomes for people who live in bad areas. The focus on area differences biases policy towards the first response. This tendency is then reinforced by a spatially representative system of democracy. Unfortunately, evidence suggests this has not been successful as area effects are very persistent and policy has proved not very effective in reducing these area effects. In contrast, especially in Britain, policy has paid too little attention to house prices and amenities. As we saw in Chapters 4 and 5, planning plays a key role in determining area differences in cost of living. This means that planning decisions play a key role in generating area disparities because people and firms sort in response to both wages and local costs (particularly housing). Similarly disparities in amenities matter because high quality of life compensates people if wages are low relative to the cost of living. Local policymakers have control over policies that directly affect house prices and amenities and relatively few that affect wages and employment.

3. AREA-BASED INITIATIVES

There are many policies that may impact on urban economies. In this chapter we will focus specifically on those that directly, or indirectly, target local employment and growth. Within this broad set of policies we are particularly interested in those that are 'area-based', that is, have objectives that are specifically framed in terms of improving area outcomes. This chapter is, therefore, necessarily selective and does not cover everything. Instead, we try to draw out the lessons that emerge when we think about the impact of urban policy using the insights and evidence presented so far in this book.

Area-based initiatives (ABIs) are policy initiatives aimed at tightly defined geographical areas. They are very popular, in many countries, as a tool for tackling problems where there is relative or absolute decline. The policy mix may vary considerably according to the specific ABI being considered but we might usefully characterise the different components as targeting firms, households or the physical and built environment of the area itself. Some policies tend to focus on only one of these dimensions, others may target multiple dimensions.

ABIs Aimed at Firms

One popular policy, often referred to as 'enterprise zones' (or similar), sees firms receive tax breaks and other incentives to locate or expand in specific areas. For example in 2011 the UK government announced the creation of 21 enterprise zones (subsequently expanded to 24 zones).[2] These enterprise zones (EZ) offer firms five-year rebates on business rates (the UK's business property tax), planning regulations will be simplified, local authorities will be able to keep business rate growth and government will ensure superfast broadband is available. The location of specific zones was proposed by Local Enterprise Partnerships (see Chapter 7), but the

---

[2] http://enterprisezones.communities.gov.uk/

government wants the zones to 'support real growth opportunities', not simply remedy local dereliction. Unfortunately it is hard to reconcile this objective with the available evidence.

Bartik (2004) provides a useful summary of earlier US evidence. This suggests that the incentives offered in US schemes (usually in the form of tax breaks) are effective at redistributing within urban areas, but do not appear to be very effective at redistributing across urban areas. More recent evidence (for example Einio and Overman 2013; Hanson and Rohlin 2013; Mayer et al. 2013), suggest that this redistribution may be occurring at quite small spatial scales with areas just outside the zone losing employment to areas just inside the zone. Why should this be the case? Urban economics provides an answer. As discussed in Chapters 2 and 3, households make location decisions trading off incomes, costs and amenities. The same is true for firms. When they think about where to locate they are trading off the benefits and costs of producing in different places. When places are very similar in terms of costs and benefits – as might be the case for two neighbouring office developments – anything that lowers costs will have a big impact in terms of attracting new firms (or encouraging the expansion of existing firms). This explains why these policies may be effective at redistributing within urban areas.

However, once we start thinking about comparisons across different cities any tax breaks (or other financial incentives) provided in poorer cities, and may be easily offset if productivity in those cities is too low or if labour or land costs are too high (for example due to national pay setting or local land regulations). This then makes the policy ineffective at larger spatial scales. As the cost of providing tax breaks can be quite large, these policies can be quite a costly way of shifting employment relatively small distances. If labour markets are very local then even these shifts may benefit local residents within the zone. If labour markets are relatively large compared to zones, then this shifting employment may have no impact on employment for residents living within the zone. Consistent with this, most recent evaluations of existing zones find evidence of positive employment effects, driven by displacement with relatively little impact on the employment rates of residents (ibid.). Busso et al. (2013) provide a noticeable exception – they do find beneficial effects for residents when considering US EZ schemes that impose a residency requirement on firms in terms of who they can employ (that is, they have to employ a certain percentage of people from within the zone to be eligible for tax breaks). It is not clear whether this institutional difference explains why their findings diverge from those in other countries or whether there is some other explanation – for example in terms of the methodological approach adopted. Other US studies that are similarly robust do not tend to find this positive effect. Despite this rather mixed evidence, enterprise zones continue to be popular with many governments.

To understand the overall impact of these type of policies it is useful to distinguish between the effect on national employment and growth and what happens in the enterprise zone. In areas with strong economies, as discussed in Chapters 4 and 5, planning often acts as a break on business expansion and development and local governments may have few incentives to allow more development. In these circumstances, EZ type reforms could help encourage growth. Some of this growth would come at the expense of other areas in the UK, but much of it could be additional. Overall, we might reasonably expect both local and national employment and growth to increase. Arguably, this has been the case with Britain's most ambitious ABI: the development of London Docklands, now the home of much of the UK's financial services sector but in the 1980s a mainly derelict port area.

However, EZs, in Britain as elsewhere, usually make these changes in areas with weak economies. Here, the fundamental problem is that these are unproductive places for business investment. Five-year rebates on business rates and relaxed planning regimes can attempt to offset these disadvantages for businesses but they do not address the fundamental problems such as the educational level of the local labour force. As we have just discussed, in these poorer cities the evidence on whether EZs have any effect on local employment is fairly weak. Even if they do, it is highly likely that much of this growth would come at the expense of other areas in Britain – most likely in the form of displacement from other areas very close by. Overall, we might hope for some small impact on local employment but should expect little, if any, impact on national employment and growth.

As discussed extensively in Chapters 4 and 5, there are many reasons to think that the British planning system acts as a break on growth. Unfortunately, reform in local zones does little to treat this problem and it is hard to see this having much, if any, impact on growth. In short, theoretical reasoning and empirical evidence warns us that EZs often involve spending money (or equivalently foregoing taxes) to shuffle employment around within cities. In some specific circumstances, this may be a useful policy outcome, but it will do little to improve overall urban economic performance.

In short, both theory and evidence urges caution in thinking about the impact of spatially targeted interventions that provide tax breaks (or other financial or regulatory incentives) to firms to locate in small geographical areas. There is a real risk of displacement from the surrounding area – a phenomenon that (much of the) empirical evidence suggests happens in practice. One way to mitigate this displacement effect is to have the policy apply at a larger geographical scale. Of course, the problem with this is that unconditional support across a large geographical scale would soon become very expensive.[3] One solution is to make support 'selective', perhaps conditional on characteristics of the firm (for example they mainly serve national or international markets) or of the business case for support. Preliminary work on the UK's Regional Selective Assistance Scheme by Criscuolo et al. (2012) suggests that such selective assistance can have a positive net impact on firm and area employment, although there appears to be little impact on productivity.

Another way to make such policies selective is to target small- to medium-size enterprises (SMEs). Such policies are certainly very popular and are often justified on the basis that these firms often face credit constraints when trying to expand. Unfortunately, governments are often unable to fix the information asymmetries that underlie these credit constraints meaning that such schemes often end up supporting a large number of businesses that go on to fail (Lerner 2009). Further, at least conceptually, urban economics warns us that the case for targeting small businesses *per se* is further undermined if most sell locally meaning that displacement from other local businesses is a real risk (Moretti 2010).

To summarise, the evidence suggests that we should exercise extreme caution in the design and implementation of ABIs aimed at firms. In most circumstances, such schemes appear to be costly ways of generating a limited number of additional jobs.

ABIs Aimed at Households

In contrast to subsidies for firms, urban economics provides no *a priori* reasons to worry about ABIs that target the characteristics and skills of households (for example to improve education or labour market participation – attempts to force 'mixed communities' are discussed in section 3.3). In fact, some of the classic contributions of urban economics to public finance make the case for localism, as we saw in Chapter 7. So the main issue with ABIs aimed at households is about the effectiveness of such policies. Once again, the evidence is mixed – although it is worrying that, in Britain at least, some fairly substantial ABIs appear to have had relatively little impact. The UK Labour government that was in power

---

[3] Another is that when tried, the newly re-locating firms tended to concentrate close to the border near the most prosperous area. When restrictions were placed on building new industrial premises in the South East – most relocating firms did not go to the assisted regions but to East Anglia (Twomey and Taylor, 1985).

from 1997 to 2010 introduced various policies aimed at improving neighbourhood outcomes. The National Strategy for Neighbourhood Renewal focused on deprived neighbourhoods, aiming to ensure that within 10–20 years no one would be seriously disadvantaged by where they live. As well as directing mainstream funding, specific programmes were associated with this objective: the New Deal for Communities, the Neighbourhood Renewal Fund, and the Working Neighbourhoods Fund.[4]

Working out the impact of these policies on deprived neighbourhoods is difficult. In addition to support for households in terms of education and training, these programmes often provided public goods to deprived areas, for example, through improved social housing and public spaces. Improved social housing clearly benefits those who live in social housing, while improving the physical environment of neighbourhoods benefits all residents. There is a question about whether benefits exceed costs (which we cannot answer) and a related question about who, exactly, benefits (which we consider further below). But, regardless, this kind of public good provision clearly delivers *some* benefits.

The wider economic benefits of the programmes are, unfortunately, not so easy to identify. Indeed, aside from the consumption value of the public goods provided through these programmes, there has been little progress in narrowing the gap between economic outcomes for the most disadvantaged individuals living in these areas and the rest.[5] As discussed in the introduction it is, of course, possible that things may have been worse without these policies. This highlights the crucial role that high quality evaluation evidence might play in helping us determine the impact of these programmes. Unfortunately, as with many urban policy interventions, few of these programmes have been rigorously evaluated (Gibbons et al. 2012b).

From the selection of government-commissioned evaluations of recent programmes, that for the New Deal for Communities (NDC) is arguably the most rigorous.[6] The NDC spent £400 per household per year between 1998 and 2011 in 39 of the most deprived areas of England. Evidence on its impact is, however, underwhelming. According to the summary report of the government evaluation (written in 2009, when the policy was still active):[7]

---

[4] http://webarchive.nationalarchives.gov.uk/20061009151514/neighbourhood.gov.uk/page. asp?id=903

[5] National Equality Panel (2010).

[6] See http://extra.shu.ac.uk/ndc/.

[7] http://www.communities.gov.uk/publications/communities/afinalassessment.

NDC areas are experiencing positive change, some of which is over and above that occurring in the comparator areas. After controlling for base characteristics, residents in NDC areas have on average seen statistically greater positive change in relation to their satisfaction with the area compared with comparator residents . . . This is not, however, the case when a respondent's initial level of satisfaction is included.

That is, satisfaction with the neighbourhood is improving (which may not be that surprising). Unfortunately, in the full report, controlling for socio-demographic factors individuals in NDC areas did worse on two to seven out of 15 indicators and no better on the remainder. In other words, based on the evidence to date, this reasonably well-funded area policy did not, on average, improve individual outcomes in targeted areas.

Reaching broader conclusions on the effectiveness of these policies would require more systematic review of the existing literature – a task which is beyond the scope of this chapter.[8] But the evaluation for NDC certainly suggests caution when thinking about the impact of ABIs on household incomes. It also holds some broader lessons about the problems of evaluating the impact of ABIs. As with many such policies the programme was structured in such a way as to make evaluation difficult (no piloting, coverage of all deprived areas). More rigorous evaluation techniques were not considered as part of the official evaluation with an emphasis instead on fairly simplistic regression analysis. Worse, basic data problems made it hard to apply even these more simple techniques. For example, because neighbourhood interventions are not well documented in the UK (as in many other countries) there may be other (that is non-NDC) ABIs active in comparison areas. If these other ABIs are as successful as NDC then this would explain why the NDC evaluation could find no effect. This is clearly a problem, although it is highly unlikely that these other ABIs could be as costly as NDC which was the major government programme at this time.[9] It was also, at the time of the evaluation, early days for NDC – another common problem for official evaluations where ministers push for evaluations at a stage when impacts are unlikely to be fully realised. That said, for NDC specifically, the evaluation itself suggests that the largest gains came first which might justify early evaluation.

One crucial issue, discussed in Section 2 of this chapter and nicely

---

[8] Such systematic reviews will be undertaken by the What Works Centre for Local Economic Growth, part of a new What Works initiative, partly funded by the British government and aimed at improving the use of evidence in policy making.

[9] Evaluation is made even more complex by the fact that large national, non-area-based spending programmes (such as investment in early years and primary education) were also in effect at the same time, and are likely to have influenced many of NDC-relevant outcomes.

illustrated by the evaluation of NDC, is whether policymakers should care about the impact on areas or households. What exactly would we view as a successful outcome for NDC? According to the NDC official evaluation there can be no assumption that 'success' is best measured in relation to what happens to individuals as opposed to what happens to these areas over time. Given the broad level objectives of the UK government's neighbourhood policy at the time ('within 10–20 years, no one would be seriously disadvantaged by where they live') this is puzzling. If such policies have equity objectives – for example helping the disadvantaged – then as discussed above we surely care about what happens to individuals, not areas. This is especially true if successful interventions increase the flow of people moving in and out of neighbourhoods. When that happens success may be measured in terms of the improved characteristics of the incomers who have been attracted by the neighbourhood improvements who may have displaced the very people the policy was targeted at. That the NDC evaluation suggests we should care about area outcomes serves to highlight the confusion about what policy could and should try to achieve.

The more general point that applies to all ABIs of this type is that that the effect of the policy is complicated by the fact that neighbourhood composition is not fixed; like buses, people get in and out all the time. Indeed, some of the poorest neighbourhoods can see some of the highest levels of churn (Bolster et al. 2007). Further, as discussed in Chapter 3, urban economics tells us that neighbourhood composition is not arbitrarily determined. Instead, it is the result of many different households making more or less constrained decisions about where to live. As a result, if an ABI is successful in raising educational outcomes or improving labour market activity it is possible that beneficiaries may choose to move away from the area, leaving area level outcomes unchanged – worse, even, if the outward migration was selective. Of course, it is possible that we might prefer it if people who benefit from the ABI subsequently stayed in the neighbourhood. This is particularly the case if we believe that there are feedbacks from neighbourhood composition to individual outcomes. However, as discussed in Chapter 3, the evidence for such effects is weak, suggesting that improvements to individual outcomes should be seen as beneficial even if they are associated with out mobility from the neighbourhood.

The question raised by the evaluation of NDC – what constitutes success – is a slightly different version of this issue. If area level outcomes are what matters for policymakers then attracting in new households with 'better' socio-economic outcomes is viewed as a policy success – even if none of the existing residents benefit. In practice, this definition of success is often implicitly (or sometimes explicitly) predicated on a belief that mixing neighbourhoods is a desirable policy objective. Again, as discussed in Chapter 3, it is not clear that this is the case. Like most of us, policy-makers also tend to find it easier to think about (relatively simple) area outcomes than about (more complex) individual level outcomes, which need to allow for the fact that neighbourhood composition changes as a result of the intervention. In short, neighbourhood dynamics significantly complicate our attempts to understand the impact of ABIs aimed at improving household outcomes.

If there is some confusion around composition on ABIs aimed at house-holds, that confusion often becomes outright muddle when considering the impact of regeneration policies that are aimed at the built environ-ment or other neighbourhood characteristics. It is to this issue that we now turn.

ABIs Aimed at the Built Environment

This section is divided into two parts. First, we look at the effect of physical regeneration policies (henceforth 'regeneration') on the neighbourhoods they are implemented in. Second, we take a look at the city-wide effects of these policies though (a) improving the commercial space available and (b) attracting more skilled labour.

Neighbourhood effects

As discussed above, at their simplest, regeneration policies involve the upgrading of social housing provision for the poor. If government has relatively strong mechanisms for controlling who lives in the upgraded housing units, then urban economics provides little additional insight on the impact of these policies. In contrast, urban economics holds impor-tant lessons for situations where government improves either housing or the built environment at the neighbourhood level, in situations where it cannot directly control who lives in the improved neighbourhoods.

Because housing is durable, falling demand lowers prices (rather than immediately reducing supply) so housing is cheaper in less desirable areas of cities. Cheaper housing is relatively attractive to low-paid people – hence the sorting across neighbourhoods that we describe in detail in Chapter 3. Urban economics tells us that regeneration policy that directly affects the supply of housing in less desirable neighbourhoods – through social housing build, refurbishment or improvement programmes, for instance – will change prices and thus the composition of the neighbour-hood. Upgrading or improving transport links to poor neighbourhoods will have similar effects.

For example, increasing the supply of housing in poorer neighbourhoods will, all else equal, decrease the price of housing in the neighbourhood.

Thus increased supply of housing in unpopular locations reinforces relative house price effects and increases the over-representation of the low-skilled in the area. Offsetting this relies on the new housing somehow increasing the attractiveness of the neighbourhood (so that additional supply positively influences demand). This is possible if, for example, new housing is of higher quality or if it replaces derelict buildings.

Note, however, that if policy does succeed in improving the attractiveness of an area sufficiently that prices rise, then poorer families will eventually be priced out of the area as costs rise to reflect improved local amenities. For poorer families to gain from such price increases they must either be owner occupiers (so they get the capital gains from rising prices) or they must live in non-market (or social) housing where rents are not related to the quality of the neighbourhood (so they can benefit from the improved neighbourhood without having to pay higher rents). When these two conditions do not hold, the adverse price effects from neighbourhood improvements will eventually force poorer families out of the neighbourhood. This is also the self-reinforcing mechanism that underpins the dynamics of gentrification – if for some reason an area becomes more desirable, price rises change the neighbourhood composition in favour of wealthier families and this, in turn, makes the area more desirable, leading to further price rises (Ahlfeldt et al. 2013).

Aside from these issues relating to composition, many regeneration policies also rely on conventional wisdom that is largely untested. For example, in the UK as in many OECD countries, policy has placed strong emphasis on increasing densities and changing the composition of local housing to encourage income and tenure mixing. It is argued that higher densities support local shops and public transport. It is also claimed that higher densities are better for the environment. Income and tenure mixing are said to be more in keeping with historical patterns, to deliver benefits to poorer households and to improve the functioning of the neighbourhood (and by extrapolation the city itself). As we saw in Chapters 3 and 5, all of these claims are open to challenge and ignore the costs that come from mixing and higher densities. To recap the arguments we made in more detail there, spatial segregation by income is highly persistent and greater integration goes against historical trends, not with them. There is precious little hard evidence that mixed neighbourhoods deliver positive benefits to poorer residents and 'mixing' fails to take account of the fact that there are also costs (for example in the loss of retail services targeted at the poor). Richer individuals demonstrate strong preferences against mixing. Once again it is striking that policy has accepted one set of arguments (mixing good) without disentangling these effects and thinking through the implications for the functioning of the city.

For example, in disadvantaged areas planned mixing makes new developments less attractive to the higher skilled than they otherwise would be, which works against the objective of attracting higher-skilled residents to these developments. The strong emphasis on encouraging mixing through what gets built – especially in Britain by means of Section 106 Agreements requiring a significant proportion of 'affordable' social housing in new developments – has also meant that other methods for encouraging mixing – for example through the provision of public spaces, educational facilities and other amenities – have received much less attention, so that we have little idea of the relative merits of different interventions in achieving policy objectives, that is on the assumption that the policy priority is to achieve mixing irrespective of any evidence that this benefits poorer households.

Overall, the balance of evidence suggests that all else equal, dense mixed tenure housing is less popular. In Britain, as elsewhere, such developments can also be more expensive to build, particularly if social housing is built to similar standards as private or on previously derelict land that needs to be remediated. In addition the resulting multi-unit developments are also less popular with relatively wealthy households (Song and Knaap 2003). In short, when regeneration policy emphasises high density, mixed tenure, multi-unit housing on expensive to develop sites (as it has done in Britain for some time) it provides developments that are likely to be both relatively high cost and unpopular with the people who have a choice about their location (high-density student halls are a growing market in the UK, but they are definitely not mixed tenure). Ironically, when these higher density developments are created by the demolition of existing housing these policies often prove unpopular with poorer residents who already live in these neighbourhoods (Power and Houghton 2010). This is particularly true when policy involves government identifying specific areas to be subject to redevelopment with little regard to small-scale spatial variations within those neighbourhoods.

An area where more evidence is still needed is on the role of the housing market in linking general income inequality with residential segregation. Research to date has touched on these issues and, as we argue in Chapter 3, the existing evidence supports the idea that patterns of residential segregation as well as their incidence are largely a spatial manifestation of societal income inequality. But many questions remain. Do trends in residential segregation and its incidence really follow those in personal income inequality, and is this played out through increasing polarisation of housing prices across communities?

We also need to know more about the role of social housing and affordable housing in this process. Do traditional forms of social housing exacerbate inequalities by concentrating the poor in particular areas – as is the case in London – or would the market equilibrium without social housing be even more polarised? There is much more scope now to answer many of these questions by linking house price data, information on earnings and planning outcomes at small geographic scales. These data potentially allow us to observe how the dispersion in housing prices moves with changes in local income and its distribution, or how prices change and residential composition changes with construction of new housing developments or the destruction of older concentrated forms of social housing (for example tower blocks).

In addition, there would be real benefits to both our understanding of how cities function and how policy could best improve outcomes if there was more research on the benefits of living in more specialised neighbourhoods – both of the 'consumption/quality of life' and 'production/life chance' types. This is a tough research challenge, made more difficult in the past by the lack of geographical identifiers for individuals' place of residence or workplace in those large-scale datasets available to the research community. The availability of these identifiers in new administrative and survey datasets does offer some way forward, though distinguishing reliably between 'causal' impacts of neighbourhoods from effects of residential sorting (on unrecorded personal characteristics) still remains problematic.

So, while ABIs aimed at the built environment provide public goods such as social housing and public spaces that have a (possibly large) consumption value, there is no compelling evidence of any further indirect impact on other economic outcomes and hence the objectives of narrowing the economic gap between disadvantaged individuals and the rest. Indeed, in a world where people can sort across neighbourhoods, these public goods do not necessarily end up benefiting the intended targets. As we discussed above, these consequences of sorting also extend to the impact of ABI interventions aimed at households or at firms.

City-wide effects

We now turn to the issue of the extent to which physical regeneration may play a wider role in improving economic performance at the city level. We start by considering the impact of policies aimed at improving the commercial property on offer before considering the role of improvements to the physical environment in attracting higher skilled workers to a city. This allows us to touch on some of the broader policy interventions that might be used to target skilled workers and highlight further lessons from the economic literature (drawing partly on the material presented in Chapters 2 and 3).

(a) Improved commercial space   In many declining cities, authorities invest considerable resources in trying to improve commercial developments. Some of these interventions have been 'transformative' in terms of both the quality of the individual developments and the more general improvements in the public realm associated with them. Why, then, do cities that have undertaken these developments continue to underperform on so many headline economic indicators? One possibility is that 'more needs to be done' (Tyler 2011). It would appear that this is the interpretation favoured by a large number of local policymakers. If this explanation is the right one, then the main challenge for local policymakers is often the absence of funding to help support development.

Before reaching this conclusion, however, it is important to assess alternative explanations as to why a significantly improved built environment has not translated into better economic outcomes. One worrying possibility is that traditional regeneration policy may have overstated the extent to which improvements to buildings and increases in commercial supply have a beneficial impact on local economic performance.

As a result of the underlying structural weaknesses of poorly performing cities the demand for commercial space in the city as a whole is relatively inelastic (that is, demand for space from firms is not very responsive to the price of that space). At the same time, high vacancy rates and availability of land for development mean that the supply of space is relatively elastic (that is increases in price tend to feed through to a reasonably large increase in available space). In such markets, further expansions in supply (either through new development or upgrading of stock) will tend to lead to area-wide falls in price rather than increases in occupancy. In contrast, in booming areas (for example, in the UK, London and the South East) supply is relatively inelastic. In such markets, expansions in supply tend to lead to increased occupancy, rather than lower prices. Of course, falls in price would be desirable if firms were likely to be attracted to lower price sites. But it is clear that already low prices, by UK standards, are insufficient to offset other structural disadvantages firms face when locating in poorly performing cities. At the same time, as discussed in detail in Chapters 4 and 5, costs are relatively high by international standards. In short, the ability of general land supply increases to further increase the amount of local economic activity in poorly performing cities is limited.

If falls in price are insufficient to attract firms, it is still possible that firms may be very responsive to improvements in the quality of the stock and other improvements in the general built environment associated with new developments. Indeed, at small spatial scales (for example shopping centres), local demand can be very responsive to improvements because firms can move to the improved location from elsewhere in the region.

That is, such schemes can generate high demand responses because they displace activity from yet to be improved sites elsewhere in the city (or broader region). But at larger, city or regional scales, such displacement is essentially zero-sum, so strong demand effects are highly unlikely to materialise (they require displacement from other parts of the country or internationally). In short, region-wide increases in supply will tend to drive down regional prices and mainly reshuffle employment from existing to improved sites. This suggests that schemes like Newcastle waterfront may be good for the city but ineffective (or even detrimental) for the wider region. It also helps explain why such schemes are popular with individual local authorities and are heavily pushed by individual developers. Note that arguments about the need for the 'right type of development' to attract high value added activity similarly overstate the responsiveness of demand with respect to quality and ignore the displacement issues high-lighted above. The deadweight cost of such policies is likely to be substantial (as improvements are costly) and little new employment is generated. The use of occupancy rates to assess the success of supported developments tends to disguise this effect because it ignores the (unintended) side-effect of increased vacancies in existing sites.

To summarise: in strong urban economies, additional commercial floor space may have positive effects (although in most cases you would expect supply to be provided by the private sector subject to the problems of tight constraints discussed in Chapters 4 and 5). In weaker urban economies, the overall problem is one of demand rather than supply. New or improved office space is certainly likely to be occupied (especially if rents are subsidised), but this is likely to be mostly at the expense of rising vacancy rates in other (non-improved) commercial buildings in the wider area. Of course, some additional employment may be generated (it is conceivable, for example, that foreign investors are very sensitive to building quality) but most of the effect is likely to come from displacement from other nearby locations. As with EZs more generally, shuffling employment around may be a useful policy outcome in some circumstances, but the effect on the city economy as a whole are likely to be extremely limited. Consistent with this, in preliminary work looking at the impact of commercial buildings as part of the UK's Single Regeneration Budget, Gibbons et al. (2013) provide evidence that new buildings do shift employment, but with no measurable effect on employment rates for nearby residents.[10]

---

[10] A similar effect occurs for residential development to the extent that new higher-end developments chase a small and fairly fixed population of higher income households. That said, in contrast to commercial development, where we care mostly about the impact of

Area-based interventions that facilitate redevelopment may provide important public goods. They help improve the built environment and the quality of the housing stock. They may help improve affordability to the extent they offset supply constraints. Often, however, the case for such intervention is based on arguments about likely improvements in local economic performance, not these public good aspects. This economic case is much weaker than traditionally supposed, suggesting that the balance of existing expenditure may have been too heavily skewed towards policy intervention in land markets as a means of improving local economic performance in declining places. In seeking to determine funding priorities it is important to recognise that the historical focus on supply-side issues in land markets as a means of reversing decline may have distracted attention and resources from areas such as education and skills, that represent far more fundamental supply-side barriers to economic growth in poorly performing areas.

(b) Attracting skilled labour   As we discussed in Chapter 2, places with large numbers of skilled people do better, respond better to shocks, and so on. This has led to a wave of policy prescriptions based on attracting skilled people as a means of improving the fortunes of poorer performing cities. This raises two central questions – how might this be achieved and what are the implications for existing residents?

Regeneration of city centres to improve city living is one commonly suggested policy lever. We know of no rigorous evaluation of this policy approach (and, indeed, it may be very difficult to rigorously evaluate the impact). But, as with ABIs, basic reasoning from urban economics urges caution that the regeneration potential of city centre living should not be exaggerated. In the UK, at least for some cities, there has certainly been an increase in the number of highly skilled people living in previously run down city centres. Evidence from the US and elsewhere suggests that the same is true of some cities in many developed countries (see, for example, Rybczynski 2009). This increased demand for city centre living likely reflects a number of factors: improvements in levels of crime, the built environment and other amenities as well as the fact that structural shifts in the economy have shifted employment back to city centres in activities that benefit from agglomeration economies (see Chapter 2).

building quality on output and employment, for housing we care about quality and affordability per se. For housing, supply responses at the middle to upper end of the market should help improve area-wide quality and drive down the area-wide price of land to make housing more affordable. In areas with critical skill shortages they could even help with labour supply since the price of housing and the quality of the environment is a significant factor in migration decisions.

Other demand-side factors may also play a role. In the UK, for example, it has been suggested that four additional demand-side factors may matter: empty-nesters choosing city centres for consumption reasons, people delaying forming families, 'power couples' maximising job choices and increased participation in higher education (Costa and Kahn 2000; Nathan and Urwin 2006). For some cities (for example Leeds, London, Manchester and Newcastle) the result has been that central locations have attracted more skilled people. In all of these places, government-funded interventions in improving the built environment have clearly played some role in driving or reinforcing this trend.

In the majority of places, however, central locations remain highly unattractive because the amenities they offer in terms of accessibility to employment and consumption are not sufficient to offset other negative factors. This is particularly true for families as single-family homes remain much more popular than any of the multi-family urban housing options (as we know from the kind of hedonic analysis described in Chapter 3). These preferences mean that while city-centre improvements may bring benefits to existing residents (including the poor) the usefulness of this policy as a means of attracting highly skilled workers to declining places is certainly overstated.

Moving beyond city centres, it is certainly the case that cities that offer improved amenities will be more attractive to the higher skilled. This has led some to suggest the provision of cultural amenities as a mechanism for attracting high-skilled workers (Florida 2002). Again, rigorous evaluation of the impacts of doing so are in seriously short supply (see, for example, discussion in Nathan 2007; Storper and Scott 2009; Nathan 2012). Aside from these consumption amenities, the (hedonic pricing) evidence points to willingness to pay for easy access to jobs, better education, lower crime, more open space and good transportation. There is also evidence from both the US and Europe that climate provides an important environmental quality – but this is not easily manipulated by policy. Recent policy in Britain has emphasised density, public transport and spaces (for example parks) to supply the latter two amenities. Public open space is important in dense neighbourhoods (because private open space is minimal) and good public transport is one reason why low-income households (without access to a car) favour larger cities. Unfortunately, this does not change the fact that willingness to pay is higher for private space and transportation. Of course, people are willing to trade private space for good access to jobs and amenities. When cities can offer good access to jobs and other amenities (as in London) then these benefits can outweigh those of more private space and better transportation in the suburbs. Such places will tend to be higher density and this higher density may then offer additional benefits.

Note, however, that the causality runs from attractiveness to density. Simply increasing density in unpopular places is unlikely to deliver benefits that outweigh the disadvantages. Emphasis on brownfield and higher densities in low-amenity locations works against the objective of attracting the high-skilled.

An alternative to trying to attract skilled people through better amenities is to attract them through lower house prices for big houses in nice neighbourhoods. In the US, and elsewhere, one can certainly think of places (for example Atlanta) that have successfully pursued this approach to attracting more skilled workers. As we saw in Chapters 4 and 5, however, this is not an approach that has been used in Britain with its strong restrictions on housing supply, especially in greener locations and at lower densities. Unfortunately, conventional regeneration policies have often exacerbated these problems. National policies that place a strong emphasis on brownfield land, high density and mixed use make new development relatively expensive and lead to characteristics that are not popular with many households. As declining places have a relatively abundant supply of housing, net additions that follow these policies also exacerbate problems of lower house prices in the area. When there are no net additions but redevelopment improves the overall quality of stock, there will be a positive effect on prices (from the composition effect of improved quality) that offset the negative effects. When development follows demolition these policies contribute to the dissatisfaction that comes from local disruption, if new build replaces housing that had characteristics that are preferred by most households (for example lower density owner-occupied terraces).

So far, we have focused on amenities and costs of living as an area where policy may affect the relative attractiveness of a place to skilled workers. The alternative, of course, is to consider the other part of the trade-off and to focus on increasing incomes by raising the demand for high skilled workers in declining places. Indeed, some authors have argued that focusing on costs and amenities is pointless in the absence of jobs (for example, Storper and Scott, 2009). Unfortunately, however, the evidence suggests that it can be difficult for policy to increase demand for high skilled workers in struggling places. To do this, it somehow needs to increase productivity or make an area more attractive to firms that employ high skilled workers. Neither of these is easy to achieve as we discussed above, in the context of ABIs and we also discuss further below.

Even if policy is successful in attracting high-skilled workers, does this necessarily improve outcomes for the lower skilled? As we saw in Chapter 3, positive spillovers from high- to low-skilled workers are limited – seemingly absent – at the neighbourhood level. At the city level, however, there is some evidence of beneficial spillovers from high- to low-skilled, at least in terms of productivity or wages (see for example Kaplanis (2010) for the UK; Moretti (2012) for the US). Urban economics reminds us, however, that we also need to think about the effects on costs of living that might offset these productivity benefits. If policies aimed at particular types of people are successful in attracting those with higher incomes, and if the productivity benefits are not large, then rising house prices may mean that lower skilled people are overall worse off. That is, in the absence of strong spillovers from skilled to unskilled at the city level, policies to attract skilled people may improve area averages while making the lower skilled worse off. One needs only to look at deprived areas within London to see that these negative cost effects can be significant.

One final argument that attracting high-skilled workers might benefit the poor relies on the idea that it allows for local redistribution from rich to poor. Once again, urban economics urges caution: first, because the scope for redistribution is limited by mobility, and second, because attracting skilled workers may change the balance of power away from politicians who favour the poor (Glaeser and Schleifer 2005).

In short, using physical or cultural amenities to attract skilled people has been pushed by a number of policy advocates and has proved highly appealing to policymakers. However, it is hard to see the policy succeeding for any but a small number of places that are already attractive to skilled people. Even when successful the benefits of the policy to existing (poorer) residents in declining places are almost certainly overstated and possibly negative.

4. IMPROVING AREA PRODUCTIVITY AND ATTRACTING FIRMS

If policies aimed at directly attracting skilled workers are difficult to implement and only of limited relevance for many places, what about policies aimed at attracting firms or improving area productivity? We have already considered the role of (selective) financial assistance and improved commercial property offers in Section 2. Here, we consider two other popular measures, starting with policy interventions that target clusters and then considering the provision of infrastructure.

Clusters

Many of the firm-specific measures that we have discussed so far can be applied either horizontally (focusing on the general conditions affecting industry – for example the supply of quality office space) or vertically (targeting particular firms and sectors – for example selective financial assistance). In contrast, cluster policies combine elements of the horizontal and vertical with measures focused on particular places but targeting groups of co-located firms that are in competitive/collaborative relationships. Such policies may include fiscal incentives aimed at particular types of firms (for example support for high tech) or commercial land use provision that is similarly targeted (for example the provision of science parks). But the range of interventions can go far beyond this to include, for example, decisions around universities, research funding and government employment. At the time of writing a number of major new initiatives, including Regional Innovation Clusters in the US, the European Commission's adoption of 'smart specialisation' regional policies, and (closer to home) the UK's Tech City initiative, all have strong cluster components.

In their overview of the field, Nathan and Overman (forthcoming) pick out two important paradoxes about cluster policy. First, as discussed in Chapter 2, there is certainly good empirical evidence that agglomeration and co-location matter a great deal in understanding the economic performance of firms and cities. But in moving from this general observation to specific policy recommendations, advocates of cluster policies draw on conceptual frameworks which are very fuzzy – both in terms of providing a tool for analysis and for developing specific policy interventions (a point echoed by Chatterji et al. 2013).This would not matter so much if we had good evidence on which policy interventions were effective. But this brings us to the second paradox (cluster policies appear to be generally ineffective and have been robustly debunked in the academic literature) see Martin and Sunley (2003) and Duranton (2011) – yet remain very popular with policymakers.

Even if cluster policies could be made more effective, urban economics once again urges caution on their likely impact. Just as with other policies to attract highly skilled workers to an area it is not clear to what extent existing workers benefit (for reasons we described above). When local cluster policy targets 'high-tech' employment, two additional complications arise. First, if the aim of policy is to densify activity, this may improve the level of knowledge spillovers within the cluster; but by encouraging entry it will also increase costs and competitors for incumbent firms. Greater competition may be innovation-enhancing on the aggregate (Aghion et al. 2009), but has substantial distributional consequences. Second, if policymakers aim to create new clusters, there is the additional complication that spreading out high-tech employment across several locations may be bad for innovation at a national level. Loss of concentration may affect both knowledge production and the operation of highly specialised job markets. The evidence suggests these benefits are important which means that spatial redistribution may end up having negative effects on innovation.

While cluster policies tend to target particular firms or sectors, an alternative approach is to try to improve the 'business environment' with the hope that this will improve overall productivity of all sectors. One way of doing this is through policies – such as business support and mentoring – targeted directly at trying to improve the way in which firms are run or to encourage entrepreneurial activity and start-ups. Other direct support might come in the form of funding for research and development (R&D) programmes that try to make firms more innovative.

Because of the quasi-public goods nature of R&D – some of the benefits may spill over to other firms or people who do not bear all the costs of the initial R&D – economic principles provide some support for the principle of public subsidy to R&D (Jaffe 1996). However, empirical evidence on the success of many of these policies is mixed. R&D subsidies appear to have positive impacts on innovation rates but much direct public support for R&D has involved directing funds to areas identified by public agencies as future 'winners' but in practice anything but (Lerner 2009; Acemoglu et al. 2013). Research remains to some extent something to support in general – so there are many initiatives – and then winners can emerge from that process in the appropriate institutional and financial setting (Rodrik 2004).

Many public efforts aimed at directly boosting entrepreneurship have failed. The same is true for many publically supported schemes that seek to provide financial support (either directly, or through venture capital type arrangements). Lerner (2009) provides a highly readable review of the existing evidence. Somewhat surprisingly, urban economics researchers have only recently begun to focus directly on questions of entrepreneurship and the city. Similarly, while the link between innovation and agglomeration has long been recognised the policy implications of this have received surprisingly little attention in the urban economics literature.

Infrastructure

In contrast, urban economics has much more to say on the impact of improving area 'fundamentals' that indirectly feed through into improved productivity. One major focus is on improving the level of skills, discussed below. Another is on the role of improving infrastructure. This is the issue which we briefly consider here. There are two ways of structuring our thinking about the likely impact of infrastructure investments. The first views public sector infrastructure investment as providing a capital stock that is complementary to private sector physical capital (that is machines and buildings) and to human capital (that is skills). The second thinks of infrastructure as providing a network that connects different places so that public sector investment reduces the transport costs between places. There are equally two basic types of policies: the first is that policy can find ways of increasing the 'quantity' of infrastructure; the second is that policy can find ways to improve the efficiency with which existing infrastructure is used. Because of the nature of congestion (of transport, communications networks or environmental 'goods') – it represents a problem of market failure – so urban economics may have a more clear-cut message on the second of these two policy types than the first.

The first way of thinking about infrastructure suggests that providing additional infrastructure will always improve area level productivity. However, it is important to remember that infrastructure can be very expensive and that the productivity benefits might well be outweighed by the costs of infrastructure provision. A good example of this problem would be Detroit's People Mover.[11] But everyone can think of brand new roads, railways, and so on that were very expensive but are underused. This problem is particularly acute when public infrastructure is used to try to turn around declining places. One of the basic insights of traditional (or neo-classical) growth theory is that public and private sector investments in physical capital are likely to be subject to diminishing marginal returns. This means that, when a place has lots of physical capital per person adding extra physical capital will not do much to increase output per person (that is productivity). Because infrastructure is durable, places that have seen stagnant or declining population and falling employment will tend to have large amounts of capital relative to employment. The concrete manifestation of this, when it comes to infrastructure, are relatively low congestion levels on the transport network in poorly performing cities. Basic economics tells us that adding further transport investment in those places will not do much to improve productivity. In contrast, investing in congested and growing places will deliver much higher returns because the congestion reflects the fact that these places have low (effective) infrastructure capital per person.

Of course, dealing with congestion does not necessarily require new infrastructure in congested and growing places. Along with most urban economists we would also advocate the application of congestion charging in a way which directly reflects the marginal social costs of using networks (transport most commonly but with applications elsewhere). The economic case for this is well developed (for a recent statement see

---

[11] http://en.wikipedia.org/wiki/Detroit_People_Mover.

Eddington (2006)) but the politics remain very challenging. Attempts to date to introduce congestion charging have mainly been blunt instruments such as London's toll system (whose zonal charge is unable to reflect actual congestion in different areas at a particular (peak) time). Technically it would not be challenging to develop systems which much more accurately required payment for actual congestion, but politically this is very difficult. In part at least this seems to be because of the unwillingness of many finance ministries to tolerate 'hypothecated' taxes; that is, taxes the revenues of which are applied to specific defined uses. Congestion charges would be much more politically acceptable if citizens thought that the revenues raised would be applied to improving network capacity. The attraction of congestion charges is that they would ensure more efficient use of transport systems in just those places where transport capacity is economically most useful.

The second way of thinking about infrastructure – as a network that connects different places – provides more mixed messages, particularly when it comes to better connecting rich and poor regions. One way to think about these types of transport investment is to view enhanced integration as a way of increasing the effective size of the local economies that benefit from the new infrastructure. As a larger local economy means higher agglomeration economies this should help firms be more productive. It is for this reason that some commentators focus on improving transport between richer and poorer cities as a means of driving growth in the poorer cities. Unfortunately, there is one important caveat to this conclusion – as considered in detail in the New Economic Geography models first developed by Paul Krugman, lower transport costs change the balance between agglomeration and congestion forces in ways that may encourage firms to move into the richer market and serve their customers from there.

This 'two way roads problem'[12] is poorly understood by many policymakers, leading them to focus solely on the benefits to the poorer market of better connections rather than thinking through the 'threats' these pose from greater competition. Recent discussion of Britain's proposed new High Speed 2 line between London, Birmingham, Manchester and Leeds provides a good case study of this effect in action. That particular scheme also highlights the importance of distinguishing between situations where the improvement in connection is large (for example a previously very badly served place is added to the network) and those, like HS2, where

---

[12] Originally and most elegantly put by the great German spatial economist Launhardt in 1885: 'the best protection for a backward region is a bad road'. Thanks to Professor J. Bröcker for this quote.

the effect represents a more marginal improvement with respect to existing networks. For example, looking at two completely new stops on a new high-speed line between Cologne and Frankfurt, Ahlfeldt and Fedderson (2010) find quite large positive productivity effects. In contrast, Gibbons et al. (2012a) could find little evidence of strong productivity effects when looking at the impact of all the main road network and of road construction schemes carried out in Britain between 1998 and 2007.

More empirical work remains to be done on the impact of network improvements on poorer regions. Theoretical analysis certainly urges caution. For example, modelling by Baldwin et al. (2005) strongly suggests that focusing on intra-city transport schemes may often be more beneficial than focusing on inter-city projects. But remember, from our discussion above, that even these schemes may not deliver large benefits in declining cities that already have high amounts of infrastructure capital per person. In short, while infrastructure investment may be vitally important for growing cities, its role in reversing decline is easily overstated.

5.   PUBLIC SECTOR RELOCATION

An alternative to trying to improve local employment via productivity improvements as a result of infrastructure provision or cluster promotion is to use public sector relocation to achieve a similar objective. One well-known conceptual problem with this approach is that public sector employment in disadvantaged areas may crowd out private sector employment (particularly if pay in the public sector is set nationally). Until recently, we had little if any evidence on how these two offsetting forces played out in practice. In a recent paper, however, Faggio and Overman (2013) look at local authority employment in the early to mid-2000s to figure out what, if any, impact public sector employment has on private sector employment. Looking at British data for a relatively short period of time (2003–07) they find that growing public sector employment has little impact on overall private sector employment. But this does not mean public sector employment has no effects. Estimates suggest that each 100 extra public sector jobs in a local authority 'creates' 50 additional jobs in (non-tradable) services, but 'destroys' 40 jobs in manufacturing. In short, increasing public sector employment is bad for local manufacturing, but good for local services.

This difference makes intuitive sense. Local restaurants and shops benefit from the spending of public sector workers, local cleaning firms benefit from demand from organisations that employ those workers. Neither public sector workers nor organisations buy much from local manufacturing firms. There are at least two possible channels that explain the negative effect on manufacturing. First, increasing local public sector employment pushes up wages and house prices. This is bad news if you are a local manufacturing firm trying to compete with China. Second, higher public sector pay attracts away good administrators, accountants and entrepreneurs who would otherwise work in the private sector. Again, this is bad news for local manufacturing. Faggio and Overman (2013) cannot say which of those channels are at work, but anecdotal evidence suggests that both probably play some role. Over a longer time period, 1999–2007, different (slightly weaker) data suggests the negative effects on manufacturing are even stronger (they lose about 80 jobs for every additional 100 public sector workers). Again, this makes sense – the channels through which manufacturing gets hurt take time to work through, while the loss of local manufacturing employment offsets the increase in public sector employment so there no longer a beneficial effect on local services. In short, over longer time periods public sector employment may crowd out private sector employment. More work is needed on the role of public sector employment as a prop to disadvantaged areas. But as the Lyons and Smith reviews make clear, local pay setting is crucial to realising any benefits. Faggio (2013) provides further discussion, finding that the net employment gains from the Lyons Review were very small, with significant displacement effects.

6.   IMPROVING THE LOCAL SKILLS BASE

We can think of traditional regional development and regeneration policies as targeting negative area effects in disadvantaged places. As discussed above low house prices mean a disproportionate number of low-skilled people live in these places. Instead of trying to negate area effects, policy could focus instead on changing skill composition either through increasing skills of existing residents or by attracting new higher-skilled people. We have already discussed the issues around attracting more skilled workers and saw that there are questions about the extent to which this kind of policy benefits existing residents. In contrast, if policy is focused on existing residents then the main insight from urban economics is that successful policy may lead people to move away, so what is good for the individual is not necessarily good for the area. We discussed this issue above, which leaves the main question: what should policy do?

From a spatial perspective there are several open questions relating to education and skills policy. Should we better join up skills policy (sometimes devolved) and employment policy (often not devolved)? For example, could there be better coordination between work programmes and education programmes, particularly for people frequently shifting employment status? Should skills policy be devolved and providers incentivised to respond to local demand or should the focus be on skills? This question of the local demand responsiveness of policy is a poorly understood issue. In many circumstance there is an (implicit) bias towards addressing local sector skill needs. However, we do not know if this is best for individuals. Who should and how should we deliver and fund local training? As discussed above, a central issue is that people may move elsewhere once trained. This has implications for who should pay for funding (it argues against purely local funding) and also suggests local policy-makers may not have strong incentives to improve individual skills. This is another good example of an issue where focusing on area outcomes is a very poor way to assess policy.

Turning from skills to education, similar questions can be asked about the best way of improving schooling outcomes in poorer areas. A key question is the role of school system reform versus extra expenditure. There is evidence that a pupil 'premium' attached to poor pupils would help to address inequalities because between LA funding is more redistributive than within LA funding. At larger spatial scales this may be less of an issue (as redistribution occurs via LA funding). There is also some evidence that attracting higher quality teachers would enhance outcomes (Marshall 2013). Declining areas have an advantage as national pay scales and low house prices mean they pay high real wages but this appears to be insufficient to offset the negative non-pecuniary costs (for example stress) of teaching in deprived areas. The evidence on a link between choice and achievement (which would be addressed by the coalition government's academies and free school policy) is weaker.

In short, while we have some reasonable evidence on the effectiveness of particular forms of intervention (see, for example, the evidence summaries provided by the Educational Endowment Foundation) we have very limited understanding of what role, if any, local flexibility in improving education and skills might play in improving outcomes. Indeed, as we showed in Chapter 7, these uncertainties over the benefits of decentralisation extend to a huge range of issues. It is for this reason that we believe that little progress can be made on the abstract question of the appropriate degree of decentralisation. Instead, we feel that future work should focus on understanding what kind of policy interventions work in particular contexts (such as skills and transport provision) and then understanding what kind of arrangements are most appropriate for delivering effective interventions.

7. ENCOURAGING LABOUR MARKET ACTIVITY AND MOBILITY

Shifting our focus from the impact of policy on places to the impact of policy on people raises the issue of how best to encourage greater labour market participation and whether to facilitate more mobility from declining places to more successful ones. As we discussed in Chapter 2, any attempt to encourage greater mobility also raises the highly controversial question of how best to 'manage decline'.

Urban economics gives us some idea of the channels, challenges and difficulties involved. For example, we saw in Chapters 4 and 5 that planning can increase house prices. In turn, high house prices act as a very significant barrier to migration. Social, cultural and family attachments to particular places are, clearly, often very important as are financial constraints on moving. But high house price differentials are arguably the largest economic barrier to migration from declining to more successful places. Economic theory tells us that moving from a declining to a more successful area improves labour market outcomes at the expense of higher cost of living: it also identifies two changes that can help address this barrier. First, increase the supply of housing in successful places. We dealt with these issues in Chapter 2 in our discussion on 'building on success'. Second, remove institutional barriers to moving and working (for example for those in the social housing sector).

Even if government could encourage increased housing supply in more successful areas, however, it would still be important to understand how benefits, social housing and local conditions interact to affect the incentives to migrate and to work. High worklessness rates in some London wards remind us that labour market problems remain an issue even in our most successful cities. We need to do more to understand how the benefit and social housing systems interact with local economic conditions to affect incentives to work. These problems are clearly more acute in areas where private sector housing costs are high relative to the non-market sector.

Public policy would also need to address the negative consequences of out-mobility. The policy changes outlined above would allow households to move away from declining cities if they wanted to, which is likely to exacerbate economic and social problems for at least some (possibly many) of those who stay. Falling house prices and vacant properties are a visible manifestation of this problem. The impact on local labour markets is harder to gauge. While the evidence on agglomeration economies suggests that local employment has some effect on local wages, it is easy to overstate the magnitude of these effects. In declining places the big problem is a lack of employment opportunities relative to population. As we have argued above, traditional policy has not proved very successful at addressing the problem of a lack of demand for workers, suggesting that some shift of emphasis to the supply (that is population) side of this imbalance may be warranted.

8.   CONCLUSIONS

This chapter challenges many aspects of the 'place-based' approach to helping declining places. It argues that focusing public expenditure on 'turning around' the economies of declining places has had little success: and specifically, many popular policy interventions have had little economic effect.

Given the current need to cut public expenditure, we have to identify priority areas of expenditure and consider more radical changes – in areas such as land use planning – to help address issues arising from spatial disparities. We have argued that these interventions should be judged on the extent to which they benefit people living in declining places. We have also argued that urban economics provides plenty of theory and evidence to help improve policy making in this area.

What, then, should be the main focus of urban policy in tackling decline and promoting growth? Given what we know about the causes of spatial disparities, and the effectiveness and impact of different policies we have argued that the high level approach needs to be on improving skills in declining places, and on investing in infrastructure and housing in more successful places.

In terms of skills, we have argued that the focus should be on increasing individual skill levels rather than increasing area-level skills (through attracting higher skilled people, for example). On infrastructure and housing we have argued that, in many countries, there needs to be far better recognition that land use policy is an important factor in urban economic performance. Perhaps more controversially, given what we know about the causes of spatial disparities and the relative effectiveness of policy, we would argue for a greater focus on encouraging labour market activity and removing barriers to mobility. In practice, this will require a better understanding of the three-way interaction between the benefit system and the housing and labour markets and the expansion of housing supply and reduction of costs of living in relatively successful places. We discussed some of the ways in which the latter could be achieved in Chapter 6. It will also require serious thinking about how to manage the negative consequences of mobility away from 'declining places' for those who stay in those places.

Beyond these broad level prescriptions, and some more detailed recommendations discussed in previous chapters, we know depressingly little about the detailed interventions required to help achieve urban policy objectives. Some of this reflects the complexity of formulating good urban policy. But equally as important is the appalling track record of governments (of all kinds) in effectively evaluating the impact of different urban policy interventions. As we have argued elsewhere (Overman 2013) effective evaluation of urban policy is possible. It certainly requires patience and also a recognition that evaluation needs to be embedded at the policy design stage. Unfortunately, these requirements are infrequently met in practice, with the result that much official evaluation of government policy boils down to little more than self-justification. Theory and evidence provided by urban economic researchers can help us formulate better urban policy, but only rigorous evaluation will tell us whether this policy ultimately helps achieve our objectives.

REFERENCES

Acemoglu, Daron, Ufuk Akcigit, Nicholas Bloom and William R. Kerr. 2013. 'Innovation, Reallocation and Growth', National Bureau of Economic Research Working Paper 18993. Cambridge, MA: NBER.

Aghion, Philippe, Richard Blundell, Rachel Griffith, Peter Howitt and Susanne Prantl. 2009. 'The effects of entry on incumbent innovation and productivity'. *Review of Economics and Statistics* 91, 20–32.

Ahlfeldt, G.M. and A. Fedderson. 2010. 'From Periphery to Core: Economic Adjustments to High Speed Rail'. Available at: http://eprints.lse.ac.uk/29430/, LSE and University of Hamburg (unpublished).

Ahlfeldt, Gabriel M., Kristoffer Möller, Sevrin Waights and Nicolai Wendland. 2013. 'Game of Zones: The Economics of Conservation Areas', SERC Discussion Paper 143. London: SERC.

Baldwin, Richard, Rikard Forslid, Philippe Martin, Gianmarco Ottaviano and Frederic Robert-Nicoud. 2005. *Economic Geography and Public Policy*. Princeton, NJ: Princeton University Press.

Bartik, T. 2004. 'Economic Development', in *Managememnt Policies in Local Government Finance*. Kalamazoo, MI: W.E. Upjohn Institute for Employment Research, pp. 355–390.

Bolster, Anne, Simon Burgess, Ron Johnston, Kelvyn Jones, Carol Propper and Rebecca Sarker. 2007. 'Neighbourhoods, households and income dynamics: A semi-parametric investigation of neighbourhood effects'. *Journal of Economic Geography* 7, 1–38.

Busso, M., J. Gregory and P. Kline. 2013. 'Assessing the incidence and efficiency of a prominent place based policy'. *American Economic Review Papers and Proceedings* 103, 897–947.

Chatterji, A., E.L. Glaeser et al. 2013. 'Clusters of Entrepreneurship and Innovation', National Bureau of Economic Research Working Paper Series, No. 19013. Cambridge, MA: NBER.

Combes, Pierre-Philippe, Gilles Duranton and Laurent Gobillon. 2008. 'Spatial wage disparities: Sorting matters!' *Journal of Urban Economics* 63, 723–742.

Costa, Dora L. and Matthew E. Kahn. 2000. 'Power couples: changes in the locational choice of the college educated, 1940–1990'. *Quarterly Journal of Economics* 115, 1287–1315.

Criscuolo, Chiara, Ralf Martin, Henry G. Overman and John Van Reenen. 2012. 'The Causal Effects of an Industrial Policy', SERC Discussion Paper 0098. London: SERC.

Duranton, Gilles. 2011. 'California dreamin': the feeble case for cluster policies'. *Review of Economic Analysis* 3, 3–45.

Eddington, R. 2006. 'The Eddington Transport Study: The Case for Action'. London, HM Treasury on behalf of HMSO.

Einio, Elias and H.G. Overman. 2013. 'The Effects of Spatially Targeted Enterprise Initiatives: Evidence from UK LEGI', manuscript, LSE.

Faggio, Giulia. 2013. 'Relocation of Public Sector Workers: The local labour market impact of the Lyons Review', in *ESSLE 2013*. Amersee: IZA.

Faggio, Giulia and Henry Overman. 2013. 'The Effect of Public Sector Employment on Local Labour Markets', SERC Discussion Paper 111. London: SERC.

Florida, Richard. 2002. *The Rise of the Creative Class*. New York: Basic Books.

Gibbons, S. and H. Overman. 2012. 'The Decomposition of Variance into Individual and Group Components with an Application to Area Disparities'. Mimeo. London: LSE.

Gibbons, Stephen, Henry G. Overman and Guilherme Resende. 2011. 'Real Earnings Disparities in Britain', SERC Discussion Paper 0065. London: SERC

Gibbons, S., T. Lyytikäinen, H.G. Overman and R. Sanchis-Guarner. 2012a. 'New Road Infrastructure: The Effects on Firms', SERC Discussion Paper 0117. London: SERC.

Gibbons, Stephen, Sandra McNally and H.G. Overman. 2012b. 'Review of Government Evaluations: A Report for the NAO'. London: LSE.

Gibbons, S., H.G. Overman and P. Pelkonen. 2013. 'Area disparities in Britain: understanding the contribution of people vs. place through variance decompositions'. *Oxford Bulletin of Economics and Statistics*. Doi: 10.1111/obes.12043.

Glaeser, E. and A. Schleifer. 2005. 'The curly effect: the economics of shaping the electorate'. *Journal of Law, Economics and Organization* 21, 1–19.

Hanson, A. and S. Rohlin. 2013. 'Do spatially targeted redevelopment programs spillover?' *Regional Science and Urban Economics* 43, 86–100.

Jaffe, A. 1996. 'Economic analysis of research spillovers: implications for the Advanced Technology Program'. *Economic Analysis* 1–14.

Kaplanis, Ioannis. 2010. 'Wage Effects from Changes in Local Human Capital in Britain', SERC Discussion Paper 0039. London: SERC.

Lerner, Josh. 2009. *Boulevard of Broken Dreams*. Princeton, NJ: Princeton University Press.

Marshall, P. 2013. *The Tail: How England's Schools Fail One Child in Five and What Can Be Done*. London: Profile.

Martin, Ron and Peter Sunley. 2003. 'Deconstructing clusters: chaotic concept or policy panacea?' *Journal of Economic Geography* 3, 5–35.

Mayer, T., F. Mayneris and L. Py. 2013. 'The impact of Urban Enterprise Zones on establishment location decisions: evidence from French ZFUs', CEPR Discussion Paper 9074, London: CEPR.

Moretti, E. 2010. 'Local multipliers'. *American Economic Review Papers and Proceedings* 100, 1–7.

Moretti, Enrico. 2012. *The New Geography of Jobs*. Boston: Haughton Mifflin Harcourt.

Nathan, Max. 2007. 'The wrong stuff? Creative class theory and economic performance in UK cities'. *Canadian Journal of Regional Science* XXX, 433–450.

Nathan, Max. 2012. 'After Florida: towards an economics of diversity'. *European Urban and Regional Studies* Online First.

Nathan, Max and Henry Overman. Forthcoming. 'Agglomeration, clusters and industrial policy'. *Oxford Review of Economic Policy*.

Nathan, Max and Chris Urwin. 2006. 'City People: City Centre Living in the UK'. London:Centre for Cities.

National Equality Panel. 2010. *An Anatomy of Economic Inequality in the UK.* London: CASE.

Overman, H. 2013. 'Geographical Economics and Policy', in M.M. Fischer and P. Nijkamp (eds), *Handbook of Regional Science*. Heidelberg/New York/Dordrecht/London: Springer, pp. 527–538.

Parkinson, Michael. 2009. 'The Credit Crunch and Regeneration: Impact and Implications'. London: DCLG.

Power, Anne and John Houghton. 2010. *Jigsaw Cities: Big Places, Small Spaces.* Bristol: Policy Press.

Rodrik, Dani. 2004. 'Industrial Policy for the Twenty-First Century', CEPR Discussion Paper 4767. London: Centre for Economic Policy Research.

Rybczynski, W. 2009. 'The Design of the Urban Environment', in R.P. Inman (ed.), *Making Cities Work*. Princeton, NJ: Princeton University Press.

Song, Y. and G. Knaap. 2003. 'New urbanism and housing values: a disaggregate assessment'. *Journal of Urban Economics* 54, 218–238.

Storper, Michael and Allen Scott. 2009. 'Rethinking human capital, creativity and urban growth'. *Journal of Economic Geography* 9, 147–167.

Twomey, J. and J. Taylor. 1985. 'Regional policy and the interregional movement of manufacturing industry in Great Britain'. *Scottish Journal of Political Economy* 32, 257–277.

Tyler, P. 2011. 'Strategies for Underperforming Places', SERC Policy Paper 006. London: SERC.

PART IV

Conclusions: what conventional policy
wisdoms do we challenge?

9. Conclusions

The importance of cities in shaping and enhancing the lives of billions makes understanding how they work vitally important. It also makes good urban policy vitally important. And urban policy is likely to neither be good nor achieve its objectives unless it is informed by an understanding of how cities work.[1]

This is true whether one is faced with the problems of the rapid growth of mega-cities in many less developed countries, or the more varied patterns of urban change we observe in Organisation for Economic Co-operation and Development (OECD) countries. This book is focused mainly on cities in more developed countries and particularly Britain. There, as we show in Chapter 2, we have seen an urban resurgence over the last decade. But resurgence is not everywhere. It is concentrated in some of the larger cities and in cities with more skilled populations. In general, cities in the south-east have 'outperformed' those further north in terms of population, wages and employment growth, and most of the older industrial cities have not done so well as administrative centres or old historic cities such as York. But even in the set of older industrial cities we observe substantial variation, with strongly performing cities (Manchester, Leeds or Newcastle) close to weakly performing ones (Liverpool, Bradford or Sunderland).

As we explained in Chapter 2, these outcomes are partly explained by global trends and policy choices (new technologies, labour market reforms and global economic integration) and how these play out spatially. But individual cities and urban systems are not simply 'passive' objects acted upon by exogenous global trends. Instead, what happens in cities is one crucial determinant of national outcomes and global trends. In other words, the local, national and global are interconnected. It is important to understand these interconnections better; especially before we intervene in economic and social organisms as important as cities.

We know that history is important. It has long been understood that a city's industrial structure is important. The inherited structure of activities and associated skills influence how a city's economy responds to new

---

[1] Even definitions matter: here and throughout this book we do not mean the word 'city' to refer to an administratively defined unit but a functionally defined one – see Chapter 7.

forces such as technological innovation or to changes in global patterns of comparative advantage. Since Marshall, we have known about the importance of agglomeration economies in shaping urban growth and change. More recently, researchers have begun to precisely quantify these effects. The evidence is now clear that people, firms and the public sector are more productive in bigger cities just because they are bigger. We are also beginning to get evidence on how much these agglomeration economies vary across sectors: much more important in service activities than in manufacturing and – maybe surprising – most important of all in the public sector. This is another explanation for the different performance of our cities over the past generation. The loss of comparative advantage in manufacturing in rich, high-wage countries was an important factor in the decline of the old manufacturing cities; but then differences in agglomeration economies and the growth in demand for many services boosted the performance of larger and skill-rich cities.

Another lesson emerging from recent research is just how important agglomeration economies are in explaining spatial patterns of consumption. As some have called it – the 'consumer city' (Glaeser et al. 2001). Bigger cities offer more of everything, particularly of variety; of cultural activities, spectator events and, as we argue in Chapter 3, choice of neighbours. In a large city you can choose to live with compatible neighbours in compatible neighbourhoods with facilities that cater for your tastes and demographic. The bigger the city, the more variety and choice there is. Of course, more popular neighbourhoods cost more to live in. So there is a concentration of richer people in such neighbourhoods. We still need more evidence here but already there seem to be strong lessons for policy.

This is related to another topic central to this book: how people sort across space, the channels through which people and firms respond to economic or environmental differences. Here, also, there seem to be important implications for policy. As we show in Chapter 2, the international evidence strongly suggests that when one is very careful to control for other factors, most 'disparities' between different cities that appear 'spatial' are in fact explained either by differences between individuals, variation in prices or environmental characteristics. When we look at differences across neighbourhoods within cities, in Chapter 3, the evidence is even stronger. People sort spatially and differences in opportunities for people of given characteristics are largely or entirely eroded between neighbourhoods within cities. The problems of distressed neighbourhoods are very largely explained by differences between people – even more so than are the differences in measured outcomes (for example unemployment or incomes) across different cities.

Policymakers are naturally concerned with raising urban economic 'performance', to meet two objectives: first, to improve the wellbeing of those who live in cities, and second to maximise the contribution of cities to the national economy. As we noted in the introduction, in the pursuit of these dual objectives they face two dilemmas. First, raising overall economic growth may require a focus on relatively more successful cities in the national system. This, in turn will widen rather than narrow spatial disparities. Second, policy also needs to allow for the huge variation in local economic performance between cities physically close to each other.

Traditionally, many discussions of urban policy try to solve these dilemmas by calling for policy to focus on 'turning around' less successful cities. Unfortunately, as we argue throughout this book, area-based policy is often ineffective in the face of strong market forces that drive spatial unevenness. The policy dilemma is very real.

All is not lost, however, if we recognise that the ultimate objective of urban policy is to improve outcomes for people rather than places; for individuals and families rather than buildings. This is not to say that we should stop caring about what is happening in different cities and neighbourhoods but serves to remind us that improving places is a means to an end, rather than an end in itself. Viewed through this lens, the central dilemma is weakened. Yes, there will be winners and losers from urban policy that builds on success, but gains for the winners should outweigh losses for the losers. Further, the spatial distribution of these gains and losses is complex and plays out across the urban system in ways that are far more nuanced than would be suggested if we focussed only on what is happening to places. Indeed, one significant policy failure to date is in our ability to manage decline in a way which minimises the hurt to individuals that such decline causes.

Implications for Urban Policy

The discussion above highlights three central themes in this book:

- The need for realism in the face of strong market forces that produce persistent spatial disparities;
- The ineffectiveness of many current urban policies in tackling these disparities – including some that achieve the exact opposite of what policy intends;
- The importance of focusing on outcomes for people not places.

What does this imply for urban economic policy? What are our challenges to conventional wisdom?

We set out our basic messages below. As we have pointed out through-out this book, urban policymaking is extremely challenging. And despite many improvements in the evidence base in recent years, we are still some way from understanding many important aspects of urban economies and urban life. So what follows is based on the theory and evidence we have – not perfect knowledge. We should also be clear that our proposals are largely focused on improving economic outcomes in cities: particularly productivity, wages and employment. As Paul Krugman (1992, p. 9) has said: 'productivity isn't everything, but in the long run it's almost every-thing'. But of course national policymakers and city leaders will want to balance economic, social and environmental goals. These imply some trade-offs, and we highlight some of these below.

Cities in the national system
A spatial economy framework suggests that we focus policy attention on places with potential – some bigger cities plus faster growing smaller cities with high-skilled populations – and equally, policy will need to provide support for structural adjustment in less successful places. Particularly when it comes to declining areas, central government will often need to work with local leaders, rather than dictating change from the centre. The experience of the UK's hugely controversial Housing Market Renewal Programme shows this very clearly – as both its advocates and critics acknowledge (Macleod and Johnstone 2012; Leather and Nevin 2013).

Intervening directly to change urban industrial structures is not straight-forward; may not even, in the end, be possible at all. The evidence on the effectiveness of cluster policies aimed at particular sectors is weak. Government can directly influence public sector employment, but evi-dence we have indicates complex interactions between public and private sectors, with increases in the public sector workforce having a halo effect on private services, but leading to some crowding out of local manufactur-ing. However, there is no evidence as yet that public sector relocation has substantial positive externalities in relocation destinations.[2]

Conversely, we have good evidence that improving the urban skills base both helps aggregate urban economic performance and raises individual economic welfare. Upskilling helps people and, if they stay where they are, helps their local economy. Even if they do not stay, however, provid-ing people with better opportunities wherever they might occur should surely be the central focus of government policy. Time spent living in cities

---

[2] It is also possible that major relocation programmes have negative externalities on the economies of source cities because of the substantial agglomeration economies in public sector activity.

can help further enhance those opportunities – evidence suggests that movers from bigger cities take their skills and an urban wage premium with them. This implies being more ready to help people move around the urban system. Reducing regional house price differentials by relaxing planning restrictions in high demand regions would have the double advantage of both helping people move and allowing greater exploitation of agglomeration economies.

Urban economic strategy
Urban economic strategies for cities should work with the grain of agglomeration economies: that is, seeking to raise benefits of urban location (for example by improving people's skills) and cutting costs and diseconomies of urban location (for example through interventions in the planning system, land supply and transport). In turn, this implies moving away from many traditional area-based interventions, especially since the evidence suggests they are not effective.

The evidence presented in this book suggests policymakers concerned with the overall economic performance of their city should also move away from area-based interventions aimed at 'micro-managing' location for firms. Area-based subsidies to firms either directly (for example tax breaks) or indirectly (subsidised commercial development) may benefit the small areas directly treated, but rather less the wider urban economy that the programmes are intended to assist. The evidence to date suggests that programmes to treat firms – rather than areas – can boost employment a little, though not productivity.

The economic evidence also suggests policymakers should be more relaxed about residential segregation in cities, but much *less* relaxed about inequality or poor education. The economic case for mixed communities is weak, with no evidence of substantial areas effects at neighbourhood level: the social evidence may be slightly more mixed. More importantly, it is very clear that individual factors matter more than area effects for explaining economic and social wellbeing, so the case for reducing inequality in cities implies helping people.

Conversely, policy can have a major impact on urban costs. We focus in this book on the planning system because this is such a major issue. But many of the lessons that we develop apply much more generally. In the case of the UK, the evidence suggests we should at the very least experiment with a shift from our system of development control towards the systems used in other European countries such as Germany and the Netherlands. This would be a rule-based system: local plans drawn up according to national guidelines and approved democratically by the local community. Would-be developers would then have virtual certainty that so long as what they wanted to do conformed to the plans and rules they could go ahead.

Changes to national guidelines would involve relaxing urban containment policies, moving from forcing development to legally defined brownfield sites and prohibiting it on legally identified Greenbelt land to deciding where to build – on the basis of the wider environmental amenity and social value of land, as well as by where people wanted to live and firms locate. Instead of Greenbelts, we need more green 'wedges' of higher amenity land with guaranteed public access and policy which effectively protects the areas that are environmentally most valuable. We need to relax both land supply restrictions and height restrictions except where there are amenity reasons not do so (conservation areas or views to protect).

It also seems from the evidence surveyed in Chapter 5 that micromanaging the locations of retail to particular sites in town centres selected by planners rather than retailers has very high costs in terms of output and productivity in an important economic sector. It also appears from other evidence that these Town Centre First policies, far from increasing town centre retail employment, reduce it. While it is not yet clear what, if any, environmental benefits these policies bring, there is certainly a strong case for revising such restrictive micromanagement of locational choice.

The evidence also suggests that effective planning systems need to make strong use of incentives and compensation systems for losers. In the UK context, this implies requiring the planning system to use price signals in a more prescriptive ways. Land price discontinuities should be a 'material consideration' with a presumption in favour of development being permitted unless (an important unless) the wider environmental or amenity values of the land in its current use justify preservation. In short, we need to regulate the land markets and patterns of development but only for some wider social or environmental purpose. Evidence does not suggest the present system is achieving much of either. How such a change could be implemented is discussed in Chapter 6.

We also favour decentralising the property tax system to provide stronger economic incentives for city leaders.[3] Specifically, incentives in the forms of (a) retention of a proportion of taxes on both business and residential property by local government which would be exempt from the national system of revenue equalisation; and (b) impact fees. As Chapter

---

[3] It should go without saying we favour updating valuations for Council Tax and increasing the range of the bands, as well as abolishing relief for second homes and relief from inheritance tax for agricultural land. These are such obvious anomalies that it is all but incredible they still endure especially in a world where urban economic research has demonstrated it is perfectly practicable to model values for millions of homes statistically more accurately than by traditional methods and at a tiny fraction of the cost.

7 sets out, such devolutionary moves need to be set at the correct urban scale, a point we return to below.

As any observer of the British scene will understand some of these proposals would meet fierce and bitter political resistance. We think the evidence of the economic and welfare – even environmental – damage done by Britain's current planning system is overwhelming, however, and that the impact will get progressively more damaging over time since supply of space is ossified but demand develops. The political problem is that while we desperately need reform it is never now that we desperately need it. The problem is that any radical reforms are politically unpalatable: but no alternative strategy will work.

No less controversial, it seems, would be a more sensible approach to infrastructure policy. Here, we have argued that the evidence is quite clear that *grands projets* and other expensive investment schemes have little chance at turning around declining cities already well endowed with high levels of infrastructure per person and correspondingly low congestion levels. Conversely, in growing cities with high levels of congestion, additional infrastructure investment would be far more successful if accompanied by effective congestion charging. High political support for infrastructure investment as a way of turning around declining places, with low political support for congestion charging, show us just how far there is to go in improving urban infrastructure policy.

Urban governance
We have laid out a large number of challenges to conventional wisdom in terms of what urban policy should do. Our thoughts on how urban policy should be formulated are, perhaps, less controversial (although certainly still highly contested in a very centralised British system). In particular, the evidence suggests that matching decision-making functions to the scale at which costs and benefits are incurred can improve policy outcomes. We also think that there is a strong conceptual case that this would also allow better use of local knowledge, and greater policy innovation and experimentation. The empirical evidence on this, however, is less clear cut. It is unlikely that the UK post-2010 coalition government's localism measures will provide us with much additional evidence on the value of localism per se. But it is possible that they might allow us to better evaluate the impact of specific policy interventions. Central to this, however, is the need to encourage experimentation and to embed evaluation at the start of policy development (indeed, failure to do this explains why this experiment is unlikely to tell us much about the overall benefits of localism). Finally, as we have noted above, empowered local leaders surely could have a central role to play in resolving some of the

most difficult policy dilemmas around the questions of managing and minimising the negative effects of decline.

In many countries – including the UK – theory and evidence imply that central government should devolve greater economic and fiscal power to local levels, typically metro-level covering the functional 'city-region'. It is important to recognise, however, that there is a real risk that devolution raises disparities, with the more economically constrained, less capable local governments left worse off. As we have argued time and again throughout this book whether this is a problem depends on the impact of these changes on people not places. This is arguably the area where it is most important to retain a focus on that central message, as we debate possible reforms.

Making better policies

A consistent theme in this book is that urban economics helps provide a better understanding of how cities work and offers many lessons that could help improve urban policy. But it is also important to recognise that our understanding of how cities work remains partial at best. So too our understanding of the likely impact of alternative urban policies.

Much of this book has focused on how urban economics research should feed into urban policy development. But we also strongly believe that the effective evaluation of existing interventions (however formulated) has a vital role to play in improving urban policy. Unfortunately, the vast majority of urban policy evaluations are of poor quality. Moreover the history of urban policy is full of examples where policies are introduced and then radically changed before they could reasonably have had much effect on anything except the costs of setting them up. This makes it very hard for national and local policymakers to design effective evaluations. As we discussed in Chapter 8, effective evaluation of urban policy is possible. It requires patience and a recognition that evaluation (using high quality design such as randomised control trials or quasi-experiments) needs to be embedded at the policy design stage. Unfortunately, these requirements are very seldom met in practice, and until they are, our understanding of the impact of urban policy will remain, at best, partial, leaving most policies contestable. Theory and evidence provided by urban economic researchers can help us formulate better urban policy, but only rigorous evaluation will tell us whether this policy ultimately helps achieve even its stated objectives let alone those of society at large. One final problem with evaluation is that too often policies are devised without any clearly stated objectives by which they could be evaluated anyway, even within their own terms.

Perhaps above all, our message is that cities are too important to be treated as sandpits for policymakers. We need to take them seriously and that requires understanding them much better. Perhaps caution is in order. Over history, cities have evolved rather like natural systems: changes and innovations were introduced in just one or two cities and, if they worked – like market places, public spaces, parks, sewerage or mass transit systems – they spread. If they stopped being useful – like city walls – they disappeared. Over the past two generations policy has begun to introduce changes across all cities at the same time, almost never with any prior understanding of what the long-term impact will be. This is very dangerous. Ideally, we need to go back to a world where we allow cities to experiment, but where the burden of proof should almost be reversed. If governments or policymakers wish to implement significant new urban policies across the board, they should be required to provide serious evidence as to what effect they will have and why. Policy needs to be more sceptical in its mindset. We should encourage policy innovation but on a small scale. If the results are good then more can and will adopt them.

REFERENCES

Glaeser, Edward L., Jed Kolko and Albert Saiz. 2001. 'Consumer city'. *Journal of Economic Geography* 1, 27–50.

Krugman, Paul. 1992. *The Age of Diminished Expectations: US Economic Policy in the 1980s*. Cambridge, MA: MIT Press.

Leather, Philip and Brendan Nevin. 2013. 'The housing market renewal programme: origins, outcomes and the effectiveness of public policy interventions in a volatile market'. *Urban Studies* 50, 856–875.

Macleod, Gordon and Craig Johnstone. 2012. 'Stretching urban renaissance: privatizing space, civilizing place, summoning "community"'. *International Journal of Urban and Regional Research* 36, 1–28.

Index